D0497504

HEART!

Fully Forming

Your Professional Life

as a Teacher and Leader

Timothy D. Kanold

Solution Tree | Press

a division of

Solution Tree

555 North Morton Street
Bloomington, IN 47404
800.733.6786 (toll free) / 812.336.7700
FAX: 812.336.7790

email: info@SolutionTree.com
SolutionTree.com

Visit **go.SolutionTree.com/HEART** to access materials related to this book.

Printed in the United States of America

21 20 19 18   8 9 10

FSC
www.fsc.org
MIX
Paper from
responsible sources
FSC® C011935

Library of Congress Cataloging-in-Publication Data

Names: Kanold, Timothy D., author.
Title: Heart! : fully forming your professional life as a teacher and leader
   / Timothy D. Kanold.
Description: Bloomington, IN : Solution Tree Press, [2017] | Includes
   bibliographical references.
Identifiers: LCCN 2016055488 | ISBN 9781943874439 (perfect bound)
Subjects: LCSH: Teachers--Professional relationships. | Educational
   leadership.
Classification: LCC LB1775 .K28 2017 | DDC 371.2/011--dc23 LC record available at
https://lccn.loc.gov/2016055488

Solution Tree
Jeffrey C. Jones, CEO
Edmund M. Ackerman, President

Solution Tree Press
President and Publisher: Douglas M. Rife
Editorial Director: Sarah Payne-Mills
Managing Production Editor: Caroline Weiss
Senior Production Editor: Christine Hood
Senior Editor: Amy Rubenstein
Copy Editor: Sarah Payne-Mills
Proofreader: Elisabeth Abrams
Text and Cover Designer: Laura Cox
Editorial Assistants: Jessi Finn and Kendra Slayton

This book is dedicated to Rick DuFour: practitioner, teacher, leader, colleague, and friend, whose heartprint on education exists deep within the potential of future generations.

Visit **go.SolutionTree.com/HEART** to access materials related to this book.

Table of Contents

About the Author

 **Timothy D. Kanold, PhD,** is an award-winning educator, author, and consultant. He is former director of mathematics and science and served as superintendent of Adlai E. Stevenson High School District 125, a model professional learning community district in Lincolnshire, Illinois.

Dr. Kanold is committed to equity and excellence for students, faculty, and school administrators. He conducts highly motivational professional development leadership seminars worldwide with a focus on turning school vision into realized action that creates greater equity for students through the effective delivery of professional learning communities for faculty and administrators.

He is a past president of the National Council of Supervisors of Mathematics (NCSM) and coauthor of several best-selling mathematics textbooks over several decades. He also has served on writing commissions for the National Council of Teachers of Mathematics (NCTM) and has authored numerous articles and chapters on school leadership and development for education publications since 2006.

Dr. Kanold received the prestigious international 2010 Damen Award for outstanding contributions to the leadership field of education from Loyola University Chicago, 1986 Presidential Award for Excellence in Mathematics and Science Teaching, and 1994 Outstanding Administrator Award (from the Illinois State Board of Education). He serves as an adjunct faculty member for the graduate school at Loyola University Chicago.

Dr. Kanold earned a bachelor's degree in education and a master's degree in mathematics from Illinois State University. He also completed a master's degree in educational administration at the University of Illinois and received a doctorate in educational leadership and counseling psychology from Loyola University Chicago.

To learn more about Timothy D. Kanold's professional work, visit his blog, Turning Vision Into Action (www.turningvisionintoaction.today).

To book Timothy D. Kanold for professional development, contact pd@SolutionTree.com.

Why I Wrote *HEART!*

I remember the moment like it was yesterday—July 17, 2002, 10:03 a.m. I was in my office interviewing a candidate for our director of instructional technology position. Usually a high-energy kind of guy, I was trying hard to listen to his responses to my interview questions, but I could not focus. And, I had been superintendent for all of sixteen days.

I knew something was very wrong.

It was hard to breathe, and my chest felt like it was going to constrict and collapse, like someone was sitting on top of me. I quickly finished the interview, quietly slipped out of my office, and drove to the local hospital. I called no one. Why panic?

Within ten minutes of entering the emergency room, I was on an operating table, and a few hours later had two coronary artery stents inserted near my heart, eliminating two severe blockages. According to the cardiologist, I was a month or two away from a full-blown heart attack.

And I had no idea.

I was reasonably young at the time. And you have to wonder, how did it come to that? What had caused me to not take better care of my heart? Or, how could I be so clueless about the actual condition of my heart?

Worse yet, it was mostly my fault. After years of playing baseball and softball, running marathons, and doing the types of "eat, move, sleep" behaviors that are good for the heart, I had drifted through a decade of actions and behaviors that gradually ate away at my heart health.

I justified that decade of course, like we all do. I was going back to school to work on an advanced degree; I was coaching my children in their sports; and my high-pressure work as an educator and author demanded more and more of my time. I had moved further out in the suburbs for more affordable housing and extended my daily drive to twenty-six miles one way each day. I ate mostly fast food, often in the car, and even worse—I had no time left for much exercise. I sat. A lot.

And then July 17, 2002, happened to me. My heart had had enough. It called me out. It was tired of the damage I was doing to myself. And, although it took five years to get it completely right, it is fifteen years later as I write this book, and I am still learning how to keep my healthier heart—every day, each day, one day at a time.

So, why tell you this story?

Soon enough, I realized my personal heart experience served as a metaphor for my work life as well. How well did I really understand my own heart for teaching and leading? Were the contributing elements of my work life gradually inspiring or destroying me and my colleagues, my students, and the school culture we were trying to build?

After all, our heart is at the center of our personal and professional lives.

It was in the recovery room at the hospital (and the subsequent next five years of often difficult follow-up procedures) that my desire to write this book began. More than ever, I realized how fragile life could be. The heart of our classrooms, our school, and our district seems to be the way we should measure our professional journey. Otherwise, why would we choose such a relationally intense profession, a profession that calls for understanding the role our heart plays?

Like me, you too may or may not be drifting into patterns of behavior that will damage your heart for educating students and colleagues. It depends on the personal and professional school season you are in. Maybe you have lost your passion for the work. Maybe your personality seems a bit edgy these days. Maybe you are tired of the constant preparation and follow-up work required. Maybe you are just tired. Maybe your perseverance meter ran out. Maybe you hide it so well that sadly, like me, no one from your professional or personal life will notice until it might be too late.

The day will come in your career when you will pack up all your boxes and wonder, "Did I make a difference?" "Was my heart right for the work I did?" "Did my work life matter?" And most important, you will ask, "What is the residue of my work life and effort on the students and colleagues I left (and am leaving) behind?"

And, how will you know?

Well, I suppose that's the point of reading this book. It's why I wrote it. I want you to know. I want you to connect and reconnect to and be mindful of your choices in doing the complex work of an educator.

Have you and I chosen wisely?

I have tried to approach this book with humor, research, experiences, reflection, hope, mindfulness, and meaningfulness—which are, of course, in the eye and the practice of the reader.

Teaching, when properly understood as a career of positive emotion and action, is such a wonderful gift you can give—a gift of your heart and your life to others. I hope this book can be a gift to your heart, a gift that both enriches your natural talent and helps you to become more intentional about your own professional practice for the personal marathon of your professional teaching life.

Václav Havel says, "The salvation of this human world lies nowhere else than in the human heart, in the human power to reflect, in human meekness and human responsibility."[1] This book is about the very human heart for our work as educators. It is about feeling and seeing the genius in every child. It is about deeper reflection. It is about a happy and healthy humility of spirit combined with a passion for our responsibility to help each and every student and colleague that joins us along our career path.

Introduction

This book is quite a ride! You will learn about parts of my professional journey while reflecting upon and discovering your own journey as well. You will explore and find your heart as an educator and examine contributing factors to becoming more deeply connected to your profession.

The book is different! It is not exactly linear, meaning there is a natural flow to the reading, but you can dive into almost any of your favorite parts or chapters that interest you and then use the book reflectively as you deem fit.

The book is more informal! It is written as if we were in class together having a conversation. I provide references at the end of each part of the book, and as endnotes and online, so as not to disrupt the flow of your thoughts and reflections as you read.

Each part of the book ends with a final thoughts section. These summary reflections bring each part to a close and offer a brief set of resources connected to the topic. I hope these resources are helpful as you explore ideas from thought leaders and experts who understand these ideas at a much deeper level than I can ever offer.

When I reference you in this book, I am including all adults responsible for educating students in your school or in the district. I am referencing each adult working in the school system—faculty, support staff, administrators, and board members—all the adults who have chosen the education profession.

Regardless of your position or job title, you are leading students and influencing each other for good or for bad, one way or the other. Thus, when I use the phrase *teacher and leader*, I am referring to the three and a half million K–12 public and private school faculty members (of which more than 350,000 are in their first or second year of teaching) as well as the half-million school administrators. I consider the heartprint you and your colleagues are leaving on each other, and on the fifty-four million K–12 students you serve.[2]

You have most likely heard of the word footprint. One *Merriam-Webster* definition of footprint is "a marked effect, impression, or impact," as in the footprint you leave on others.[3]

To this effect, in this book, I use a new word: *heartprint*.

You won't find *heartprint* in *Merriam-Webster*, but you will find a form of the word in the book *The Heart-Led Leader* by Tommy Spaulding.[4] Using the word, and combining it with *Merriam-Webster's* *footprint* definition, I define your heartprint as the distinctive impression and marked impact your heart leaves on others—your students and your colleagues, as your career and your school seasons unfold.

HEART! provides insight supported by research and various experts about ideas for pursuing a deeply mindful teaching and leading school life and professional career as an educator. It is my desire to ensure the ideas are much bigger than just my personal thoughts and experiences. By experts, I include thought leaders outside of our education profession who have much to teach us about our work. For example, you may or may not know these names: Grant and Tichy, Rath and Conchie, Goleman and Collins, Brown and Kahneman, Loehr and Schwartz, Seppälä and Spaulding, Kotter and Cohen, Sanborn and Segar, Duckworth and DePree, and Abelin and Benkler. You will meet them from time to time throughout this book.

I also include reflections and wisdom from more than forty teachers and leaders in our profession. You will meet them all during your journey through *HEART!*

Each part of the book represents one of five unique aspects for developing your heart for our profession. The five unique parts derive from the word heart, as the title indicates: finding happiness through engagement in meaningful alliances while taking focused risks using intelligent thought and wisdom. Each part answers an essential question.

- ◆ **Part 1: H**appiness—Are you a person of passion, positive impact, and perseverance for the education profession?
- ◆ **Part 2: E**ngagement—Are you an inspiring person with the day-to-day energy required to be fully engaged in your work life?
- ◆ **Part 3: A**lliances—Are you a person open to influence and shared values, able to become relationally intelligent and collaboratively interdependent with others?
- ◆ **Part 4: R**isk—Are you a person of vision-focused risks for sustainable change, with a growth and data-driven mindset for learning and life?
- ◆ **Part 5: T**hought—Are you a person with surface and deep knowledge capacity, thought, and wisdom?

I believe all five of these *HEART!* elements are essential to deeper connections to your work over the lifetime of your professional career. You might be strong in one element but weak in another. You might be great at taking risks but not very emotionally positive and happy (and no one may really know). You might be positively passionate and happy in your work but lack the engagement and energy to bring the best of yourself to work each day. You might be awesome at developing your own knowledge but not very adept at creating alliances and being part of an effective collaborative team (so your great thoughts and wisdom are not shared and ultimately have limited benefit to your school and its students).

Your heartprint matters! Knowing the heartprint you are leaving on others is a reflective activity. So I ask you to be mindful of the ninety-plus My Heartprint reflections that occur throughout the book.

MY HEARTPRINT 🩶

I suggest reading one to two chapters per week—not too quickly! My personal improvement as a teacher mostly came as a result of becoming a more reflective and mindful practitioner and by learning from and embracing my mistakes along the way.

It is my hope that *HEART!* will be both affirming and challenging as your teaching and leading career unfolds. No matter where you may be in the wonderful journey of this remarkably rewarding and sometimes frustrating profession, I hope the book will touch the story and the humanity of your professional life.

Please complete this book by writing in your own story along the way. Perhaps use the book in group study and discussions with colleagues. As you do so, you will discover your personal heartprint and realize the power you have to touch the hearts of all the students and colleagues in your school community and professional life.

These spaces or margins are places to write your responses and tell your story as you read your way through the book and reflect on your career progress. Use the spaces as you deem fit for your personality and style. The chapters are reasonably brief and provide space for you to take notes and be more reflective as you read, if you so choose.

DEVELOPING **HEART**

H

Is for Happiness

Essential Heartprint Question:
Are you a person of passion, positive impact, and perseverance for the education profession?

There is no passion to be found playing small—in settling for a life that is less than the one you are capable of living.

—Nelson Mandela

In part 1 of this book, we explore the role happiness plays in our pursuit of a fully formed professional life. We explore the happiness—positive emotion-passion connection—in our day-to-day teaching and leading life, and we explore the role of compassion and love in living a more meaningful professional life.

Without passion for the profession or the desire to become a person of positive influence, character, and perseverance, your heartprint on others could result in settling for a life that is less than the one you are capable of living, as Nelson Mandela reminds us in the opening quote.[5]

You should carefully consider the role of happiness in the workplace as you join the teaching profession. Does our profession fire you up and align your personal passion with the nature of an educator's work life? Does your positive emotional state serve you well through the grind of each and every day?

In this first part of the book, we explore the elements of the happiness research, what it feels like to become a wholehearted teacher of others, with the essential and necessary challenge of providing compassion, hope, and stability to others.

You will be asked about the love you have for your work and the issues in your life worth weeping over. We examine what experts can tell us about happiness and then try to apply it to the journey of our professional work and life.

If you teach young elementary school students or are in a stage of your personal life that includes younger children, you most likely know Pharrell Williams's song "Happy." First released as part of the *Despicable Me 2* movie soundtrack, the words seem relevant to the context for this part of the book.

Here are two lines from the chorus:

> Because I'm happy
>
> Clap along if you feel like a room without a roof[6]

You can almost hear the tune in your head and sing along, right? If not, go to iTunes (www.apple.com/itunes) and check it out! This specific part of the chorus resonated with my heart the loudest: "Clap along if you feel like a room without a roof." You see, in order to be meaningful, our professional life needs to feel like a room without a roof: unlimited potential and possibilities as we grow together. No ceiling on our potential and our achievement as educators, no limits to how expert we could become as practitioners within a profession we love.

In part 1, "H Is for Happiness," we examine actions that help us to reconnect to the meaning of our life and our career as educators and professionals. We examine steps to stay connected to our calling toward the profession and maintain joy in the journey—a joy that makes it so much more than just a job—as the days unfold, the seasons come and go, and the promise of a great career rests in the rearview mirror. The following chapters describe how to find and maintain that joy!

The Happiness Dilemma

H   E   A   R   T

Folks are usually about as happy as they make their minds up to be.

—Abraham Lincoln

Emma Seppälä is someone you should get to know. She serves as the science director at the Center for Compassion and Altruism Research and Education at Stanford University. In her book *The Happiness Track*, she defines *happiness* as "a state of heightened positive emotion" and elaborates further: "[Happiness] increases our emotional and social intelligence, boosts our productivity, and heightens our influence over peers."[7]

Happiness is about your state of being. It is about the heartprint of positive emotion we leave at school each and every day. We either walk into work in a positive emotional state or we don't. Alternatively, we are either creating an emotional drag on our students and colleagues, or we are not.

You and I make an impact each day: one way or the other and no matter the circumstances of our lives. The students also need us to be at our best, which on some days can be very difficult to achieve.

We each have a story—your teaching career consists of a sequence of school years or seasons, generally starting in August and ending in late May or early June. Our lives and our careers revolve around one season after another. These seasons stack up one upon the other, each with a unique path in its own way, year after year, eventually stringing together the real-life chapters of what will become your professional career for good or for bad.

It is in the daily grind that our school seasons unfold. And it is in our school seasons that our professional life unfolds.

Identify your current

professional moment in time as you read this. Place a date on the page and the actual time right now. List your school season number and the current time of year in that season. It affects your frame of mind and provides context when you look back at what you were thinking as you read this part of the book. Add your location as you write this.

_____

_____

_____

_____

_____

_____

_____

_____

_____

_____

_____

_____

_____

_____

_____

_____

_____

What's happiness got to do with it? According to Seppälä, quite a bit. It maximizes your resilience at work, your creativity for your lessons, and your interactions with others, your productivity, and even your charisma factor![8]

All your former students and the trail of colleagues that intersect with the wake of your work will remember your *happiness state* season after season. It becomes part of your reputation in the community and among your colleagues.

Speaking of seasons, which season number is this for you, as you read this first part of the book? What school year are you in (for example, 2019–2020)? And, is this school season number one, five, twelve, or twenty-five for you? Or is it some other number? What time of the year is it? First quarter, third quarter, or is it the off season (usually summer) as you read these words?

 # MY HEARTPRINT

For the eighth season of my teaching career, I chose a job at Community High School District 94 in West Chicago, Illinois. We started the school year twelve days late due to a teacher strike (I had not yet set foot in the door, and I was already walking a picket line). As we started the school year—the new season—I was in a department of teachers that was not in a positive emotional state. Department meetings were contentious. We experienced disagreements about what to teach and how to teach it. We prepared lessons but with minimal effort and planning. We had lost two weeks of pay, and everyone and everything seemed to be suffering.

Where was the happiness? There . . . was . . . none.

And the students felt the brunt of it.

It was a rough start to this new and eighth season of my career as well as for all my colleagues. However, I was strangely living outside of this state of negative emotion. A positive person by nature, I did not have emotional attachment to the events leading up to the strike. Later in my career, I would serve as a faculty union president and as a school district superintendent. But at the moment, I was mostly detached from the strike issues. I just wanted to teach!

This brings me to a *happiness dilemma*. Based on these circumstances, should there then be no happiness? You might know that a dilemma is a usually undesirable or unpleasant choice. Being unhappy seems to me to be an unpleasant choice. I have never been part of or observed an unhappy school culture that was successful.

Enter Barry (not his real name). Barry was a teacher in our department perpetually in a state of heightened negative emotion. He was the exact opposite of Seppälä's definition of happiness. He was very unhappy. His students felt it and for sure his colleagues felt his wrath as well. No one dared cross his path. Not even those adults "to his north," such as our department chair. He was an angry person and wanted to be left alone. For him, the teacher strike had given him fuel and an enemy for his state of unhappiness. It was a happiness dilemma, for sure.

Is there someone like this in your school or office? Is there a negative, unhappy person residing within the path of your work? If so, think about him or her. Imagine this person in your mind. How do you approach someone like that?

I asked around to see if there was ever a time in Barry's teaching life when he was happy. Not too many could remember. I was sure he did not just wake up this way. We tend to drift to a place of unhappiness and for whatever reasons, both Barry and his colleagues allowed him to drift too far, so far in fact that now it seemed no one could touch him and bring him back to a place of happiness.

His heartprint was negative, and his legacy was trending as not so good. It bothered me but not enough to do anything about it. After all, wasn't that someone else's job to help him, like the principal?

Then in the early winter of his eighteenth season (my eighth), our department went on a curriculum retreat at a former Baptist center in the middle of rural Wisconsin. We all shared a large house and also had to share rooms (like in a hotel).

Barry was my roommate.

"Why did I get this assignment?" I thought. I just knew I was headed for a long weekend. The first day proved me correct, as Barry's emotional state was peppered with complaints about the why, what, and where of the entire retreat event. He was leaving a trail of negative emotion on each of us.

It appeared to me that teaching was no longer his calling. It was for him, at best, a way to get a paycheck every two weeks. I was not sure which season of teaching he could reconnect to and remember why he became a teacher in the first place, but I knew it was not a season close enough for him to remember.

Deep down, I sensed Barry had a teddy bear–like quality. He could actually be funny at times despite all of that cynicism. But somewhere along the way, he got burned out. On the second day we were there, it started snowing and the two of us set out to find some firewood for the house as the sun started to set.

So, back to my happiness dilemma: *the usually undesirable or unpleasant choice.*

When searching for firewood, I wondered, Should I ask Barry why he is so negative and unhappy all the time? Do I face this undesirable choice of aggravating him further in light of the circumstances? Do I lean in to this angry person? To go on receiving his negativity was not a good choice for my happiness or the happiness of our school culture. Professionals do not act this way, I kept thinking. They face the happiness dilemma and work their way through it.

And at the moment I had my own dilemma: to speak or not to speak. So, I quietly decided, yes. I'll face the happiness dilemma that was like a cancer to our team and department. I will face my own personal dilemma and say something. But what should I say? What would you say?

As we were walking, I asked him a simple yet complex question: "Why do you hide behind this wall of unhappiness? What happened to you?"

Silence. I repeated my question and waited. You could hear our footsteps crackling in the snow.

His eventual response was revealing in so many ways. Barry told me that it was just easier than dealing with the reality of what his students don't know. Essentially, he had lost his desire to do battle. He could not slog through another season of students failing. It wasn't just the teacher strike. Essentially, he no longer found meaning in his work, and for him it was just easier to blame his problems on the students, the administration, and sometimes his colleagues—like me.

I asked him if teaching was his passion. He wasn't sure anymore. I asked him if he wanted to stop being so negative. He said *no.* So, I stopped talking for a while. Eventually, we returned to the house and talked long into the night. He didn't bite my head off, but it was difficult at times, because he seemed so angry with me. I knew it wasn't about me, but it was still hard to listen and not take it personally or not tell him I thought he was rude sometimes. We became what I would term cautious colleagues over the next few years.

I won't get into more details, because it was a personal journey for Barry, but I will say he reconnected with owning his own emotional state, becoming more aware of his negative impact on others, and finding some love for his students once again. It took him time, but his heartprint gradually began to change. I don't think he ever reconnected with his original passion for the work. He also thought my positive outlook was not acceptable given the teaching conditions that caused the strike.

MY HEARTPRINT ♥

In the end, I told him I thought he had those endearing and funny traits of the better teachers I have known. He had, however, just forgotten what it meant to join and commit to the teaching and learning profession. It was okay to search for his happiness in his work. It was okay to find joy in the journey. It was okay to connect to students and colleagues with grace and, as we will discover later, something called *grit*.

It was his choice after all. Just as it was my choice too.

Think about Seppälä's definition of *happiness* again: "A state of heightened positive emotion."[9] In the space provided, write about some of the actions you take at school or home to maintain your positive emotional state with your students and colleagues, even on the toughest of days.

Do you have a happiness dilemma that needs to be resolved? Do you have a work relationship that is draining you? Are you avoiding that colleague or student? Do you need to make the choice to lean into and engage a colleague who needs a happiness checkup?

Name the colleague (keep it to yourself—you do not want to offend someone, even if you need to lean into him or her), and decide the action you are able to take after you read chapter 2. For additional support with this type of happiness dilemma, see also chapter 19 in part 3, "A is for Alliances."

HOW do you and your colleagues generally exhibit a positive emotional commitment to your students, each other, and your work? Be descriptive with your response.

_____

_____

_____

_____

_____

_____

_____

_____

_____

_____

_____

_____

_____

_____

_____

_____

_____

_____

_____

_____

_____

_____

_____

_____

_____

_____

_____

_____

It is possible that you will be able to reconnect that person to his or her passion for the profession. This connection, in turn, may just be what this person needs to help him or her find elements of happiness in professional life once again.

The Happiness-Passion Connection

H E A R T

Passion makes the difference between something common and something special.

—Mark Sanborn

You are special. That might sound trite, but it is not. You chose this profession. That alone makes you special in my eyes and the eyes of the hundreds of students who pass through your life. And, according to Mark Sanborn, author of the *New York Times* bestseller *The Fred Factor*, your passion is part of what makes you special.[10]

I recovered from sometimes difficult school seasons mostly because of my deep passion for teaching and because of colleagues, students, and family members who took the time to reconnect me to my deep passion for the work.

That is an interesting phrase, right? *Deep passion for the work.*

What does it mean to have a passion for teaching? *Passion* is an impactful word and yet, it is tough to measure or define. As I was writing this chapter, I thought back to when I first *knew*.

It was revealed in one of those singular moments in time—when with great clarity while sitting in an eleventh-grade mathematics class at Addison Trail High School in Illinois, I just flat out knew I wanted to become a teacher—and maybe someday a fully formed educator. Teaching was what I was meant to do with my work life!

When did you know? Can you remember? Why did you choose education as your profession? Was it the influence of a parent, colleague, teacher, or child? Was it, like me, a singular moment of clarity while learning from my favorite teacher, Al Foster? How did you know teaching children was a choice you would fully embrace? How did you know it was your passion?

Why did you choose education as your profession?

Write about what a passion for education means to you. Start with *Passion is* . . .

_____

_____

_____

_____

_____

_____

_____

_____

_____

_____

_____

_____

_____

_____

_____

_____

_____

_____

_____

_____

_____

_____

_____

_____

To tap into this idea of passion, I decided to ask hundreds of educators who have made the choice to join our ranks.

In the summer of 2016, during Solution Tree's PLC institutes, I asked more than five hundred educators, just like you and me, to define what passion in the workplace means.

Here are the primary categories of responses I received.

Passion is . . .

Passion is what I feel.

Passion is what I love, and I love to teach.

Passion is to be fully energized in my work.

Passion is the emotion I bring to work every day.

Passion is what helps me to inspire my students.

Passion is what serves me when I get tired.

Passion is what sustains me in
my moments of doubt.

Passion is my burning desire
to help difficult children.

Passion is what motivates me to
right the wrongs I see in my school.

Passion is just my style.

Merriam-Webster offers up a solid definition of *passion*: "a strong *feeling* of enthusiasm or excitement for something or about doing something."[11]

 # MY HEARTPRINT

Hmm, passion is a strong *feeling*. Moreover, passion is a feeling of enthusiasm or excitement. And I am supposed to feel this way every day? Not just at the start of the school year? What about February when the year seems to be dragging along, even then?

Seems like a tough request—but not for Lee Maciejewski. Lee *who*, you ask? I hadn't really thought much about my passion as a teacher of students and eventually as a teacher of my colleagues until I met teacher and coach Lee Maciejewski.

"What is your secret?" I asked him.

"What do you mean?" Lee responded as we rode back from Glenbard East High School.

It was on a quiet school bus on a Saturday night after another loss. We were almost to the end of a very long high school basketball season. I was the sophomore boys' basketball coach, and Lee was the junior varsity (JV) coach—the main assistant for our varsity team. Our varsity team was not having a very good season, and a small community revolt was mounting against the current varsity head coach. And, by association, against Lee as the JV coach too.

The secret I was referring to, when I asked Lee the question on the bus, was related to his incredible passion for his job as the JV coach. Despite a losing season, despite a team of athletes, which was not all that athletic, despite our head coach, who was very difficult to get along with, and despite the responsibilities of raising his own young family, Lee brought a passion to his work that was infectious. Lee was the type of teacher, coach, and leader who made you want to give him the best you had.

It did not matter to him that he was not in the starring role. He wasn't the head coach, and his input was not often valued. Lee was a few years older than me, but he seemed to have wisdom far greater than mine. His answer to my question that night on the bus, when I asked him how he brought that passion and love for his work day after day—work for which he was never outwardly recognized, or where he was sometimes told to keep his thoughts to himself or asked to do jobs that were not part of his job description, and especially on the days that were not all that great—left a heartprint on me I never forgot.

Lee quietly said to me, "I just decided that no matter what I do in this life, I will bring the best of me to that job every day. Today I am the JV coach. So today, *I will be the best damn JV coach I can be.* The boys deserve no less. My family deserves no less. I deserve no less. And no matter what my job is in this school, I will give it everything I have."

Funny, there I was all of thirty-two years old, and that single phrase *I will be the best damn JV coach I can be* stopped me in my tracks. Lee actually went on to say a few more words, but I did not hear them. It became even quieter on that bus ride home, and his words made me realize that I was not *always* the best teacher I could be. His words, along with the phrase *carpe diem*, became my family's mantras for years to come.

From that day forward, I made no excuses. I decided that as long as I was in this profession, I would be more like Lee Maciejewski.

Hit the pause button for a moment. How does Lee's story connect to your own perspective on life and work? To your passion and purpose?

_____

_____

_____

_____

_____

_____

_____

_____

_____

_____

_____

_____

_____

_____

_____

_____

_____

I would be the best damn teacher and leader, father and husband, and colleague and friend I could be: in the moment, every day. I did not and will not always succeed, but it would not be for lack of effort.

MY HEARTPRINT

To understand the impact of the story with my colleague, Lee, is to also understand that Lee and I were very different in personality, style, and perspective. Lee was a lifer as a coach. It was his deep passion and love. I really enjoyed coaching, but I also had a deep passion for teaching and leading other adults, not only students; and eventually, that would become my role as a professional educator. Lee saw me as a bit of a "square," maybe even a bit of an egghead. For example, I would never say the word *damn*, except in the context of this book. Let's just say Lee was more flamboyant! Passion manifests itself in lots of ways!

Over the years, in my family, when any one of us would complain about our station in life, chores that needed to get done, or unhappiness with our current workload, you would hear someone echo the phrase, "Be the best damn JV coach you can be!" This was our way of saying to buck up and get the work done—no matter how big or how small you think the job is.

Lee's passion served him well. Teaching was his calling. It gave him meaning far more than a paycheck or health benefits ever could. He went on to have an extremely long tenure as a teacher and a great career coaching football, girls' softball, and boys' basketball in the suburban Chicago area.

Part of knowing if you are measuring high on the passion index is to decide whether or not you will be the best damn educator you can be! Think about it. Teachers are *the* major players in the education process. That means you and me. *We matter!* Our daily choices matter! We have so much power and influence over students, more than we realize sometimes.

Educational researcher John Hattie claims that high-effect or high-impact teachers are passionate and inspired. Hattie describes how expert teachers show a passionate belief that all students can reach the success criteria and that intelligence is changeable.[12]

Passion, therefore, is so much more than enthusiasm. Hattie quotes Christopher Day, a professor of education at the University of Nottingham:

> All effective teachers have a passion for their subject, a passion for their pupils and *a passionate belief [in] who they are and how the teacher can make a difference* [emphasis added] in their pupils' lives, both in the moment of teaching and in the days, weeks, months and even years afterward.[13]

It is the third element (italicized) of Day's description that causes me to stumble a bit. How about you? I have always had a love for my subject (in my case, mathematics) and a love for my students. However, I'm not sure that in every teaching moment, or in every day, week, month, or season of my teaching life I have had a passionate belief in myself to make a difference (by the way, for those of you old enough to remember, this is what was once referenced in the education genre as high expectations). Could I really win with every student?

MY HEARTPRINT 💜

Why did you place the X where you did? At the writing of this book, my X would be about 82 percent. I have been trying to close the "belief in myself to help each child learn" gap for years. I often see both weakness and strength in my work. Can you and I close the gap? Can we close the gap between our X and the top of the line at 100 percent? I believe we can! To close the gap requires us to act with compassion and love, live with hope in our journey, and become more gritty and grateful.

In the next chapter, we explore the love required to become a *wholehearted* teacher. Let's take a look at how to make it happen!

Draw a vertical line. At the bottom write 0 percent. At the top write 100 percent. Now, draw an X on the percent line that represents your *passionate belief in yourself* that you can make a difference in the lives of every one of your students.

_____

_____

_____

_____

_____

_____

_____

_____

_____

_____

_____

_____

_____

_____

_____

_____

_____

_____

_____

_____

_____

_____

_____

_____

What's Love Got to Do With It?

H E A R T

Great teaching is always a form of love.

—John Ortberg

Think of the best teacher you have ever known (you may or may not have been his or her student).

MY HEARTPRINT 💙

Great teaching is always a form of love.

Think about those words for a moment. Do you agree? Can you think of one great teacher you have known who did not demonstrate love? Every parent knows when a teacher loves his or her child. Every child knows when there is an atmosphere of love in the classroom. And yet, it is one of the hardest emotions we share. We so easily fall in and out of love with our work, our students, and our colleagues. We use our love to inspire joy and sometimes to cause harm.

Great educators do so much more than share information; teach ideas, concepts, and facts; and give and grade assignments. Great teachers—most likely the person you named in that box—saw (or sees) beyond your failures and frailties. Great teachers and leaders see beyond your predisposed rough edges. They open you up—your mind and your heart—to a world of

Name this teacher. Then list three characteristics that describe what this person contributed or contributes to your life as a student or colleague. Is there a favorite memory or experience you remember having with this teacher?

_____

_____

_____

_____

_____

_____

_____

_____

_____

_____

_____

_____

Take a moment to connect to Brown's view of wholehearted living by thinking about your current professional role in your school. What is your response to her words for you and for your students?

_____

_____

_____

_____

_____

_____

_____

_____

_____

_____

_____

_____

_____

_____

_____

_____

_____

_____

_____

_____

_____

_____

_____

_____

_____

learning and new meaning. They teach you with a *whole heart*.

Brené Brown is a research professor at the University of Houston graduate college of social work. As of this writing, her TED talk at Ted.com is one of the top ten most viewed with over six million viewers. She is the author of three *New York Times* bestsellers, including *Daring Greatly* in 2012. In the book, she defines *wholehearted living* as follows:

> Wholehearted living is about engaging in our lives from a place of worthiness. It means cultivating the courage, compassion, and connection to wake up in the morning and think, *No matter what gets done and how much is left undone, I am enough.* It's going to bed at night thinking, *Yes, I am imperfect and vulnerable and sometimes afraid, but that doesn't change the truth that I am also brave and worthy of love and belonging.*[14]

 # MY HEARTPRINT

It was the day after Christmas as I wrote my final blog entry for 2013. Looking back, I wish I had not taken her life for granted quite so much. I suppose we always think we can make life really matter a little bit more in the next season of our professional lives. And there is always next year, a next school season, right?

Not always.

That morning, December 26, the most wholehearted teacher I ever knew unexpectedly passed away. Mary Layco was beloved. Joyful. Smart. Grace filled. Lover of mathematics. Lover of students. Completely engaged from a place of worthiness.

Mary was humble but confident. Fair but tough. Her gift in life was teaching. She taught algebra and calculus for thirty-five years to all kinds of rough-edged students. And they loved her right back. She belongs in the mathematics teacher hall of fame. Mary was a pro's pro—a natural. And she maximized every ounce of her teaching talent, with double the effort of most colleagues, in an attempt to become great for her students.

Teaching was definitely her calling. She had a love affair with her work every day, every week, every month, every year. If Mary was having a bad moment, you didn't know it.

She was a popular teacher for all the right reasons. As a student in her class, you would find rigor, wisdom, teamwork, ways to think creatively, confidence that you could do it, and, perhaps most important, you would have fun! Fun with algebra and fun with calculus! Imagine.

Over the years at Adlai E. Stevenson High School in Lincolnshire, Illinois, I am pretty sure we had hundreds of students take calculus just for a shot at being in Mary's class. One year, I taught calculus just so I could be on her teaching team. She taught me how to sing songs to get students to remember important rules, like the duet we created around Aretha Franklin's "Chain of Fools" as we taught the chain rule for derivatives to our classes.

Unexpectedly, Mary became seriously ill. The outpouring of love for her was amazing, and I am sure for her family—heartfelt, real, kind, and, perhaps too, a bit overwhelming. Events like this reveal a visceral response of thanks, gratefulness, and an inner desire to say, "Do you know how much we really love you?"

And there had been this deep and sudden sadness. You stop your life for a moment and allow yourself to weep for such sadness. Knowing that the next season—in this case the 2014–2015 season—would not come for our local hero.

When I first met Mary, she did not think she was such a hero. She did not think she was worthy to teach calculus. Similar to how a second-grade teacher might not think she can teach fifth grade, Mary thought the content was beyond her knowledge base. She exemplified, however, the second part of Brené Brown's quote: "Yes, I am imperfect and vulnerable and sometimes afraid, but that doesn't change the truth that I am also brave and worthy of love and belonging."[15]

Over the years, she would write to me (I was her boss, so to speak) and tell me about how I had been her coach, mentor, and inspiration to become the best teacher she could be. In the end, I would tell her she had it backward. Mary was my coach, my mentor, and my inspiration. She made me want to be the best teacher and leader and best person I could be. I was the one who was imperfect and vulnerable, and she let me know I could be brave and worthy of love and belonging. She had that kind of effect on her students and her colleagues.

It is why love is at the heart of your happiness in this profession.

Mary was a legacy-building, inspirational teacher and friend. She lives in the memories of all of us blessed enough to know her. She

You know the heartprint you are leaving on others. You know the real residue of your work life and effort. What do you hope that residue will be? How do you hope your students and colleagues will describe you?

_____

_____

_____

_____

_____

_____

_____

_____

_____

_____

_____

_____

_____

_____

_____

_____

_____

_____

_____

_____

_____

_____

_____

did not get to name or claim the school season in which her career would end. For her and her students, it was cut short before she and they were ready. This teacher, who loved students beyond reason, did not get to open up a new school season. And all who knew her suffered for it.

Fast-forward eight months to the start of the 2014–2015 school season. "Will it be a good one or not?" we asked. Mary was not there to respond, however. Then, before you know it, all of a sudden here comes your next season, and your next one—you blink and it is the 2028–2029 season. Graduation for the kindergarten students of 2016–2017! And for some of you reading this book, that will be it. Your final season! No more chances to get it really right!

Take a moment. Think way ahead. Remember too, that like Mary, sometimes we do not always get to name our final school season. That is why making sure this current school season of your life matters and is so important. What would you like to be able to look back on and say you accomplished?

♥ MY HEARTPRINT

Mary was passionate about making every season of her teaching career really count. She believed in PMA—*positive mental attitude*—and thought every one of her colleagues and students should exhibit PMA every day (sounds very similar to Seppälä's 2016 definition of *happiness*,[16] right?).

As the 2014–2015 school year was about to start, I had an opportunity to work with a great California school district as part of the start-of-the-school-year activities. Mary was on my mind, as I was very aware she would not be back in my school district for her thirty-sixth season.

As I walked out of the three-hour session, a veteran teacher and someone I suspect has worked hard for a long time to be more like Mary, stopped me to say thanks. His words did give me pause though, as he said, "It was so great for you to be honest with us and not give a *!#@! about our reaction, good or bad.

Thank you for saying what we needed to hear. It was tough, but it was done with a spirit of love."

You know, I thought a lot about what he said when I got into my car. I suppose on that day, I was a bit more direct than I normally am, perhaps too direct with these wonderful teachers about to start a new school season. I tried to understand why I was so direct. As I sat in my car, I realized why. For several minutes, there were quiet tears. The tears were for my love of Mary. She didn't get to start a new season like all the teachers I had just had the privilege to interact with. The tears were for my own inability to deeply impact those who get the privilege of another season, and somehow wishing I could have given her more. I think too the tears were for the students who deserve for their teachers to demonstrate love for each of them and to have great seasons just like Mary, every year.

Teachers and leaders just like you.

Find your inner Mary Layco and go for it in this school season of your professional life. Bring an increased understanding of love to your work, your colleagues, and your students. Don't let any form of cynicism win the day.

Work together, learn from one another, and give it everything you've got. There really is nothing to lose—other than the privilege of that next school season.

MY HEARTPRINT ♥

At the start of this chapter, I asked you to name the best teacher you have ever known and three characteristics that describe what this person contributed or contributes to your life.

As you end this chapter, I would like you to turn the heartprint task around and think about one colleague at work who needs you to be someone who loves him or her (in the sense that you are going to pay attention to that person more) enough that you become a person he or she looks to as a positive contributor to his or her life.

Remember, this is not something you will declare to your colleague, "I have chosen to notice you more this

Are you still in love with your work? And your colleagues and students? How do you know?

Name a colleague or student and write out a few actions you might take to be more fully present for him or her. Start your commitment with *I will* . . .

_____

_____

_____

_____

_____

_____

_____

_____

_____

_____

_____

_____

_____

_____

_____

_____

_____

_____

_____

_____

_____

year!" Think of it as just a more quiet and subtle way to improve the culture of love for the colleagues in your workplace each day.

To some extent, as you complete the My Heartprint, you will notice it requires a certain amount of compassion for your colleague. Happiness in our profession and in the school workplace requires a personal compassion check—time and time again, over and over and over.

What does it mean to experience a compassionate workplace? And what exactly is the compassion connection to happiness? That is next.

Got Compassion? Check!

If you want others to be happy, practice compassion. If you want to be happy, practice compassion.

—Dalai Lama

A fully formed heart—a heart that pursues happiness in its work for students, for colleagues, and for you—finds completeness in its compassion.

Don't read too fast. Read that sentence again.

A fully formed heart—a heart that pursues happiness in its work for students, for colleagues, and for you—finds completeness in its compassion.

MY HEARTPRINT

Run a Google images search for the word *compassion*, and you'll see several images with a heart in them. To become a teacher whom a child or colleague would follow and to become an administrator whom a teacher or colleague would follow, we demonstrate and develop a culture of compassion. It becomes part of our heartprint over time.

She was a colleague of mine. We taught many of the same classes together. She taught in Room 212. I taught in Room 210. This was before the professional

How would you define *compassion*? What does the word *compassion* mean to you?

How does a fully formed heart exhibit compassion?

_____

_____

_____

_____

_____

_____

_____

_____

_____

_____

_____

_____

_____

_____

_____

learning community (PLC) era. She was older than I, and I did not know too much about her. We mostly lived in different worlds: my life filled with teaching, coaching, and my own young children; her life filled with friends and activities outside of school. We did not work on school activities or lesson planning together.

Then one day I entered her room before school, because I could hear her crying. She sat at her desk sobbing. Her dog had died the night before. Yet, here she was at work. I knelt down by her side and hugged her for what seemed like a really long time, maybe three minutes. And it seemed a bit awkward, hugging an older female colleague.

But at that moment, she needed me to mourn with her. She needed me to provide her with my compassion. She needed me to allow her loss to enter into my being. And I do not know why I felt that way. I wasn't sophisticated enough to think, "Oh, she needs compassion right now, so give her some." It just seemed to be the right thing to do.

A few years later, I needed a small amount of money for a family emergency. She heard about my dilemma from another colleague. Without reproach or request, she wrote me a check. She said she knew I would repay her. She said she had never forgotten my act of compassion on the day her dog died. Again, I was too young to understand, but her act of compassion on that day was her way of identifying and owning with me my family emergency. Her kindness overwhelmed me.

Compassion means being there for the students and colleagues that intersect your path. It means you *identify* with them. You are *cheering* for them. You celebrate victories with them, no matter how small, and more important, you *mourn* their setbacks. It means you always and sincerely wish them well in your heart. You lean into them, even when it is difficult to do so.

You and I have a lot of power. Think about the words used thus far: We *demonstrate* compassion. We *mourn* setbacks. We *cheer* on victories. We *identify*.

We can also choose not to do these things.

We can choose to withhold compassion. Over the years, I refused to allow my colleagues to hide behind or allow others to hide behind the words, "I am just not a very compassionate person."

Yes, you are.

Do not let your colleagues get away with this mindset either. Compassion is a choice. To identify with another person is a choice. Passing judgment that someone does not deserve your compassion, and withholding it, is also a choice you can make.

Gallup asked workers over the age of eighteen the question, "What leader has the most positive influence in your daily life? And, "What three words best describe what this person contributes to your life?" The workers produced four categories of responses. The first category was compassion. When asked what compassion meant to these respondents, the top responses were:[17]

- Compassion is about caring.
- Compassion is about friendship.
- Compassion is about love.
- Compassion is about happiness.

So, got compassion? Compassion encompasses caring, friendship, love, and happiness. It is an essential professional element of an effective workplace culture. In My Heartprint that follows, think about each compassion category and reflect on how you show compassion in the workplace.

MY HEARTPRINT 💜

Caring: You mourn the setbacks of others.
Friendship: You cheer on their victories.
Love: You do not withhold compassion.
Happiness: You model compassion for others.

How would your students or colleagues rank you on each of these four compassion characteristics? Give yourself a 1, 5, or 10, with 1 being low, 10 being awesome, and 5 meaning you are working on developing compassion in your professional life. Briefly explain your rating.

_____
_____
_____
_____
_____
_____
_____
_____
_____
_____
_____
_____
_____
_____
_____
_____
_____
_____
_____

Although compassion means being there *for* your students and your colleagues, don't confuse love and compassion with softness. Being there for someone is deeper than just wanting to spare him or her pain. If I really am there *for* the person (child or adult), then I must be ready to warn, reprove, confront, or admonish when necessary. Always do so with grace and humility, of course. Always with the understanding that to be there *for* them, to show compassion for them, may also require honest reflection with them about potential destructive behaviors.

Linda Ruesch was my final student teacher, and she was terrific during student teaching. I was moving on to my new job at Stevenson, and I begged her to join me in my new district when a teaching job opened up. We became friends and colleagues, as Linda and her husband played on our coed Friday night softball team too. She became not only a great teacher to her students but also a mentor to many of her colleagues. She had a disarming way of collaborating with others and bringing peace to the resolution of tough issues teachers face every day. She had a tough-minded compassion.

For me, she became someone I trusted implicitly. She was a model of grace and humility. I also knew I could trust her with information that might be confidential at a given moment, as I would often test out an idea with her regarding the entire scope of our division's work.

One day, I called her into my office and asked her an important question: "I am thinking about applying to be the next superintendent of our district. Give me your honest response, do you think I would be good for the job and good for the school district?"

What Linda did not know is that I had been stewing about this for about two weeks. That is usually the way it is for you too, right? By the time you actually talk to your spouse, colleagues, immediate boss, or even your students, you have already been rolling the issue over in your mind. But for them, it is new news.

I knew this was the first time Linda (or anyone other than my family) was hearing this, so her quick and immediate response took me back a bit.

Without even a second of hesitation, she said to me, "Oh, Tim, you would be perfect for that job!"

I thought, she must really want to get rid of me! What I said out loud, however, was, "Why do you think that?" And this is when I learned a lesson from this very wise teacher.

Linda said to me, "Because you are a compassionate man, but we are all just a little scared of you. You hold us accountable, but you generally do it with grace. That will serve you well."

Her response was meant to be a compliment, but I went home wondering, what was the real residue of the work life and effort I was leaving behind?

Was it a residue of fear? Compassion? Kindness? Retribution? Grace? Focus? Clarity?

MY HEARTPRINT 💟

Linda indicated that the faculty and my students knew I loved them. But they also knew I meant business, which in turn, created a small amount of compassion-based urgency to our work.

Wholeheartedness. Love. Compassion. These pursuits allow you to delight in and enjoy others. If I choose to love you, I do not do so out of obligation or duty. When you love your students and your colleagues, the thought of them should delight you, right?

Love and compassion give to and serve the one who is loved. The test of your heartprint for a fully formed heart (and this may take you a few years, as I am not sure I am completely there yet) is that you give love when there is *no expectation in return.*

This describes a type of love that takes the most ragged students who enter your path and creates value in them—so they can build value in others—forever. This is why our teaching profession is such a daunting day-to-day challenge. You have to be on your best game every day. Our profession is not for the weakhearted.

As we look at our students and our colleagues, do we see who they are intended to become? Do we see their potential? Do we understand and connect to their feelings? Do we really?

Sometimes I was so worried about my own ailments that I could not see the other persons in my professional life. I could not connect the dots of how my actions affected them. The residue of the work life and

Ask a trusted colleague, "Do I bind together compassion, humility, grace, and love with an appropriate sense of toughness? Am I too soft? Am I too hard? How could I be better at demonstrating compassion?"

_____

_____

_____

_____

_____

_____

_____

_____

_____

_____

_____

_____

_____

_____

_____

_____

_____

_____

_____

_____

_____

effort I was leaving behind was not in my rearview mirror; it was on the road right in front of me.

I just needed to look. Like when I first met Rebecca DuFour.

If you have had the pleasure to meet PLC at Work™ educational leader and author extraordinaire Rebecca DuFour, then like me, you have found her high level of compassion compelling. I went to Becky and asked her for advice on how to nurture compassion in the school culture. Here is what she had to say (R. DuFour, personal communication, May 23, 2016):

> Members of a school community—students and adults—can instill and nurture compassion in the culture of a school first and foremost by modeling compassionate behaviors. Ralph Waldo Emerson wrote, "What you are stands over you the while, and thunders so that I cannot hear what you say to the contrary."
>
> Treating others with kindness, care, concern, and consideration in our daily interactions will demonstrate what compassion "looks and feels like." But if we want those behaviors to permeate our school's culture—and we should—we can also communicate the importance of compassion in additional ways.
>
> For example:
>
> • Teach students to recognize and demonstrate compassionate behaviors during character education lessons, through shared stories, books, and real-world examples.
>
> • Celebrate and reward acts of compassion on a regular basis in classrooms and throughout the school. Create bulletin boards, showcases, sections of newsletters, awards, positive notes home to parents, and media stories that highlight specific examples of compassion within the school community.
>
> • Confront behaviors that are not congruent with compassionate acts. Help members of the school community understand that compassion is so important, you are willing to gently but firmly call attention to negative behaviors as a way of reinforcing positive ones.
>
> When compassion becomes part of a school's culture, the larger community benefits as those behaviors ultimately extend beyond the school walls.

Reflect on Becky's words about creating a more compassionate school culture, and then take the time for a final compassion, sympathy, and empathy check. Use the definition for each word.

Our passion works best when complemented by love and compassion. In Atlanta, Georgia, on February 4, 1968, as part of his final message before his assassination, "The Drum Major Instinct," Martin Luther King Jr. stated: "Everybody can be great. Because anybody can serve. . . . You only need a heart full of grace. A soul generated by love."[21]

Grace and love. Compassion and courage.

These are the elements that become the signposts of our heartprint greatness. These are not courses we take in our undergraduate teaching certification. And yet, they represent critical elements of the social justice mission and the responsibility of our work with students. They represent the life source of authentic happiness in the workplace. In the next chapter, we explore the love and hope required to achieve a school and classroom culture that sustains compassion for others.

MY HEARTPRINT ♥

Rank yourself 1, 5, or 10 on how well you understand and express these three feelings toward others during this current season of your professional life.

Compassion: "Feeling what it is like to live inside somebody else's skin."[18]

Sympathy: "The feeling that you care about and are sorry about someone else's trouble, grief, misfortune, etc."[19]

Empathy: "The feeling that you understand and share another person's experiences and emotions."[20]

Wanted: Persons of Positive Character and Hope

H   E   A   R   T

The most momentous thing in human life is the art of winning the soul to good or evil.

—Pythagoras

Your influence on others, without moral character, can lead to manipulation and inauthentic behavior. It can lead to potential actions of entitlement and selfishness. As you model the core values of the school culture, you influence your students and colleagues toward the essential voice, purpose, and the general "good" of the expected and agreed high-quality work of your school. As Pythagoras indicated, "You and I have a lot of power for good or for evil."[22]

The ability to make and keep commitments, the ability to manage your life well, and the ability to meet deadlines, to lead your students with good intentions, and to take responsibility for every area of your life represent actions of persons of positive character and maturity. Building such character requires a teachable and growth mindset.

Healthy schools are filled with adults that possess great character.

Over the years, I have learned positive character lessons from Becky DuFour. We have worked together at the Solution Tree PLC at Work Institutes since 2011. Toward the very end of a fall season of institutes, we shared some quiet time with her family and friends.

Becky shared with us a poem, "To Be of Use," from the book *Circles on the Water*, a collection of poems by Marge Piercy.[23]

Read Piercy's poem. Is there a phrase or thread that connects to you and your work as a professional educator, teacher, and leader? Mark or highlight on the poem and write about your thoughts.

_____

_____

_____

_____

_____

_____

_____

_____

_____

_____

_____

_____

_____

_____

_____

_____

_____

_____

_____

_____

_____

_____

To Be of Use

The people I love the best
jump into work head first
without dallying in the shallows
and swim off with sure strokes almost out
of sight.
They seem to become natives of that element,
the black sleek heads of seals
bouncing like half-submerged balls.

I love people who harness themselves, an ox to
a heavy cart,
who pull like water buffalo, with massive patience,
who strain in the mud and the muck to move
things forward,
who do what has to be done, again and again.

I want to be with people who submerge
in the task, who go into the fields to harvest
and work in a row and pass the bags along,
who are not parlor generals and field deserters
but move in a common rhythm
when the food must come in or the fire be put out.

The work of the world is common as mud.
Botched, it smears the hands, crumbles to dust.
But the thing worth doing well done
has a shape that satisfies, clean and evident,
Greek amphoras for wine and oil,
Hopi vases that held corn, are put in museums
but you know they were made to be used.
The pitcher cries for water to carry
and a person for work that is real.

Source: Piercy, 1982. Used with permission.

 # MY HEARTPRINT

I flew home from that meeting with Becky and our friends and immediately taped the poem to a cabinet door in my office. I wanted to use it to inspire my work every day. For me, I told Becky it was the last line: "A person [cries] for work that is real." I have wanted that kind of work my entire life.

How about you?

Is the work you do at your school every day real for you? Are you with people who want to submerge themselves into the task at hand? Can you feel that certain connectedness to your students?

In our profession, the work is too real sometimes. Just look into your students' eyes. What greater cause is there for you or for me than to give our life to the development and positive growth of children? To see them and give to them in a way that makes a difference? Our students and our colleagues represent the residue of the work life and effort we leave behind each year. Do our colleagues and our students become a greater asset to others because of us? The character development of the next generation is part of the heartprint we are leaving on the students in our classrooms or school; it is our use, as the poem title relates.

Look back at the title of this chapter: "Wanted: Persons of Positive Character and Hope." You might wonder why I intentionally use the word *persons* rather than *people*. For me and the purpose of *HEART!*, the word *people* refers to a generic group, while *persons* refers to thinking of each member of that group as an individual— a person with thoughts, feelings, and soul. The persons I refer to mean more to me than just a collection of people. They are personal to me. Hope manifests itself in the growth we experience when we positively redirect the life of so many individuals. When we choose to become teachers and leaders of positive influence and impact, we see the people we work with as more than just members of a group. We see each student and each colleague as a person with a heart and a soul just like ours.

Tom Rath of Gallup poll fame has written three international bestsellers. In one of his books, *How Full Is Your Bucket?* he provides a Positive Impact Test.[24] You can visit http://bit.ly/2atJSB4 to find the test and other resources on positive impact statements. You can also go online to take the positive impact test and see how you score! When you take the test online, respond to each statement with *yes* or *no*, and as Rath indicates, do not worry if your initial score is too low. Following are two statements from the test. When I first took the test, I could not say *yes* to either of these statements!

I have helped someone in the last twenty-four hours.

I have praised someone in the last twenty-four hours.

MY HEARTPRINT ♥

After you complete the online test, choose one specific descriptor for which you responded *no*, and work on it for the next few months. You can write about your choice and describe how you can work to make your response a *yes*! Come back to this section of the book a few months from now and see how you are improving with your positive impact effort.

_____
_____
_____
_____
_____
_____
_____
_____
_____
_____
_____
_____
_____
_____
_____
_____
_____
_____
_____
_____
_____

It's funny. *Hope* is a word we overuse quite a bit. Yet, I have learned over the years that hope indicates there is a better future ahead. We say things like "I hope to get there someday." Hope alone won't get you to your destination, but hope provides the opportunity to travel there. *Merriam-Webster* defines *hope* as follows: "To want something to happen or be true and think that it could happen or be true."[25]

I tend to think of hope more as something we *provide* to others. We provide students with the hope and the expectation of learning. We provide our colleagues with a vision of a better tomorrow and the hope of its expectations. Becky DuFour is an example of a hope provider. It is why so many educators are drawn to her work.

When Gallup asked adult workers the questions: "What leader has the most positive influence in your daily life?" and "What three words best describe what this person contributes to your life?," the respondents produced four categories of responses. One of the four primary categories was *hope*. When asked what hope meant to them, respondents indicated three general categories.[26]

1. Hope is about direction—where are you taking me?
2. Hope is about faith—you know where to take me.
3. Hope is about guidance—you will help me own how to get there.

MY HEART PRINT ♥

Hope is about direction—where are you taking me?

Hope is about faith—you know where to take me.

Hope is about guidance—you will help me own how to get there.

Think about these three descriptors and check them off. How would your students or colleagues rank you on each of these hope characteristics? Give yourself a 1, 5, or 10, with 1 being not very good, 10 being awesome, and 5 meaning you are working on it. Defend your rating!

I once listened for twenty-five minutes as the leadership team of a large school district in the Pacific Northwest proceeded to tell me many of the difficult issues they faced. The faculty, staff, and students were generally joyless. The onsite administration echoed a lack of faith and hope in the staff. Student achievement data had been stagnant for almost a decade. "Parents too?" I asked. "For sure," they said. "Parents have no idea how hard we work. And they are the least grateful of all for our efforts."

I had an overwhelming feeling there was no hope. If all was lost, if there was no hope, why try? So, I interrupted their monologue and asked, "Is there no hope?"

Without blinking or hesitation, they responded, "Yes! Of course!"

I responded, "Well, it does not sound like it to me. You speak as if there is no hope. You speak without joy. You speak without faith in your students and colleagues and community, and without a sense of guidance or direction that tomorrow could be better. If you really mean it, let's go recapture that hope and return to the joy in your work."

We then talked about how to bring hope and joy back to their school district's journey. I asked each of the leadership team members to write on poster paper three actions he or she could take to rebuild a culture of hope. In the next six weeks, what was one action for *direction*, one action for *faith*, and one for *guidance* that could impact his or her area of school leadership? Those posters, and the actions they inspired, reignited hope in their journey.

There is a very subtle comment in that last paragraph. Hope is more than some ideas on a poster. It is in the action of our work that hope finds a home; we become more empowered, and we recapture our joy in the journey.

The Joy-Gratitude-Stability Connection

 E A R T

When you express your gratitude, you will bring joy to others' lives. When others know joy, your life will be filled with happiness.

—Arthur Dobrin

Quick, who is the most joyful person you know? Write down his or her name. What makes this person so joyful day in and day out? Is he or she authentic? Real? Sincere? What other words might describe this person?

I suspect that person also works with a deep sense of gratitude. It is impossible to be joyful unless you are building gratitude into your heartprint every day. Author Brené Brown wrote the book *The Gifts of Imperfection*. In that book, she states, "Without exception, every person I interviewed who described living a joyful life or who described themselves as joyful, actively practiced gratitude and attributed their joyfulness to their gratitude practice."[27]

Notice her careful choice of the phrase *actively practiced gratitude*. That is, you and I take action and are expected to practice being grateful. We do not just talk about it or hope for it. We keep journals, we think intentionally about it, we consistently reflect on the statement *I am grateful for . . .*

Write an answer to the prompt *I am grateful for . . .* Can you connect your response to a joyful heartprint? What about the person you identified as the most joyful person you know? How would you describe his or her gratitude quotient, or GQ?

_____
_____
_____
_____
_____
_____
_____
_____
_____
_____
_____
_____
_____
_____
_____
_____
_____
_____
_____
_____
_____
_____
_____
_____
_____

 # MY HEARTPRINT

Dolores came running into my office and asked, "Are you mad at me?" I was a bit startled, and as my mind raced, I could not honestly think of any reason why I should be mad at her. She was a colleague of mine, an incredible worker with deep love for her students. She was, in fact, my answer to the most joyful teacher I knew. So, I said, "I don't think so, why do you ask?"

"You didn't place a smiley face on the note you left in my box! I figured something must be wrong." Dolores Fischer was by far one of the most motivating and inspirational teachers I knew. She had a joyful heartprint that was always obvious to others. And she was worried I was mad at her!

I assured her that my lack of a smiley face on her note was just an oversight. No worries. I had fallen into the pattern of placing smiley faces at the end of all my notes. This "retro" practice was way before the emoticon generation. I thought the work of our teaching life was hard enough that a smile, and a genuine thank you, just might boost my colleagues from time to time.

I observed this same idea at work in a positive way with students in Dolores's classes. She had a way of thanking them each day, of letting her students know how important they were and letting them know she was grateful to be their teacher. She found joy even for those students with difficult behaviors who at the moment "haven't to deserve it," as Dolores would say.

It was quite extraordinary. Dolores thought her job was to bring joy to the journey of others, which, in turn, brought great joy and happiness to her and, as you can imagine, her students.

Be careful not to assume that Dolores had some grand and great happiness in life. She did not. She was a single mom for much of her career and raised two great children. Life was not always easy for her, but her *choice* of gratitude sustained her. She was one of those silent heroes. She was a person who chose not to act like a victim. She chose joy, she practiced gratitude, and her students and colleagues returned the favor. She was forever young with her ideas to create lessons that would be fun for her students, while keeping the rigor bar high toward the essential learning standards.

Placing smiley faces on notes may not be what works for you. What needs to work is any way you show gratefulness and find joy that is genuine in your heart. Ultimately, only *you* know your true intent. My only advice is to make sure you show gratitude out of a desire to respect and show care for your students and colleagues.

Ultimately, if you do not practice a grateful heart during this school season, then your positive heartprint will start to fade and slowly erode the joy in your professional journey. Can you find the peace that comes with a youthful heart and spirit no matter what age you are and what bridge you need to cross each year? The answer lies partly in understanding the role you play as a stable force in the life of your students and your colleagues.

Joy and gratitude are connected to stability as well. This joy-gratitude-stability connection serves happiness in our daily work.

When Gallup asked adults the questions, "What leader has the most positive influence in your daily life?" and "What three words best describe what this person contributes to your life?," respondents produced four categories of responses, such as *compassion* and *hope*. A third major category was *stability*. When asked what stability meant to them, respondents indicated three general characteristics: (1) strength, (2) support, and (3) peace.[28]

MY HEARTPRINT ♥

Reflect about evidence of these three characteristics of stability in your work life.

Stability is about strength—
We can do this!

Stability is about support—
I will be there when you fail.

Stability is about peace—
I will demonstrate gratitude and joy toward you.

How would your students or colleagues rank you on each of these stability characteristics? Give yourself a 1, 5, or 10, with 1 being not very well, 10 being awesome, and 5 meaning you are working on it.

Answer *yes or no to* each of the previous stability questions, and think through why you might have responded *yes* to any of them.

What is your strategy to stay in a place of stability, supporting others while not letting them rob you of your day-to-day joy?

_____

_____

_____

_____

_____

_____

_____

_____

_____

_____

_____

_____

_____

_____

_____

_____

_____

_____

_____

_____

_____

_____

_____

_____

Ultimately, you are constructing your professional life as each season of your career unfolds. As I have mentioned, the quality of the choices you make determines the quality of your character and thus, your positive emotional impact on others. You can determine if your character is one of *stability* for the students and colleagues influenced by your actions and choices by considering these questions.

- Am I overly eager to please? Do I find myself looking for others' approval to validate my choices?
- Do I struggle to make good decisions? Do I lack clarity and hesitate to commit to what I think is right or good?
- Am I anxious when I receive a little criticism from the wrong source? Does it leave me feeling defeated and not wholehearted?
- Do I sometimes lack integrity? Instead of freely saying what I believe, do I calculate and adjust my words to fit more closely with what I think the other person wants to hear?

♥ MY HEARTPRINT

In general, the joy-gratitude-stability connection leads to greater happiness and creates an impact on your achievement as a teacher and leader. And by achievement, I mean your overall effectiveness and impact on student learning.

There is one more heartprint happiness issue to address throughout your career. It may seem odd, because it means understanding what is worthy of being *unhappy* about.

What are the events in your professional life that are worthy of your tears?

Why Should We Weep?

H E A R T

When you are sorrowful look again in your heart, and you shall see that in truth you are weeping for that which has been your delight.

—Kahlil Gibran

This chapter title may seem like a strange question. As professional educators, what makes us weep? Perhaps you might think I am referencing the figurative sense. But I am not. I do mean this literally. When is the last time you shed tears over your students or your colleagues?

Merriam-Webster defines the word *weep* as just that: "To express deep sorrow for [something] usually by shedding tears."[29] The definition doesn't state whether it is public or private, but for me, there have been three occasions when I felt the deep need to weep as a professional. Two were private, and one was public.

In every case, as Gibran indicates in the opening quote,[30] I was weeping because I knew better, meaning I knew what could be and wept at the stubborn absence of the possibility. In the following text, I explain one example and then ask you to write your personal story. By definition, weeping requires deep sorrow in our professional life, not shallow sorrow or the everyday annoyances. I think, too, weeping requires a certain degree of deep caring.

I sat in the parking lot in my car. It was 11:18 a.m. I called my wife Susan, who was, at the time, working two time zones away from me. She too was often on the road for her job, and it was one of those rare during-the-day moments when I just needed to connect with her. This was something we normally did not do during the day, as over the years, we fell into the habit of connecting at the end of our workdays. I prayed she would pick up, and she did. All I could do was cry. I could not even muster a *hello*.

Giving me some space, she eventually asked, "Everything okay?" My sadness seemed strange to me in that I did not know the persons for whom I was weeping that morning. I had never been to this poverty-stricken middle school before. The student population was mostly Latino, where English was not the primary language. And that day I was only there for about four hours. During that time, the principal described to me all the reasons why he could not get the students or staff in his school to perform better. When I asked him if there was no hope, he mostly agreed. It was spring, and he relayed to me his plan to leave for "a better building" job next year.

As I talked with the teachers, I discovered that—from their perspective—the real reasons for the lack of student success were all factors out of their control: a faulty central office (lack of support for the teachers), excessive student absenteeism, and required testing.

"The students just don't care," they told me.

"How many don't care?" I asked.

"Most of them," they replied. *Don't blame us* was their implied tone.

As I observed classes, I saw most of them filled with students. Some of them were not paying attention, but most were polite, took notes, and did exactly as they were told. Most sat in rows and quietly faded away.

I saw many things being taught that were just wrong. I took notes and left some feedback, but overall, I felt like I was applying a bandage on a gaping wound, a wound so ugly that almost 52 percent of the students were failing the classes, and the teachers were blaming the students for the failure. Feeling like victims, they asked me, "What do you expect us to do?" So, when I reached my car, I wept.

It is rare that I am so overwhelmed I don't know where to start. The culture of this school was void of hope. Both the students and the adults were suffering. The heart and soul of this school were missing. My eventual response is partially revealed in part 3, "A Is for Alliances," when we talk about the PLC life of collaboration. Collaboration is the engine that drives a school culture and ultimately the agreed-upon covenants for improving the school. At that moment, there was no collegial collaboration and certainly no covenants, agreements, or meaningfulness to the expected work of the adults.

The reason I sat weeping is because I knew better. As Gibran said, "When you are sorrowful look again in your heart, and you shall see that in truth you are weeping for that which has been your delight."[31]

I knew the delight of schools that had overcome these barriers. I wept for the reality and the shame for my profession and its service to this community.

I recently mentioned this story to my friend, colleague, and fellow author Luis Cruz, when we were working together in San Antonio. Luis, an outstanding school leader, in collaboration with a committee of teacher leaders at Baldwin Park High School (just east of Los Angeles), received California's prestigious Golden Bell Award from the California School Boards Association for significantly closing the achievement gap between the general student population and students learning English as a second language.

As an elementary, middle, and high school principal, Luis helped schools just like the one I visited on that fateful morning to find their hope and take action to overcome their language and poverty barriers. In reflection, I asked Luis if he would send me a written note of what he had said to me, as it had touched me deeply. Here is what he said:

> We have reached a point in education whereby public school educators, especially those who teach in low-income communities, must embrace the reality that we do more than just teach reading, writing, and arithmetic to students, we break kids free from the cycle and wrath of poverty. Those of us who choose to teach in ghettos and barrios must not only provide a sense of hope to a community drenched in hopelessness, but must be willing to change archaic policies, practices, and procedures in schools that were never designed to address issues related to poverty and a community's sense of helplessness. (L. Cruz, personal communication, June 10, 2016)

Take some time to dwell on his thoughts and any connection to your current school situation. If you could identify one aspect of your current school culture that fails to address issues related to poverty or a community's sense of helplessness—what would it be?

When you are connected to your heartprint for teaching and leading students and colleagues, there is a profound understanding of what it is about your students, school, and culture that is worthy of your tears. Take some time to read and respond to the My Heartprint on page 46.

Describe a time and the event when you wept for your students, your colleagues, or your school.

Describe your response in the aftermath of the event.

_____
_____
_____
_____
_____
_____
_____
_____
_____
_____
_____
_____
_____
_____
_____
_____
_____
_____
_____
_____
_____
_____
_____
_____
_____
_____

 # MY HEARTPRINT

Take a close look at your story. Compare it to the following seven types of situations we should weep for in our schools. Does your story fit one of these situations? If so, which one? If not, how might you provide a new situation for the list?

1. Students become marginalized, and no one notices them.
2. Students are viewed as interruptions to the workday.
3. Flaws in work-life conditions prevent equity or cause inequity in students' lives.
4. Teachers and leaders are more worried about data than the students (the persons) represented by the data.
5. There is a confusion between working for money versus working for meaning.
6. Inequities exist in student rigor and learning experiences because of the failure to reach agreements on learning standards, assessments, and homework expectations.
7. Teachers and leaders seek to control and not liberate student empowerment and thinking.

This takes me back to the teacher strike at Community High School District 94 that I mentioned in chapter 1. In the end, the strike had very little worth weeping over. Teachers lost a week of pay, and that hurt. For three years, my salary was frozen, and that hurt. Contract language was changed to provide some better working conditions, but you cannot legislate or contract happiness.

Eventually, pay increases and better working conditions were helpful. But none of those things caused or were rooted in the happiness of our teachers and leaders. Getting paid really well in a culturally dead place like the middle school I described is still a really bad job.

Getting paid well enough to work in a place that understands the conditions of happiness and the motivations of change based on actions worth weeping over—that is a culture worthy of your time, energy, and effort.

Why? It means you are contributing to a professional workplace culture that embraces the heartprint of teaching and leading each other and your students—a workplace culture that although never perfect, finds happiness in the colleagues and the students that come together every day.

FINAL THOUGHTS

The World Happiness Report

 E A R T

The ending of this part of the book is about eudaimonia.

Eudaimonia? What is that?

Persons who are emotionally more positive and thus happier, who generally have more satisfying lives, and who live in happier communities, are more likely both now and later to be healthy, productive, and socially connected.

The *World Happiness Report 2013* reveals:

> Subjective well-being has an objective impact across a broad range of behavioral traits and life outcomes, and does not simply follow from them. They observe the existence of a dynamic relationship between happiness and other important aspects of life with the effects running in both directions.[32]

The report goes on to state:

> In the great pre-modern traditions concerning happiness, whether Buddhism in the East, Aristotelianism in the West, or the great religious traditions, happiness is determined not by an individual's material conditions (wealth, poverty, health, illness) but by the individual's moral character. Aristotle spoke of virtue as the key to eudaimonia, loosely translated as "thriving." Yet that tradition was almost lost in the modern era after 1800, when happiness became associated with material conditions, especially income and consumption.

> This chapter explores that transition in thinking, and what has been lost as a result. It advocates a return to "virtue ethics" as one part of the strategy to raise (evaluative) happiness in society.[33]

Happiness in our professional workplace is a positive emotional state of being, a state your students and colleagues need you to be in every day. But it is not nirvana. And it is not free. It comes with a price. It is a tax on your energy, engagement, and ability to respond when all you really want to do is rest and, sometimes, weep.

Passion, love, compassion, hope, joy, gratitude, and stability—these are all elements of happiness and a better present. There is a balance of emotions, perseverance, and purpose for finding happiness and achievement in your work and in connecting or reconnecting to your calling as a teacher and leader of others—students, parents, and colleagues.

MY HEARTPRINT ♥

Reflect on part 1 and the past seven chapters. What are your primary takeaways?

Include two or three possible actions you can take as you continue your journey in this important aspect of your work life.

Think of the next steps as *I will* . . . statements, and write them down as you measure your personal heartprint during this stage of your career.

Know there will never be enough time to meet the demands and all that is required in your daily professional work as a teacher and leader. A person who delivers above and beyond the norm as a normal way of professional life understands that time is a *constant*. It is a fixed quantity—twenty-four hours in one day.

That same person, however, also understands that energy is a key ingredient to full engagement at work. Your energy is as variable as you allow it to be, and your engagement in your work is a choice. Your energy becomes the secret ingredient to your engagement in work and in life.

The following resources are instrumental in the support of our work together in part 1. Depending on your personal interests, you may use these resources as you continue to expand your knowledge base and the knowledge base of your colleagues. You may also visit **go.SolutionTree.com/HEART** to access direct links to the websites and download three additional chapters related to part 1.

Part 1: H Is for Happiness

Resources

Brown, B. (2012). *Daring greatly: How the courage to be vulnerable transforms the way we live, love, parent, and lead.* New York: Penguin.

Grant, A. (2014). *Give and take: Why helping others drives our success.* New York: Penguin.

Hattie, J. (2012). *Visible learning for teachers: Maximizing impact on learning.* New York: Routledge.

Rath, T., & Clifton, D. O. (2004). *How full is your bucket? Positive strategies for work and life.* New York: Gallup Press.

Seppälä, E. (2016). *The happiness track: How to apply the science of happiness to accelerate your success.* New York: HarperCollins.

Additional Resources

- Brené Brown's website: www.brenebrown.com
- Emma Seppälä's website: www.emmaseppala.com
- *The World Happiness Report 2013*: http://unsdsn.org/wp-content /uploads/2014/02/WorldHappinessReport2013_online.pdf
- *The World Happiness Report 2016*: http://worldhappiness.report
- More on student demographics and populations from the National Center for Education Statistics: http://nces.ed.gov/fastfacts/display.asp?id=28
- The Positive Impact Test and more resources on positive impact statements: http://bit.ly/2atJSB4
- More on John Hattie's work: http://visible-learning.org
- More on Adlai E. Stevenson HSD 125's story: www.d125.org/about

PART 2

DEVELOPING HEART

E

Is for Engagement

Essential Heartprint Question: Are you an inspiring person with the day-to-day energy required to be fully engaged in your work life?

We cannot dream of a utopia in which all arrangements are ideal and everyone is flawless. Life is tumultuous—an endless losing and regaining of balance, a continuous struggle, never an assured victory. . . . Every important battle is fought and re-fought. We need to develop a resilient, indomitable morale that enables us to face those realities and still strive for every ounce of energy to prevail.

—John W. Gardner

In part 2, "E Is for Engagement," we explore the role that energy and effort play in your pursuit of a fully formed and exceptional professional life. What are the heartprint actions you can take and the conditions you create if you choose to be fully engaged in your work life every day? Will you choose to fight and re-fight every battle? Will you choose to use and reuse every ounce of energy and effort necessary to positively impact children and adults? Will you choose to become great at managing your energy resources?

Will you choose?

You and I have a lot of influence. That influence manifests itself in the person we become and the high positive energy we bring to work each day. In the following seven chapters, you will discover that energy and not time is the human capital you need to develop and protect if you wish to live a fully engaged and grace-filled work life.

And, you might be surprised, but you will discover that the vast majority of adults in our profession is not fully engaged in its work. This can damage the culture for learning in your school or district. In a 2014 report, Gallup states:

> Disengaged teachers are less likely to bring the energy, insights, and resilience that effective teaching requires to the classroom. They are less likely to build the kind of positive, caring relationships with their students that form the emotional core of the learning process.[34]

In other words, full engagement, effort, and positive energy at work are necessary and never-ending improvement pursuits for every one of us when we choose education as our profession. This includes administrators too. Imagine if we rewrote the Gallup quote and just changed a few words (italicized):

"Disengaged *administrators* are less likely to bring the energy, insights, and resilience that effective teaching requires for the school culture. They are less likely to build the kind of positive, caring relationships with their *teachers* that form the emotional core of the learning process."

If you and I are not currently able to locate a positive, high-energy state in our daily teaching and leading lives, then we are expected to be mindful of it, nurture it, and define it until it becomes part of who we are as professionals. It is my intent in these chapters to provide some insight into how to grow in your full and positive engagement as an educator—each and every day.

As we lead a more purposeful professional life, a life committed to some of the happiness factors listed in part 1, we are more likely to move toward a fully engaged professional life. Strangely, however, you can score yourself high on the happiness criteria, find yourself somewhat satisfied by your work as a teacher and leader, and still be noncommittal toward high engagement with your work life.

MY HEART PRINT 🩶

Thus, part 2 provides a road map to help you stay emotionally connected to the work of your profession.

Do you wonder from time to time what would possibly compel students or colleagues to follow you? I know I did. Early in my teaching career, I distinctly remember sitting in my classroom late one night after a basketball practice, imagining I was a student in my own class and wondering, "Would I even enjoy being led by me? Am I really an engaging and inspiring teacher to my students?" The answer at the time was a little frustrating. I just wasn't completely sure I could say *yes*. I liked teaching, but the job often overwhelmed me.

In the next seven chapters, we will go on a journey in pursuit of the energy balance necessary to pursue a professional life that becomes inspiring to others.

We will connect to strategies that prevent our drift away from full engagement at work, clarify the time-energy dilemma faced in the pressure and pace of daily life, learn to become grittier, and examine how to use our own personal stories to inspire others.

After all, it is why we became teachers and leaders, is it not?

To get started, consider two work engagement questions.

1. Do you care so much about teaching students well that you are willing to stay committed to teaching and give it your best energy and effort every day?

2. Are you still in love with teaching and leading others? More important, do you believe you are currently fully engaged in your work?

_____

_____

_____

_____

_____

_____

_____

_____

_____

_____

_____

_____

_____

_____

_____

_____

_____

_____

_____

_____

_____

_____

Full Engagement *Not* Ahead

H   A   R   T

Throw yourself into some work you believe in with all your heart, live for it, die for it, and you will find happiness that you had thought could never be yours.

—Dale Carnegie

The title of this chapter may give away the answer, but take a guess by estimating what you believe is the percentage of teachers actively engaged in their work at your school. Think of all of the educators: teachers, administrators, and staff who are part of your professional work life.

MY HEARTPRINT ♥

Where exactly do you go to find such information? The Gallup polls, of course! You may not know it, but Gallup polls (named after George Gallup from Princeton) began in 1935[35]. The reputation of the Gallup polls and surveys over the years continues to bring insight and focus into the professional life of educators. So, back to our question: *What percentage of U.S. K–12 teachers do you think is fully engaged in its daily work?* In a 2015 Gallup report on engagement among U.S. teachers, respondents indicated whether they were *engaged, not engaged, or actively disengaged* at work based on responses to questions about workplace

What percentage of your colleagues do you think is actively engaged in its work each day? Describe your reasoning. How would you define *actively engaged*?

_____
_____
_____
_____
_____
_____
_____
_____
_____
_____
_____
_____
_____
_____

elements with proven links to performance outcomes.[36] Gallup described three categories of engagement as follows.

1. *Engaged* teachers are involved with, enthusiastic about, and committed to their work. They know the scope of their jobs and constantly look for new and better ways to achieve outcomes. (30 percent of all respondents)

2. *Not engaged* teachers may be satisfied with their jobs, but they are not emotionally connected to their workplaces and are unlikely to devote much discretionary effort to their work. Discretionary effort is a hallmark of measuring the teaching profession as meeting your passion and purpose. (57 percent of respondents)

3. *Actively disengaged* teachers are not only unhappy, but also act out their unhappiness in ways that undermine what their coworkers accomplish. (13 percent of respondents)[37]

Overall, only 31.4 percent or so of U.S. teachers fall into the *engaged in their work* category, matching the national average for all types of workers. It seems our profession is no better or worse than other professions in general. Only one problem—our work impacts the next generation of workers—our students.

Do these results surprise you?

I know I was surprised—shocked would be more like it. Our students need us to come to work every day fully engaged with a fully formed heart for the work. If only about 30 percent of the teaching workforce is fully engaged, what is happening to the students in the other 70 percent of classrooms? How have we fallen so short of the expectations and the hope provided by the heartprint our students and colleagues deserve from each of us?

Gallup uses a very interesting term to distinguish these three types of engagement: *discretionary effort.* Think about the colleagues you identified as actively engaged at work. Can you describe their willingness to give discretionary effort to their work each day? The following teachers, Mrs. V. and Mr. W., represent two examples from my life as a parent—one positive and one not so much.

When my daughter was in fifth grade, she had a veteran teacher we dubbed Mrs. V. (not the actual letter of her last name). Mrs. V. also had a previous career as a biologist, so she was a little bit older than most teachers in her thirteenth teaching season. From the very beginning of this new season, it was apparent our daughter loved Mrs. V., and she loved her students in return. *Great teaching is always a form of love* makes me think of Mrs. V.

At an open house a few weeks into the school season, you could sense a certain energy and excitement in her work. In a quick moment as the open house ended, I went back to her room. I asked her why she left her job as a biologist to teach elementary school and why she was teaching fifth grade. (This was the No Child Left Behind era, and a lot of pressure was placed on fifth-grade teachers.)

Her response was enlightening. She said, "My most highly energetic moments at work in the lab occurred for me when I was teaching others. We also had a student intern program with the local high school, and I always volunteered to take that person into my lab."

"Why fifth grade then?" I repeated.

"I just knew that was where my heart was. I wanted to be with kids this age," she replied.

Throughout the year, I had many conversations with Mrs. V., partly because she drove me crazy as the new authority in my household. Whenever a topic would come up at the dinner table, both my wife and I would give our (or so we thought) very learned thoughts and opinions. Then our eleven-year-old daughter would jump in and say, "But Mrs. V. says it is like this!" For a full year, we had no knowledge credibility with our own daughter, as compared to the likable Mrs. V.

One final note about Mrs. V. is that she was well on her way to becoming a fully formed professional. She did not yet understand the unintentional inequities she caused for the students in her school, because she worked in isolation from the other fifth-grade teachers. She excelled at the H and E elements of her heart for teaching and would eventually pursue that same excellence in the A and R parts, as she and the culture of her elementary school began to change.

As Gallup would claim though, Mrs. V. was engaged!

By contrast, in eleventh grade, my son had Mr. W. (again, not the actual letter of his last name) for a college advanced placement (AP) social studies class. Mr. W. also was a veteran teacher and had been at the school for almost twenty-four seasons. This was his first school season of teaching this AP class, however. From the beginning, our son was in angst over this class. He liked the subject but found the class disengaging and flat.

Initially, I took his complaint with a grain of salt because, after all, he was a high school junior. And then, the open house occurred. That late-August evening, I sat in the classroom in one of seven rows with several parents and listened as Mr. W. faced the screen at the front of the room, lectured parents on his rules and outline for the course, and

Take a moment and think about one of your colleagues who you believe is fully engaged in his or her work and one colleague who is not as engaged. How would you describe why he or she is or is not engaged in his or her professional work life?

_____

_____

_____

_____

_____

_____

_____

_____

_____

_____

_____

_____

_____

_____

_____

_____

_____

_____

_____

_____

_____

never once engaged with us or looked at us. This brief interaction at the open house verified what I thought might be true. Gallup would describe Mr. W. as an actively disengaged and unhappy teacher.

As the year went on, the most glaring aspect of Mr. W.'s daily work was his lack of preparation. He used the notes from another teacher of the AP course and lectured those notes to his students the entire class period. The students were to be quiet, not talk, and copy down all of the notes. My son informed me that he had stopped listening to Mr. W. and just read the book, took his own notes, and mostly spent class time on other work.

Mr. W.'s disconnect with his students further exacerbated the lack of creativity, joy, and interest in the subject matter. And, although I was not a teacher in his district (I was working in a school district about twenty-six miles away), I asked him if I could meet with him and observe a few of his classes. I wanted to verify my perceptions of his instruction, and not just rely on innuendo and hearsay from students, parents, and some of his colleagues who played on my men's softball team in town.

Here is an important school culture question: *How was Mr. W. allowed to make decisions that would not only reflect disengagement for his work each day but also promote his students' disengagement?*

MY HEARTPRINT

I am sure you are a bit bothered by my description of Mr. W.'s teaching. And, we must wonder, what on earth was the vision for instruction in the social studies department of the school? And so, when I met with Mr. W., and after my class visits verified his methods of lesson design and teaching, I asked him: "What is your vision for actively engaged student learning as part of your instruction in this course? And is your vision aligned with the vision for instruction in your department and the school?"

These questions began his social studies department on a journey of engaging one another into the purpose for and evidence of learning in the curriculum. It was a first step toward engaging Mr. W. into his work.

Engaged educators are more likely then to contribute to a professional culture where discretionary effort is the norm, and they also are more likely to view their work as being part of something bigger than themselves. Teachers and leaders who are not engaged highlight the subtle difference between satisfaction and engagement in their work. Satisfied teachers and leaders tend to answer the question, How good do I *have to* be? Engaged teachers and leaders tend to answer the question, How good *can* I be?

Gallup notes that engaged teachers in the United States enjoy a substantially higher level of purpose and well-being compared with their less-engaged colleagues.[38]

In addition to the individual benefits of an engaged teacher workforce, positive outcomes have been traced to students whom highly engaged teachers and leaders serve, as well as the school systems where they work. Gallup's report *State of America's Schools*[39] highlights a link between teacher engagement and student engagement—and thereby, student achievement. Visit http://bit.ly/1THTwjW to read the report and learn more.

There is more good news, however. Since Gallup published these 2014 findings in their 2015 report, in February 2017, Gallup reported 35.1 percent of U.S. workers were engaged based on their daily tracking of workplace engagement.[40] This was the highest level obtained up to that date.

For our profession, there does not need to be a ceiling on teacher and leader engagement at work. Is 34.1 percent really the best we can do? I know your school could score higher. I know the level of engagement we eventually experienced at Stevenson was much higher, although we never measured it. It was more of a general understanding and commitment to becoming more engaged in our work.

We can get better at our personal level of engagement at work, even on the toughest of days. The remaining chapters in part 2 help describe how we can do this.

9

Getting Engaged!

H   **E**   A   R   T

You have to want to be engaged. There has to be a deep-seated desire in your heart and mind to participate, to be involved, and to make a difference.

—Timothy Clark

Have you heard of the Elementary and Secondary Education Act (ESEA)? No Child Left Behind (NCLB)? Every Student Succeeds Act (ESSA)? The U.S. Congress legislated these acts in 1965, 2001, and 2015, respectively.

In 2001, the ESEA was reauthorized and renamed as NCLB. It became a very public and political football (mostly due to the issue of required state-level assessments) until its revision in 2015, when the original 1965 ESEA was renamed and reframed once again as ESSA.[41] Under ESSA, states now may reduce the role student assessments play in school ratings and accountability in favor of other factors, such as school climate, teacher engagement, have student access to advanced coursework.

Of all these factors, teacher engagement and, I would add, staff and administrative engagement, have the greatest potential to make a significant impact on student learning.

What exactly is teacher, administrator, and staff—adult—engagement at work?

To help answer the question, let me ask you one. Imagine you are being interviewed for a job at Stevenson, my place of work for twenty-two years. How would you answer this question? "Describe for me one of the best days you ever had at work. It is the end of a long day, you are at home, and in reflection you just knew it was a great day."

I am listening for your excitement about being authentically engaged in your work. Is there evidence of an emotional commitment that demonstrates how much you care about your work, your students, and your school? Is there evidence you are loyal to the work and

What is your personal response to the *engagement at work* definition and the voluntary discretionary effort given for improved student learning? How well does it align with your thoughts about your work effort and engagement each day?

_____
_____
_____
_____
_____
_____
_____
_____
_____
_____
_____
_____
_____
_____
_____
_____
_____
_____
_____
_____
_____
_____
_____
_____
_____
_____

to your current school's culture? Are you excited that your students "just got it" on that day you describe?

I have learned over the years that teachers and administrators deeply engaged in the nature of our professional work don't just do the work for a paycheck or just for the next promotion; instead, we work on behalf of and are willing to engage in the continuous improvement of the school's commitment to an adult and student learning process—every day.

When adults in our profession care—they are engaged in their work—they use discretionary effort and seek better solutions. They become more intimate with their work. This leads me to my personal definition for engagement at work: *the emotional energy and discretionary effort you give to students, the school, and district and to their vision for improved student learning.*

Take a minute to slow down and dwell on this *engagement at work* definition.

MY HEARTPRINT

Highly engaged educators understand their work as something bigger than themselves. They do not make excuses or place blame on others. They look in the mirror and ask what can they do differently to help students and colleagues improve learning. They take action. The engaged teacher and leader reaches out to one more student, leans into a difficult colleague, surprises a parent with a positive phone call, and demonstrates a constant awareness of others.

The engaged counselor, social worker, nurse, or teacher and leader, makes an additional call home for that struggling student, makes appointments to meet with support staff for an underachieving student, and takes a stand with colleagues against inequities in student learning, even when the principal, parent, or boss isn't watching.

The engaged principal or superintendent teacher and leader takes the time to notice and attend important events, takes the extra step needed to model the behavior expected of other adults, listens to colleagues at all levels of the organization, celebrates teacher effort and accomplishment, and builds trust via meaningful and formative feedback to all colleagues.

In general, when we are fully engaged, you and I become intimate with our work, our colleagues, and our students. We own the problems and the solutions to all that is going on around us. Many of you reading this book may know education leader Rick DuFour from his 2016 book *In Praise of American Educators* or from his more than three decades of messages from the practitioner's lens about the profound impact of the Professional Learning Communities at Work™ culture on student and adult learning. You may have seen him on the big stage, and I am sure, have been moved by his wisdom and wit.

I have often thought that what makes his words so authentic is the way he engaged—lived and led—everything from which he spoke. There are many examples I could cite, but the one I was most impressed by is what we reference at Stevenson as our Freshman Mentor Program (or FMP).

At Stevenson, we were painfully aware that like most high schools, the freshman year is critical to overall student success and engagement during all four years of high school. Our highest failure rates occurred mostly in freshman-level courses, and the transition to high school expectations was a challenge for many students.

As principal and eventually as superintendent, Rick engaged our faculty in a meaningful discussion and design around the idea of a freshman mentor program. The lunchtime homeroom program eventually became a national model and has been widely written about and adopted by high schools across the United States[42], but that is not the point here.

At the FMP's inception, Rick understood the importance of engaging many stakeholders in owning the success of the program and driving the program from the lens of what was best for the freshman students. An example of engaging stakeholders was to look for other community members to support the freshmen, such as our fourth-year senior students. We carefully selected FMP leaders through a rigorous application and leadership training process. Each senior would be assigned five freshman students and would mentor those students from the start of the school year.

Five groups (twenty-five students) assigned to the same counselor would be given an FMP period during lunchtime with a faculty advisor and five senior leaders. This allowed the counselor to use the FMP once per week and work with the freshmen on their rosters.

The FMP also had a faculty member leader who worked with other faculty, the senior students, and the counselors to create an engaging curriculum during these twenty-five-minute meetings each day. The driving force behind developing the ownership of this new program was, of course, Rick DuFour. And now for my point: *Rick DuFour, superintendent, served as an FMP advisor.*

Fifth period, twenty-five to thirty freshman students, another five senior leaders, a counselor, and Rick, leading and modeling the way for all the other faculty advisors.

The man was engaged! And he was engaged with a variety of stakeholders, including the parents of the students in his FMP. It allowed him to continue to keep his pulse on the energy and inertia of the FMP. The story reveals another quality of highly engaged educators. Like Rick, they become intimate with their work.

One way to measure if you are fully engaged in your work is to consider the engagement statements listed next in the My Heartprint. If the statements reveal that you are not fully engaged, consider the root cause of your disengagement and remember, blaming someone else, such as colleagues or students, is not an option here!

MY HEARTPRINT ♥

For each statement, rank yourself as 1 for low, 5 if you are working on it, or 10 if you are awesome at it.

- I feel stretched and challenged but not so stretched that I am overwhelmed.
- I often take the time to provide recognition and positive affirmation to others.
- I find proactive ways to update colleagues and students on progress weekly.
- I have chosen work that I love to do every day.
- I have the energy to improve on my work every day.
- I keep practicing to get better at my work over and over and over.

Take a moment to reflect on your engagement progress. Choose a statement from the list for some intentional and deliberate practice over the next month or so.

Being happy or satisfied at work does not necessarily translate to being fully engaged, however. Many schools use teacher satisfaction surveys, and administrators and teachers talk about teacher satisfaction or administrator satisfaction.

However, satisfaction as a goal is a bar set too low. A satisfied educator might show up for his or her daily eight-to-four job without complaint. But that same satisfied educator might not either want to or be able to give the discretionary effort required on his or her own, and most will likely bail out if any given school season gets too tough.

Satisfaction isn't enough—not nearly enough to take care of your professional heartprint.

In fact, the best educators I know have never been fully satisfied with their work life. Like great artists, there is always one more way the final product could be a bit better. These educators relentlessly pursue ways to make improved student life part of their improved professional learning life and experiences.

Paraphrasing Jim Harter, a scientist at Gallup research, "Engaged employees are more attentive and vigilant. They look out for the needs of their coworkers and the overall enterprise, because they personally 'own' the result of their work and that of the organization."[43]

Rick DuFour was not only attentive and vigilant when it came to the success of the FMP and the impact on our students, but he was relentlessly engaged in it as well.

I believe engagement surveys should be our future pursuit and not satisfaction surveys. If we really want to measure the strength and heart of our school culture, then we should measure our stakeholder levels of engagement. As professionals, we really should never be fully satisfied with our work. Do you agree? This is true for students and parents too. Don't measure student and school culture with satisfaction surveys, measure it with questions about levels of engagement into the life and work of the school.

Our personal solution pathway for becoming more engaged with our professional work as educators begins with our choice to come to work each day with the requisite energy to do the job. If we don't have the energy, then there is limited chance we will become fully engaged.

We explore how to pursue these energy-based behaviors in the next few chapters.

It's Energy, Not Time

H   **E**   A   R   T

*The core problem with working longer hours is that time is a
finite resource. Energy is a different story.*
— Tony Schwartz and Catherine McCarthy

Our colleagues and, most important, our students need us to be in a positive emotional state (our definition of happiness in the workplace) at school. In addition, it is our responsibility and our benefit to also be fully engaged in our work. We hope that our professional work life—our decision to become educators—serves a deeper purpose for our being and connects us to our students and colleagues for a cause worthy of our best efforts (you could argue our families need the same level of engagement from us as well).

We start losing the time and speed necessary to get everything done as the school season progresses. Good intentions in August fade by November, just as New Year's resolutions in January fade by March. There just isn't enough *time* in the day to keep all of those home, work, family, and friend plates spinning efficiently. As they stop spinning, you can begin to lose all sense of balance.

So, you go into work earlier and stay later. By the end of the day, you have worked as hard and as many hours as humanly possible. You cannot answer one more email. You have done as many tasks as you could. Yet, there are still three texts; two WhatsApp messages; four Instagram, Snapchat, or Facebook photos to look at; tweets; or some other social media app response expected. You are tired. You have nothing left in the tank.

You need to go to bed. You are out of time in this day.

And yet, the work lingers.

Family needs linger.

You. Just. Need. More. Time.

Or so you think.

Dwell on the Schwartz and McCarthy ideas just for a moment. What words connect with you?

What is your response to the idea that the energy you bring to work each day is a renewable resource? It has no limitations.

_____
_____
_____
_____
_____
_____
_____
_____
_____
_____
_____
_____
_____
_____
_____
_____
_____
_____
_____
_____
_____
_____
_____
_____

Take a closer look at what energy thought leaders and authors of our opening quote to this chapter, Tony Schwartz and Catherine McCarthy, have to say:

> Defined in physics as the capacity to work, energy comes from four main wellsprings in human beings: the body, emotions, mind, and spirit. In each, energy can be systematically expanded and regularly renewed by establishing specific rituals—behaviors that are intentionally practiced and precisely scheduled, with the goal of making them unconscious and automatic as quickly as possible.[44]

♥ MY HEARTPRINT

Take heed: unlike time, your energy is not a fixed constant of twenty-four hours a day. And more important, you can engage in specific personal practices that renew your energy, and thus, your levels of engagement, every day.

It is why some of your colleagues—maybe even you—seem to be able to spin so many plates at once. And yet, if other colleagues—maybe even yourself—are asked to do one more thing, spin one more plate, increase one more expectation, they are going to scream!

What you may not realize is that it is not a question of enough time for all of your professional work expectations to get done. Rather, engagement in your work is a question of finding the requisite energy for completing the work.

Invariably, energy depletion happens to every educator sometime during the school year. Eventually, the speed of expectations, the pace of obligations, the *simpler, better, faster* mantra catches up to you—as a professional and as a human being. Your energy and your full engagement at work start to falter, and you just can't keep all the plates spinning—at work or at home. They start to tilt and fall on you, your colleagues, and your family.

Since the pace of your work, home, and health life can be relentless, a default solution for responding to the demands and regaining your balance is the modern notion of multitasking. You try to do more things at the same time as a way of catching up with your workday.

And superficiality wins the day.

You might be multitasking right now. As you read these words, what else are you doing? Listening to music? Checking your cell phone for text messages or signal beeps for incoming email? Running a load of laundry? Wondering about an overdue bill? Stressing about an unreturned phone call? Reviewing your child's homework? Watching HGTV? Looking at Snapchat? Liking a Facebook page photo? Monitoring a homework hotline for your students?

In the book, *The Way We're Working Isn't Working*, Schwartz quotes University of Michigan researcher David Meyer regarding training for efficient multitasking: "Except in rare circumstances, you can train [for efficient multitasking] until you are blue in the face and you'd never be as good as if you focused on one thing at a time. Period. That's the bottom line."[45] Schwartz goes on to say:

> We create plenty of distractions for ourselves by juggling tasks, making ourselves perpetually available to others, opening several windows on our computers, and focusing on whatever feels most urgent at the moment without regard to whether what we are doing is really important.[46]

That last line is the killer: *Without regard to whether what we are doing is really important.*

Ouch.

And even worse, at times I am tempted to blame others for why I am so busy and don't have the energy to get it all done. How about you?

Making excuses and blaming others (external factors) for your inability to get things done are sure signs that you—or those in your sphere of influence—are drifting into an energy crisis. In his 2007 book, *The Power of Story*[47], bestselling author and psychologist Jim Loehr provides insight into how you can penetrate the veneer of excuses like, "No one else who had my current job, my current home situation, or my personal life and health situation could find happiness, either."[48]

Why do we tend to blame others, especially the mysterious they, to justify our busyness? It is so much easier to just say, "*They* won't let us do this," "*They* are making us do this," or "*They* just don't understand our problems." One quick way to check the victim speak of your life is to observe the frequency with which you use the word *they* in conversations with your colleagues, students, or family members.

So, what is it like for you and your colleagues? How frequently at your team meetings or in personal discussions does the word *they* creep into your teacher talk?

Loehr refers to this multitasking tendency as the "because I can syndrome."[49] Why do I check emails while on vacation? Why do I text during family dinner? Why do I interrupt a conversation to take another call or return a text message? Why do I work every night until midnight? Why do I answer my cell phone during my daughter's concert? Why do I skip that afternoon workout? Why do I miss breakfast (other than coffee) every morning?

Because I can.

Everyone I know has this issue. I suspect that, at one time or another, you too have taken on too many tasks and become overwhelmed. The demands of managing work, family, and your personal health (and energy) make it impossible not to skirt the edges of faulty assumptions. Eventually, one of those areas, if not all three, begins to suffer.

Let's end this chapter by slowing down for a minute. Take a moment and assess how you are currently doing with multitasking and *because I can* default thinking excuses. Does this thinking drain your energy?

Becoming aware of any tendency to make personal excuses to rationalize your behavior is a first step toward denying the energy drain often caused by the *because I can* (get away with it without being challenged by my family or my peers) syndrome.

MY HEARTPRINT ♥

Describe two to three major
excuses you use on an ongoing basis that
are of the *blame others* or *because I can*
variety. Include excuses for things such as
why you cannot pass back tests right away,
why you can't give a colleague same-day
feedback, why you are late to a team
meeting, why you don't have time to exercise, or why you can't volunteer anymore.

Now that you are more aware of potential external excuses you might make, take the time to do what I refer to as a 3 × 3 execution card. Remember the last line of the Schwartz quote: ". . . focusing on whatever feels most urgent at the moment without regard to whether what we are doing is really important."

This advice should be well heeded. Is what you are doing today urgent or important? Or is it urgent *and* important?

A 3 × 3 execution card is a personal list of the three most essential actions you need to take in the next three weeks or you will lose the full engagement battle at work or with your family. These should be actions that are both urgent and important for success in your work life. Ask a colleague on one of your teams to create his or her personal list too, and see how his or her urgent *and* important list compares to yours. How might you support one another in completing the items on each person's list?

Now for the good news: there are additional strategies you and I can take to stop our engagement and energy drain during the school year. We study these actions next as we continue our journey to becoming more highly engaged, fully formed professional educators.

Name That Energy Quadrant

H   E   A   R   T

The challenge of great performance is to manage your energy
more effectively in all dimensions to achieve your goals.
—Jim Loehr and Tony Schwartz

Sports psychologist Jim Loehr and author Tony Schwartz wrote a *New York Times* bestseller, *The Power of Full Engagement*. In the book, they discuss the energy we bring to the workplace each day and provide a helpful grid that highlights the dynamics of our daily energy state based on negative to positive energy (the horizontal axis) compared against low to high energy (the vertical axis).[50]

I used an adapted version of their grid in my 2011 book *The Five Disciplines of PLC Leaders*.[51] You can visit **go.SolutionTree.com/HEART** to download a free copy of the grid. I have discovered that this Energy State Grid, as I call it, resonates with educators today more than ever.

<table>
<tr><td colspan="2" align="center">**High Energy**</td></tr>
<tr><td align="center">**Quadrant III**</td><td align="center">**Quadrant I**</td></tr>
<tr>
<td>

High Negative
Angry
Fearful
Anxious
Defensive
Resentful
</td>
<td>

High Positive
Helpful
Hopeful
Joyful
Connected
Confident
</td>
</tr>
<tr>
<td>

Low Negative
Depressed
Exhausted
Burned Out
Hopeless
Defeated
</td>
<td>

Low Positive
Reflective
Serene
Relaxed
Tranquil
Peaceful
</td>
</tr>
<tr><td align="center">**Quadrant IV**</td><td align="center">**Quadrant II**</td></tr>
<tr><td colspan="2" align="center">**Low Energy**</td></tr>
</table>

Negative Energy (left axis)   **Positive Energy** (right axis)

Imagine your own personal Energy State Grid, and write about your current energy state. In which quadrant are you currently residing as you read the words for each description? How are you doing? Has there been a moment this school year when you could feel yourself drifting toward Quadrant III behaviors? If so, write about that as well.

_____
_____
_____
_____
_____
_____
_____
_____
_____
_____
_____
_____
_____
_____
_____
_____
_____
_____
_____
_____
_____
_____

The grid highlights four possible energy states via four distinct quadrants.

1. **Quadrant I: High positive energy**—This energy state quadrant represents your full engagement at work. It is where your students and your colleagues expect you to exist each day. They would characterize you as helpful, hopeful, joyful, connected, and confident.

2. **Quadrant II: Low positive energy**—This energy state quadrant represents where you must spend time every day, week, month, and year or you will never sustain a Quadrant I work or family life. It is best described as a place where you are reflective, serene, relaxed, tranquil, and peaceful.

3. **Quadrant III: High negative energy**—This is the energy state quadrant that makes you very unpleasant to work with, drags down your students and colleagues, and makes it very difficult for you to be a giver at work. Colleagues would characterize you as angry, fearful, anxious, defensive, and resentful.

4. **Quadrant IV: Low negative energy**—This is the energy state quadrant that makes it very difficult for you to function as a teacher and leader and as a team member. It is a place that is very difficult to transition from without help and support. Colleagues would characterize you as depressed, exhausted, burned out, hopeless, and defeated.

♥ MY HEARTPRINT

The hope is that you can become the type of teacher and leader others want to be around. This will not be the case if you are in energy state Quadrants III or IV.

The hope also is that you will go to work and experience a Quadrant I life. The energy state described in Quadrant I is where you become fully engaged and more personally satisfied with your work. _It is in Quadrant I that you and I are most likely to experience optimal professional performance._

Your energy is high and positive, and that helps you to become a teacher and leader others will want to follow.

When working and living in Quadrant I, you are more likely to influence others (students and colleagues) toward a Quadrant I work life. When you are in Quadrant I, your speed issues start to dissipate. All of those hats you are trying to wear, all of the plates you are spinning, suddenly come into focus and seem more manageable. You have more time to dig deeper into your work and become less superficial with those closest to you.

In Quadrant I, you feel and act fully engaged at work. Yes!

I have studied (in more of a field-based, informal research kind of way) the nature of the Quadrant I teachers and leaders I have encountered across the United States. They tend to shun using victim talk and laying blame on other people. They also seem to have little acceptance of colleagues and peers who act like victims.

When I had a chance to work with the school leadership team (administrators and teachers) at Sanger Unified School District in California for a few years, I was struck by how no one on the team allowed victim speak to prevail. They were open and honest with each other about progress and areas in need of improvement, yet no one was negatively criticized for an idea on the table. Everyone consistently seemed to be in a positive energy state at work.

I also noticed that the Sanger Unified team (consisting of eight to twelve adults, depending on the meeting) tended to dig in at deeper levels of insight. They were connected to others on the team and to their faculty and very aware of how their words, actions, and inactions affected others. When I asked them how they achieved this Quadrant I type of work life, they reminded me of the 2.9 to 11.6 positivity ratio I had shared with them previously.

The what?

The team's *positivity ratios* while communicating with one another.

Without getting into too much detail, Jim Loehr shares the work of researchers Barbara Fredrickson and Marcial Losada, in which they conclude that business teams flourish with a positivity ratio for communication between 2.9 and 11.6. This means the number of positive words and comments coming from your mouth should be roughly between three and twelve for every one negative comment team members might make. In a marriage, the positivity ratio should be roughly between five and eleven positive words and comments![52]

Do you believe you give out three to twelve positive comments for every one negative comment to your students or colleagues, or perhaps your family? Think about this day and the nature of your comments to others. Better yet, ask someone you trust to let you know your positivity ratio for today!

 # MY HEARTPRINT

Energy state Quadrant I is a great place to be. A high positive, fully engaged, fully energized work life. There is one major problem, however. Most educators reading this book will spend their entire professional life trying to work and live in Quadrant I while fighting the natural drift into the high negative energy state behavior of Quadrant III.

Some educators can fight the drift alone. My experience reveals that is a rare individual. Most of us (including me) not only need to be intentional about stopping the drift but need to have the support of trusted colleagues, family members, and friends that call our attention to the drift and help us along our professional journey.

Avoiding the
Quadrant III Drift

H   E   A   R   T

*If you want to make a difference—not just today, but for many
years to come—you need to put your health and energy ahead of
all else.*

—Tom Rath

While I was working on this part of the book, I could sense my energy and
behavior drifting to Quadrant III—a high negative energy state. I did not say anything to
my family, but the pressure of the deadlines and the other work on my plate was getting
to me. All the pressure was sitting with me and quietly building up inside.

And then, out of the blue, while I was in the middle of writing this very section, our
youngest daughter (a college junior) burst through my door to excitedly announce her
grades for the second semester of her sophomore year (we had been waiting to hear the
results). My response was, "Can't you see I am busy here?! You know I have to get this
done!" Without a word, she withdrew. There it was on display for her to experience. My
Quadrant III high negative energy state behavior was not beneficial to either one of us.

To note, I love her—a lot. I care about her achievements and her life. My normal
response would be to enjoy the moment for and with her. But no. Not at that moment.
My drift made me selfish—look at me, look how important I am! It's all about me, me,
me, me! (I am beating my chest with my fists as I tell you this.) I was not in the high
positive energy state of Quadrant I where I could be connected to my daughter's world,
joyful for her effort and hard work, and encouraging to her. I was not in a place of grace.

An apology was both appropriate and given and, thankfully, I was forgiven.

I should not be too hard on myself though. We all drift to a Quadrant III high negative energy state at times. We just forget about the drift sometimes or get so busy we ignore the symptoms. Why didn't I stop the drift before my actions required an apology and more? Why didn't a friend or colleague or family member notice enough to stop my drift? And so, the drifting begins, and it sneaks up on you.

Have you noticed a colleague currently drifting toward Quadrant III behavior? It shouldn't be too hard to find someone from your team, course, or grade level, or for that matter, maybe someone from your family. Have you said anything to that colleague or family member? If not, what might you choose to say and do? How can you help stop the drift?

A few heartprint signs might alert you to a Quadrant III drift in yourself or others.

First is the speed of technology in your life—email, texts, Facebook, Twitter, Snapchat, Instagram, Periscope—can you name others? How do you currently keep these technology pressures manageable? Do you feel yourself drowning in the cascade of messages and expectations for immediate response? These issues do not include your additional responsibility to use technology appropriately in your lessons every day.

Such pressure!

Second, look at the quality of your relationships with those closest to you. Think about your family and friends in your inner circle. We tend to take those relationships for granted when the pressure is on. Do I really need to tell my wife today that I love her? I did that yesterday. Do I really need to call my oldest daughter and see how her new puppy is doing? I did that last week. Do I really need to call my best friend with Alzheimer's and see how he is today, knowing it will leave me mentally exhausted?

Yes. I really do need to take those actions.

Are your relationships starting to lack depth? Do you experience weaker connections and irritations with family and friends? How do you know?

A third sign of drift is lack of energy. You are constantly late and unable to keep up with tasks and feel tired all the time. Without realizing it, you lose your moral compass as the day or week progresses. During the school day and late in the afternoon, you notice an overall drag on your stamina that a good piece of chocolate just can't fix!

It is wise to surround yourself with colleagues who love you enough to tell you (with grace) when you are drifting to Quadrant III negative energy behaviors and bring you back to the more positive high energy Quadrant I.

Can you avoid the inevitable drift out of Quadrant I and into Quadrant III? Good news! Yes. You can at least delay the drift for as long as possible by engaging in five ongoing personal practices. Even if these deliberate practices seem obvious to you, ask yourself, "Am I intentionally *doing* these behaviors every week?" If you are, then you are most likely gaining the positive energy state behaviors necessary to stay fully engaged in your work. You are becoming someone who others find *inspiring*. Here's how you can do it!

First, hang out with exceptionally inspiring people. Some people are life bringers. They inspire us to be more inspiring to others. They add energy and zip to our work and our lives. They deepen our joy, add to our hope, and bring out the best in us.

Other people are life drainers. They suck the joy right out of us. They pull us over to Quadrant III, because they want us to join them.

We should be intentional about spending time and working with exceptionally inspiring people—those who give energy, not those who take it away. The question becomes, Which person brings you new energy each day, and does he or she know it?

MY HEARTPRINT ♥

Early in my career, I realized this person was my colleague Jerry Cummins. He was the type of person who inspired others. His values and beliefs were aligned with mine, and he was someone who always seemed ahead of me in certain ways. So, I chose him to inspire me. The only problem was, he did not know it!

So we went to breakfast one morning before work, and I told him, "I have chosen you to be an exceptionally inspiring person in my life. You need to start doing your job!" We laughed about the innocence of that moment, but the reality was, I needed him to notice me and inspire me, so that I, in turn, could do it for others. I needed him to help me prevent the drift!

Name a professional colleague who is exceptionally inspiring from your point of view. Think about why it seems to you that he or she leaves a positive heartprint and acts as a positive energy giver to you.

_____

_____

_____

_____

_____

_____

_____

_____

_____

_____

_____

_____

_____

_____

_____

_____

_____

_____

_____

_____

_____

_____

_____

Think about daily or weekly events that are exceptionally inspiring to you. Write them down. Do you intentionally engage in the activity in order to reenergize your engagement, effort, and work?

_____
_____
_____
_____
_____
_____
_____
_____
_____
_____
_____
_____
_____
_____
_____
_____
_____
_____
_____
_____
_____
_____

Second, participate in events that are exceptionally inspiring to you. For me, Scott Oliver is one of the best and most inspiring teachers I have ever known. Scott was a computer science teacher, AP computer science grader, and professional developer for the College Board. He was our chess club sponsor and much more during my years at Stevenson. What is fascinating about Scott is that he is so self-effacing. To meet him or talk to him, you would never know how great his teaching really was and how he was helping to lead the shifts taking place in a field like computer science, in which change is rapid.

Once I became superintendent, there were several times that I could feel my energy draining or when I had a moment of doubt about various battles that are part of the job. So, I would head over to Scott's computer science classroom, sneak into the back of the room, and just watch his joy in teaching his students and his subject. Scott never disappointed. Not once. I would walk out of his classroom charged up and willing to fight whatever battles were needed. Scott was well worth me giving my best effort to my job.

MY HEARTPRINT

Third, pay attention to the physical disciplines of eat, move, and sleep. Tom Rath writes about this in his 2013 book, *Eat Move Sleep*.[53] It was my ignoring of these exact habits that caused many of my heart (cardiovascular) problems described in the preface.

In this age of the Fitbit technology generation, you can instantly track and monitor your daily eat, move, and sleep activities. And now with the increased focus on these factors toward supporting our high positive energy state at school, this becomes an important and very personal issue to address. If you are ready for a deep dive into these heart and health factors, I highly recommend Rath's book. I provide a brief list of his resources at the end of part 2.

Following are a few highlights from Tom Rath for us to think about.

EAT. Rath reminds us that the quality of what we eat is far more important than the quantity. His suggestion is to identify the healthiest elements of diets you have tried over the years and build them into your lifestyle for good. He also suggests to daily: "Set your sights on foods that are good for your near-term energy and long-term health."[54]

When I was working on my doctorate in the late 1990s, I completely failed to follow Rath's advice. I completely ignored my long-term health (and the effects my eating had on my energy levels) by eating fried foods, refined carbohydrates, and lots of foods with extra sugar in them. My choices were not good for my heart health.

MY HEARTPRINT ♥

Rath makes it clear that eating well does not need to be complicated and suggests that eating healthy foods is much simpler than jumping from diet to diet.

MOVE. Make inactivity your enemy. Avoid long periods of sitting. My Fitbit tells me when it is time to stand. No wonder, as sitting is the enemy of energy renewal. Thank goodness we are in a profession in which for most of the day we stand in and among our students and colleagues.

You might find the following observations from Rath surprising—I know I did:

> On average, [Americans] spend 9.3 hours sitting down each day. . . . Watching your diet, and exercising 30 minutes a day will not be enough to offset your many hours of sitting. . . . Reducing this chronic inactivity [sitting] is even more essential than brief periods of vigorous exercise. . . . Exercise clearly helps, but it will not offset several hours of sitting.[55]

What is your plan to not sit so much during the day?

If you are interested in a deeper dive into the move aspect of maintaining a high positive energy state, I recommend Michelle Segar. Segar is a behavioral scientist and serves as the director of the Sport, Health and Activity Research and Policy Center at the University of Michigan. You can visit her website (http://michellesegar.com) to find her work. She is the author of *No Sweat*, and among many ideas she provides

Give yourself a grade on the EAT factor (1, 5, or 10, like before), and write about your current progress and future expectations. How do you know which foods are "good for your near-term energy and long-term health," as Rath suggests?

_____

_____

_____

_____

_____

_____

_____

_____

_____

_____

_____

_____

_____

_____

_____

_____

_____

_____

_____

_____

_____

_____

_____

Give yourself a grade on the MOVE factor (1, 5, or 10), and write about your current progress. How do you give physical activity clout as part of your daily agenda?

_____

_____

_____

_____

_____

_____

_____

_____

_____

Give yourself a grade on the SLEEP factor (1, 5, or 10), and write about your current progress. Are you at the eight hours and thirty-six minutes of peak performers or the six hours and fifty-one minutes of the average American worker?

_____

_____

_____

_____

_____

_____

_____

_____

_____

_____

that are compelling, is her directive in the book to "give physical activity clout"[56] as part of your daily activities, which resonated with me as a daily strategy.

Instead of complaining about the long walk from

♥ **MY** HEARTPRINT

the parking space at the airport, grocery store, or mall, I embrace the walk now. If my knees keep holding up, I will continue to avoid escalators and use the stairs on most days. I want to embrace that walk or those stairs and give them some clout!

SLEEP. Sleep longer to get more done. On average, "the best performers sleep 8 hours and 36 minutes a day."[57] Really? By comparison, the average American gets six hours and fifty-one minutes on weeknights, and more than 30 percent of workers sleep less than six hours. Rath suggests that working on a task too long can actually decrease your performance.[58] When you need an extra hour of energy, add an hour of sleep. Work in bursts and take breaks as needed. The bottom line is sleep longer tonight to do more tomorrow.

Fourth, pay attention to your working environment.

♥ **MY** HEARTPRINT

Attack! Those were the posters on the wall in his office. Imagine pictures of wolves, bears, and cheetahs, all with words like _attack_ on them. Add to the fact he was the district superintendent, and it seemed a bit like an intimidating office space to me. I did not know him very well at the time, but we were working on a project together, and this was my first time in his office. I was trying to decide if I should say something to him or not. He seemed like a nice guy, but I wasn't sure based on the posters, at least.

So, I gathered up the courage to finally ask him, "What's up with all the attack posters? Seems a bit intense to me!"

His response was immediate. "Oh, that's not for you. That's to remind me to come in to work every morning and attack the day!"

Made sense to me. I suggested to him, however, that maybe he should put up another poster that says something like, "Ignore all the posters in my office; these are for my daily inspiration, and not for you!" I never had the chance to visit his office again, so I don't know if he created that extra poster or not.

My office space is very messy. My wife's office space is amazingly neat. I don't know how she does it. In each case, our working environment inspires us the way we each need it to. What about you? What is inspiring about your working environment?

MY HEARTPRINT ♥

Fifth, have an inspiring recreation outside of your work world. I play on an over-fifty softball team. It's a bunch of ragtag guys who have been playing together a long time. We are a pretty funny bunch too. String and baling wire, KT tape, braces, and bandages hold our bodies together. If you hit a home run, you just go sit in the dugout. Of the twelve guys on the team, eleven have designated runners. No one wants to play in the outfield—he might need to run after the ball!

What is best about these fellow softball junkies is this: they really do not have interest in my professional work and do not want to hear about my problems. They just want to play softball and have a good time. They inspire me exactly because they pull me away from the pressure of my work life.

To be sure, the intent of an inspiring recreation outside your work world is not that it be a sport. Recreation can be anything. Maybe you play drums in a country and western band on the weekends. Maybe you are part of a poetry jam or a bird-watching group.

If you are interested in pursuing some of the eat, move, and sleep factors described in this chapter, Rath wrote a follow-up book in 2015 titled *Are You Fully Charged? The Three Keys to Energizing Your Work and Life*, which explains in great detail both the research and the actions you can take to gain the energy you need at school and at home to be fully engaged each day.[59]

What are specific elements of your current working environment that inspire you each and every day? List them as you reflect upon why they inspire you.

_____

_____

_____

_____

_____

_____

_____

_____

_____

_____

_____

_____

_____

_____

_____

_____

_____

_____

_____

_____

_____

_____

_____

_____

_____

_____

MY HEARTPRINT

What is your inspiring recreation outside of your work world? How does it pull you away and help you balance your work-life pressures?

_____

_____

_____

_____

_____

_____

_____

_____

_____

_____

_____

_____

_____

_____

_____

_____

_____

_____

_____

_____

_____

_____

_____

_____

_____

_____

Consider fourth-grade teacher Corrine Howe, who is also my neighbor and friend. Every morning, she is up early doing some type of morning workout activity before she heads to school for the day. Her activity is validated by something Rath describes as the twelve-hour energy gain (a during-the-school-day benefit) as a result of a twenty-minute moderate intensity morning workout. Rath further advises that late-afternoon workouts (like the ones I prefer) may not be of as much benefit to you, since the twelve-hour energy and mood boost are lost during sleep.[60]

Your drift into daily Quadrant III behaviors will devastate the culture of your school and classrooms if the drift lingers and enters into your daily behavior with students and colleagues. Our profession is very relationally intense. You and your collaborative team members should avoid Quadrants III and IV at all costs—for yourself, your colleagues, and the sake of your students, your school, and your family.

In the next chapter, we examine how to live our lives in such a way as to avoid this drift.

Quadrant II Time Required

H   E   A   R   T

In the stillness of the quiet, if we listen, we can hear the whisper in the heart giving strength to weakness, courage to fear, hope to despair.

—Howard Thurman

Your heartprint, when measured, should accomplish exactly what civil rights leader and author Howard Thurman's words in the opening quote[61] challenge us to do: get quiet, and then bring strength to student weakness, bring courage to student fear, and bring hope to student despair. Our heartprint expects a lot from you and me.

How long does it take during the school year, during the season you are currently in, before your heart can no longer hear the whisper of student despair? A real danger is that if you leave your drift to negative energy state tendencies unchecked, it will take you a bit longer to get back to Quadrant I and hear that student whisper.

You must know yourself well enough to be aware of approaching the line where busy, fully engaged, and active become hurried and dispassionate. You should seek out a trusted friend or colleague and ask him or her to be crystal clear with you about your drift. Your friend will observe your unbalanced life in you long before you recognize it in yourself. The question then becomes, Will you be willing to hear it from him or her?

Is your life in a state of unbalance?

Can you hear any complaints from colleagues, students, parents, friends, and family regarding your "out of balance" life? I cannot remember a year when the issue of balancing or juggling all the pressures of school wasn't either a major or minor concern for teachers and students or their parents—and for me too.

Reflect on how you currently try to balance your life, when you feel both the pressures of school and home knocking you a bit off balance. What do you do to regain your positive energy and daily sense of balance?

_____

_____

_____

_____

_____

_____

_____

_____

_____

_____

_____

_____

_____

_____

_____

_____

_____

_____

We live in an era in which students and adults are bound by a fast-paced life, tied together by their schedules, text messages, iCalendars, computers, and smartphone apps. The demands of our schedules eat into the very essence of our existence. So, what we most seek is a balanced life—time for work, play, family, friends, travel, academic study, faith, hobbies, reflection time, and sleep.

Thus, we make a choice. We can either pursue *external* balance or *internal* balance, and the question is, which balance solution is best? Before I define these two different approaches to seeking balance in your life, first reflect on your current patterns of behavior.

MY HEARTPRINT

The pursuit of external balance as your goal for reducing stress and regaining your Quadrant I energy life assumes your problems are beyond your control. *The world will not devote itself to making you happy.*

External balance assumes that outside circumstances need to change, circumstances beyond your control as you fall prey to the plague of *if only*: *If only* the Internet didn't exist (eliminating blogs, email, Twitter, Snapchat, Google Hangouts, parent portals into your gradebook, and more); *if only* the board of education, community, and faculty didn't have such high expectations; *if only* the local press would just leave you alone; *if only* your teacher teams would be more fully functioning on their own; *if only* parents would just stop complaining and be more helpful; *if only* students would work harder; *if only* students would show up for school; *if only* we had more services for EL students.

Then, you think, you could lead a more balanced work life. *Not so.*

At home you might think: *If only* the holiday season wasn't so demanding; *if only* you didn't have to drive to and from work in dense traffic; *if only* your children weren't in so many activities; *if only* the dog wouldn't shed; *if only* your relatives were all healthy.

Then, you could lead a more balanced personal life. *Not so.*

The answer to living a fully formed professional life—a life that honors the expectation of being your Quadrant I best for your students and colleagues every day—lies not in eliminating external disorder but in seeking out the requisite Quadrant II low positive energy time that helps you to face the internal disorder of your life.

Dwell on that thought for just a minute: *the internal disorder?*

It lies in creating an internal order that allows you to focus on a few actions in your job and your life really well—and do them at a deep, reflective, and meaningful level. No superficiality in that lesson preparation and design or those discussions with colleagues and faculty members.

This is why continued training to become a reflective practitioner is a required part of the development for your heartprint. You take time every day, week, month, and year to perform internal checks. Ask yourself, "Does my behavior reflect positive character, compassion, grittiness, good intentions, and rock-solid values? Are my intentions and interactions honest, genuine, and without hidden intentions? Is my voice to others authentic and sincere? Do others trust what I say, and can they hear how I say it? Am I making intentional and mature decisions to live an internally balanced life? Do I know myself well enough to notice my drift into Quadrant III—a high negative energy state?"

So, how do you do this?

Although we work and live for the experience of a Quadrant I life, too much time in either Quadrant I or Quadrant III will send us deep into Quadrant IV.

I am going to say that again: *too much time in either Quadrant I or Quadrant III will send us deep into Quadrant IV.*

In other words, we discipline ourselves to strategically disengage from Quadrant I and intentionally engage in meaningful Quadrant II time—every day.

Although I did not know it was called Quadrant II reflection at the time, more silent moments like a quiet break for an ice-cream cone at Dairy Queen after a long day at work, a yoga class, a stop on the way home at a local park to watch a baseball game or soccer match, some quiet time by a lake, or an afternoon Starbucks stop could give me the requisite energy to reboot and walk into my house ready for the Quadrant I mindset my family deserved.

So, you discipline yourself to be fully engaged in high positive energy while strategically planning to disengage from Quadrant I into low positive energy Quadrant II time on an ongoing basis. How

Identify your favorite Quadrant II low positive energy state activity. How do you intentionally find the time to engage in this activity every week, if not each day? What can you do to improve the quality of your Quadrant II time?

_____

_____

_____

_____

_____

_____

_____

_____

_____

_____

_____

_____

_____

_____

_____

_____

_____

_____

_____

_____

much time is needed in Quadrant II depends on the individual. You have your own "enough is enough" line where the undesired energy path to Quadrant III begins. Your line that crosses over into Quadrant III behavior may or may not be the same as the students you teach or the colleagues working next to you.

As you become a model of internal balance for your colleagues, you help them also learn how to live in a Quadrant I energy state at work, while becoming intentional about taking Quadrant II low energy state quiet time for reflection and rest. The stakes are high. By pursuing daily Quadrant II time, you become more able to mobilize, focus, inspire, and regularly take action that renews the energy of students and colleagues. You become more of a professional, as you are more able to fully engage with others.

Solitude is a required aspect for Quadrant II, as it is in solitude that you slow down enough to allow introspection into your professional and personal life. Quadrant II low energy time should mostly be alone. Yet, you can also achieve solitude with a deep friendship that allows for an honest accounting and intimate discussion of how you are really doing in your daily grind.

 # MY HEARTPRINT

In 2002, when I became superintendent at Stevenson, my administrative assistant, Nancy Wagner, noticed I often scheduled a gentleman named John R. Tunis into my weekly planner, usually for an hour of time. After a few months when John failed to show up, Nancy finally asked me why Mr. Tunis kept missing his appointments. I indicated it was probably because, as a favorite childhood author of mine, he had died many years before.

What I was actually doing was seeking out a Quadrant II, low positive energy moment in my intense workday. This time for reflection and intermittent disengagement helped me to get still, be okay with the lack of intense conversation that tended to fill my day, and evaluate current progress and re-engage for the day's next activities. I was fiercely protective of this brief time for reflection within the madness of the day's work.

There are, of course, other daily routine actions you can take to slow down for some low energy, meaningful, and reflective Quadrant II time.

- During the week, plan windows of time with nothing on your schedule except reflective brainstorming.
- Purposely stand in a longer line at the store, and do not look at your smartphone.
- Take off your watch and shut down your email on the weekends. Leave an emergency contact number if needed.
- Plan to deliberately show up early while you are waiting to meet someone. While waiting, give yourself permission to do nothing but notice your surroundings.
- Most important, however, find brief periods of time for solitude and reflection—no inputs, no noise, and no voices from colleagues (unless invited in), family, or friends coming at you.

Solitude comes in many forms and not always at the same time each day. Maybe you like the quiet stillness of the early morning. Maybe you like to run, jog, or walk. Maybe you prefer to write in a journal or to just let your mind decompress as you do household chores. The key is that whatever you do to quiet your mind, do it in real solitude. Just you, your thoughts, and low positive energy. Use this solitude and silence as an opportunity to become aware of your own personal attitudes, mindsets, and beliefs about your students or colleagues and your work life in general. Use it as a chance to learn more about yourself as you renew your Quadrant I positive energy commitments to your students, colleagues, and family.

Try to get comfortable with the quiet.

Simply ask yourself, "How am I doing? Who did I forget to notice today? What are my priorities? Am I spending quality time with my family? What did I learn from that crisis today? How will or should I respond differently next time? Am I treating my students and colleagues with respect and appreciation? Am I willing to at least listen to their perspective even if I disagree with them?"

The list is endless. Quality reflection time is not about what others need to do better. It is about what you and I need to do and whom we each need to become in order to bring the correct energy, mindset, and problem-solving skills to a better tomorrow at our school or district.

Spend time reflecting on the past to impact a better future. Examine how well you are engaging others in difficult decisions without being condescending or judgmental. Use this time to become clear on the type of deliberate practice you can engage in so others most benefit from your growth as a professional educator.

In short, reflect during your Quadrant II time, refine your practice and actions, and then act on that reflection and refinement within the days and weeks ahead. Through this cycle of continual reflection and growth, you become better as an educator by growing your *grit*—the focus of the next chapter. You develop your ability to sustain the energy and engagement needed to be at your best each and every day.

Grit: Deliberate Daily Practice

We have to be willing to fail, to be wrong, to start over again with lessons learned.

—Angela Duckworth

My first teaching job was in Stillman Valley just outside of Rockford, Illinois. It is a small farming town, and I was the only mathematics teacher for grades 7–12 when I first started (we eventually grew to 2.5 teachers in the mathematics department).

I also drove a morning school bus route, sponsored the mathematics competition team, developed and supervised the sports intramural program, designed the first health education classes for the school, and coached volleyball, basketball, and varsity baseball.

While all the activities in this list might sound admirable, the truth is I was over-whelmed most of the time. I barely knew what I was doing. Every night after my sports practices, I would go to my classroom and stand at the board. This was the chalk era (but we had colorful chalk too). I would practice my first lesson for the next day using all my board space and thinking through every little detail. Then, I would practice my next lesson, then my next one, until I felt ready for the next day.

I often left the school as late as ten or eleven at night, because I did not want to be unprepared. I was young, single, and raw to the work and practice of teaching. A lot of the content was new for me, and I knew I needed to practice, practice, practice!

I learned the value of mindful and focused practice from my colleague and head boys' basketball coach, a teacher like you and me, and the grittiest person I have ever known— Reggie Murray. Reggie was an old-school tough guy, but he taught me how to prepare every single minute of every practice so there would be no wasted time or energy. He taught me how to engage the students (athletes, in this case) so that when it came to game day, they would have practiced exactly the skills and developed the understanding needed for game readiness. Reggie had been at it for a long time, and yet, he prepared and practiced his craft with great urgency and purpose.

Reggie was the first teacher and coach I had observed who seemed to understand the importance of preparation for the school season you are in. Despite years of knowledge for the game, he knew his students and athletes were too new to the learning required and expected of them. They might need different strategies of understanding and learning to be successful. Reggie modeled for me how to never rest on past performance.

The preparation he expected from me in the coaching arena transferred to my classroom. I learned early on to always be prepared for my lessons, and better yet, to make sure my students were prepared for the game; in this case, our unit exams.

If I had been wise enough to ask Reggie about his greatest fear, I suspect that, like most seasoned veterans of our profession, he would have told me his greatest fear was endurance. How do you endure, engage in, and sustain a high level of energy, hope, and positive inspiration for students and others year in and year out and keep up with the latest understanding on how students are motivated to learn and perform? Reggie never wanted to lose his impact on learning. He viewed his ongoing personal growth as a major aspect of his positive heartprint on others. Reggie knew, far before I did, that to endure as a professional educator required engaging in lots of practice for improvement. He knew instinctively that deliberate practice would impact achievement and improve the end result of student performance.

Four decades later, Angela Duckworth, a professor of psychology at the University of Pennsylvania, described the idea of grit as working on something you care about so much that you're willing to stay loyal to it.[62] I was instantly reminded of Reggie. He cared about teaching and coaching so much that he stayed loyal to his own personal improvement for forty years!

In her 2016 book *Grit: The Power of Passion and Perseverance*, Duckworth further describes the role of deliberate practice as a critical element of our own personal achievement in life. Talent matters, she points out, but deliberate practice and effort count twice as much and are a critical reveal of her message.[63] Reggie Murray was an educator with tremendous grit built on the back of deliberate practice.

What does the deliberate practice of expert teachers and leaders mean for you and me?

First, those considered experts at their profession set a stretch goal. A stretch goal creates a target of performance beyond current performance that beckons to be achieved.

Second, experts seek immediate, accurate, and specific feedback, including feedback that could be considered negative (such as feedback I received on early drafts of this manuscript).

Third, experts reflect on the results of their effort, seek out what went wrong, and start again, correcting their weaknesses as part of the next practice round.

Thus, reflection and refinement with action become your most powerful growth tools as you engage in deliberate practice around your specific job role each day.

MY HEARTPRINT

Expert educators understand there are always weak spots, so they practice over and over until those weaknesses are addressed. What happens if you finally nail the lesson, performance, or project flawlessly? What if it is perfect in both its delivery and the learning that takes place?

Accomplished educators jump in the air, click their heels, eat some cake, and then set a new stretch goal for that lesson, unit of study, performance, or project for next week, next month, or next year so they can take learning even deeper!

∞

So, what happened to me during my days at Stillman Valley? I soon realized my engagement, as a professional, was limited there. I was never going to become the expert teacher my students needed me to be if there were no opportunities for me to work with others, develop my thoughts and wisdom about the nature of my practice, and become a more accomplished practitioner at reflecting and refining my mathematics lessons around personal stretch goals. So, after six years, I left and went back to the university

Take a moment to reflect on these deliberate practice ideas, and then answer the following questions.

1. What is a *stretch goal* you might set based on your current teaching and leading performance?
2. How do you currently *receive feedback* on your daily practice for becoming a better educator?
3. What do you (or your team of colleagues) currently do each day, week, or unit to *reflect on the results* of your professional practice, take action on them, and correct any weaknesses immediately?

_____
_____
_____
_____
_____
_____
_____
_____
_____
_____
_____
_____
_____
_____
_____

to get a master's degree in mathematics. I knew I needed more base knowledge in my field to become more fully formed and of greater benefit to my students in the long term. In my case, I needed to become more practiced at both the content and the process of learning mathematics. *I needed to become more mathematically gritty!*

Near the end of her book on grit, Duckworth states:

> What we accomplish in the marathon of life depends tremendously on our grit—our passion and perseverance for long-term goals. An obsession with talent distracts us from that simple truth . . . you can grow your grit . . . you can connect your work to a purpose beyond yourself. And you can learn to hope when all seems lost.[64]

If you want to determine your level of grittiness and examine the role grit can play in your life and the life of your students, you can go to http://angeladuckworth.com/grit-scale for the Grit Scale and more. Suffice it to say that I knew I also needed to grow my grit with *others*. I needed to be engaged in deliberate practice with others. I needed to be engaged around personal reflection and refinement practices that would make a difference in student learning and help me to join the 31.4 percent of actively engaged teachers. And I did not have enough wisdom to figure out how to become more fully formed in my professional work life on my own.

I did have a certain spirit for the work. Teaching was definitely my professional journey. But I needed to learn how to engage fully with others in order to enrich and deepen my own learning.

Thankfully, my career took some twists and turns that landed me right in the middle of the place that birthed the PLC movement and helped to set the expectations of our professional work we will explore in part 3.

The MTXE Perspective

H   E   A   R   T

What is perspective? To a great extent, perspective is how we view something. The word has its origin from the Latin *perspectus*, "to look through [or] see clearly."[65] This is very hard to do when immersed in the smothering details and activities of your professional and personal life. One overriding thought is that *life is short*. Where do the time, energy, and effort of ending one school year in June and starting another one in August go? Pretty soon, all those school years become a blur of sorts. Your career becomes this connected series of school-year segments as thousands of students roll through the kaleidoscope of your work.

And one thing you know from experience—*life is uncertain*. The single adjective that best describes future events is *unexpected*. There will be unexpected stuff—illnesses, accomplishments, transfers, promotions, surgeries, triumphs, and tragedies. The events sure to follow in the next school season are, indeed, uncertain, will drain your energy, and are often only understood in reflection once the season ends.

And these issues affect your engagement levels at home and at work.

In "The Secret Ailment," presidential advisor and educational author John Gardner summed up the goal of our journey as teachers and school leaders. I used elements of this quote in the opening epigraph to part 2 of the book:

> We need to develop a resilient, indomitable morale that enables us to face those realities and still strive for every ounce of energy to prevail. . . . Every important battle . . . will need to be fought and re-fought. . . . We have to believe in ourselves, but we mustn't suppose the path will be easy. It's tough and rain falls on the just.[66]

I carried these words in my wallet for more than twenty-five years of my teaching career. The words served as a reminder on my darkest days to never, never, never give up—the professional path we choose is never easy, but it is so worth it to so many *students*.

Every important battle in your professional life must be fought and refought. What a great statement about the perseverance perspective needed to meet and embrace adversity with hope. You will build the story of how you will be remembered this coming year, every day, one brick at a time—by the way you choose to respond to the stuff of your life.

I call Gardner's challenge to us the MTXE perspective: *m*ental *t*oughness and e*x*tra *e*ffort. Students, athletes, and colleagues can earn MTXE awards with me. There is a certain toughness required to do the difficult and deliberate work of our profession, and it requires extra (think discretionary) effort. MTXE is a lot like grit.

As you discovered, high positive energy balanced by daily moments of low positive energy is the secret sauce to your engagement and discretionary effort in work and in life. Will your heartprint story join the 31.4 percent of fully engaged teachers in our profession? In her book *No Sweat*, Michelle Segar reveals just how tough we need to be when the unexpected occurs:

> No matter how carefully we plan our work, dutifully scheduling in time for exercise, we inevitably encounter an unexpected call for our attention—a sudden change in a friend's plans, an urgent last-minute request from our boss, a sick child who needs to stay home from school, a meeting we must attend. . . . In each moment, we must make choices about which calls to heed and which to disregard.[67]

Take a moment now to reflect on Segar's words and pause to reflect on all of part 2. Which chapters were most beneficial to you? How can the engagement, energy, and effort ideas of part 2 help you to join the 31.4 percent of teachers and leaders currently actively engaged at school? Or, how can the ideas expressed, and all of your reflections, help you to remain more actively engaged in your current school season?

Think of the next steps as *I will . . .* statements, and write them down as you measure your personal heartprint during this current era of your professional journey.

MY HEART PRINT ♥

The following resources are instrumental in the support of our work together in part 2. Depending on your personal interests, you may use these resources as you continue to expand your knowledge base and the knowledge base of your colleagues. You may also visit **go.SolutionTree.com/HEART** to access direct links to the websites and download three additional chapters related to part 2.

Part 2: E Is for Engagement

Resources

Duckworth, A. (2016). *Grit: The power of passion and perseverance.* New York: Simon & Schuster. (Go to http://angeladuckworth.com/grit-scale for the Grit Scale and to discover your grit score.)

DuFour, R. (2015). *In praise of American educators: And how they can become even better.* Bloomington, IN: Solution Tree Press.

Loehr, J. (2007). *The power of story: Change your story, change your destiny in business and in life.* New York: Free Press.

Rath, T. (2013). *Eat move sleep: How small choices lead to big changes.* Arlington, VA: Missionday.

Rath, T. (2015). *Are you fully charged? The three keys to energizing your work and life.* Arlington, VA: Silicon Guild.

Schwartz, T. (2010). *The way we're working isn't working: The four forgotten needs that energize great performance.* New York: Free Press.

Segar, M. (2015). *No sweat: How the simple science of motivation can bring you a lifetime of fitness.* New York: AMACOM.

Additional Resources

- Tom Rath's website: www.tomrath.org
- Tony Schwartz's website: https://theenergyproject.com
- The *State of America's Schools* report highlighting a link between teacher engagement, student engagement, and student achievement: www.gallup.com/poll/181523/engaged-teachers-enjoy-personal-professional-edge.aspx
- *The 2015 Gallup Report, The State of America's Schools:* www.gallup.com/services/178709/state-america-schools-report.aspx
- Gallup Daily: U.S. Employee Engagement: www.gallup.com/poll/180404/gallup-daily-employee-engagement.aspx
- The Gallup Employee Engagement Survey: www.gallup.com/products/170969/temp-q12-employee-engagement-center.aspx
- Gallup's "Critical Drivers of Parent Engagement in Schools": http://bit.ly/2hnlUgT

PART 3

DEVELOPING HEART

A

Is for Alliances

Essential Heartprint Question: Are you a person open to influence and shared values, able to become more relationally intelligent and interdependent with others?

The first order of business is to build a group of people who, under the influence of the institution, grow taller and become healthier, stronger, more autonomous together.
                                                            —Robert Greenleaf

In part 3 of this book, we explore the role alliances play as part of our heartprint in pursuit of an effective and fully engaged professional life. Our intentional effort to effectively collaborate and engage with our colleagues and to honor the covenants and agreements of a team helps to at best erase causes of inequity in our school, and at worse allows our teaching and leading life to expand its impact and find its full and realized potential.

What a payoff! You become both an inequity eraser for your students, and you begin the journey of maximizing the greatest potential that lies within you as a teacher of others.

The heartprint you leave on your students and colleagues begins by understanding the elements of happiness described in part 1 and discovers its personal impact in your engagement efforts revealed in part 2. The impact of your heartprint becomes *magnified* via the deep alliances and collaborative efforts with colleagues as described in the seven chapters of part 3.

We are meant to be in relationships with others. It is in the hardwiring of our human design, as you will discover. Our alliances with colleagues are, according to author Robert Greenleaf, a "first order of business."[68] And yet, there is a mystifying counterintuitive embrace of isolation in our profession, as if it is an entitlement of our job as educators. And to further complicate our collaborative work, depending on our relational intelligence and the relational intelligence of our colleagues, nurturing healthy and positive relationships with others can be a challenge!

It just isn't an easy aspect of our work in which we have had much preparation or development in the past. However, there has been a genetic breakthrough that serves the nature of our profession—an understanding by evolutionary biologists and psychologists that neural and possibly genetic evidence exists of a human predisposition to cooperate.[69] We are more cooperative and less selfish than we might believe.

My second job as a teacher was in a more urban district, where I had my own room—Room 210. I wasn't expected to form alliances with my colleagues and collaborate, nor did I really think I needed to or should collaborate with anyone else on my work. On a scale of 1 to 10, my ability and my effort to collaborate with other teachers and form alliances with others would have been pretty low. This is surprising in light of my additional responsibilities as a basketball coach, in which everything was based on working together—the coaches and the student athletes.

Part 3, "A Is for Alliances," and its expectations for living a great work life might not have been part of what you signed up for as an educator, initially. Nobody really told us this was the way of the professional life in undergraduate school, did they?

Nobody mentioned to me that working alone and privately making all my own decisions could cause rigor inequity and damage to the overall learning of every student in our school and, in the long run, limit my potential impact and journey toward becoming a fully formed professional.

Seems a bit unfair.

And yet, no matter the school or district you work in today, we now know the knowledge sharing and development of each educator in the school (urban, rural, or suburban), regardless of grade level (elementary, middle, or high), cannot be limited to a hallway happenstance.

MY HEARTPRINT

In high-impact schools, there are intentional structures in place and a relentless culture that values effective knowledge sharing by adults and students around evidence of student learning.

I know some of you have been through the collaboration process at your school and with your teams. And you know just how hard it is to solve your major work challenges together. You are expected to notice students and colleagues and give thanks to them, show grace to them, discuss the opportunities (won and lost) around the evidence for student learning with them, and to learn from them.

Whew! Alliances ask and expect a lot. They reveal joy, sorrow, and sharing from within us. In the seven chapters of part 3, we explore an understanding of the heartprint aspect of these alliances, the nature of collaboration as a bumpy road, and how to become someone others would want to collaborate with. We also explore the benefits and the costs of belonging as part of our work-life heartprint on our students and colleagues.

We will address the almost eerie silence by educators about how the PLC process serves as an inequity

Think about your current work-life situation. Give yourself a score on a scale of 1 (low) to 10 (high) about your effort, desire, and ability to effectively form alliances and collaborate with others at work around evidence of student learning. Do you believe alliances with your colleagues are important? Why do you feel that way?

_____
_____
_____
_____
_____
_____
_____
_____
_____
_____
_____
_____
_____
_____
_____
_____
_____
_____
_____
_____
_____
_____

eraser for the often-hidden social injustices from the wide variety of student learning experiences in our schools. This unequal variance is primarily caused by isolated teacher and leader decision making and team dysfunction regarding the rigor of daily task selection, student assessments, and effective instructional practices.

We will discover how the fastest way to a fully engaged workforce is the development and growth of everyone. Everyone becomes better at their profession because of their influence on one another—one of the primary benefits of belonging.

Everyone understands that the real way to become a great teacher and leader of others is to *exist in, and become part of, a great teacher and leader team.*

To do so, your heartprint should show acceptance and empathy toward others. You build your own knowledge capacity so you can serve and share with your colleagues and build a culture of trust with them and learn from them. Collaboration is then an ongoing heartprint process for building the greater knowledge capacity and effort of every faculty and staff member, every teacher and leader, and every student, no matter how strong or how weak.

And most important, your participation in deep alliances and effective collaboration celebrates great teaching in one room while successfully supporting the pursuit of great teaching in the room next door.

The Primary Purposes
of Collaboration

*Neuroscience shows that a reward circuit is triggered in our
brains when we cooperate with one another.*
—Yochai Benkler

In the mid-1990s, we were ramping up our faculty alliances and collaborative team efforts at Stevenson and leaving the era of teacher isolation in our wake. We did not completely understand the purpose of our collaborative teams. As you can imagine, this caused a few bumps along the road. It is not like we didn't know to some extent, but we were learning on the fly.

I just did not fully understand the personal benefits. I saw collaboration by our faculty (and by our students) as a social justice issue for the students. It was a way to erase rigor inconsistencies and inequities in our students' opportunities to learn. That made sense to me.

As it turns out, more than twenty years later, there is quite a bit of science that supports another and more personal reason to embrace collaboration as a professional responsibility during our careers: it serves our unselfish gene and our desire to collaborate with others. This might seem counterintuitive, since in many cases your experience might be that the selfish mindset of some colleagues is a barrier to the development of meaningful collaboration with your team.

Yet, evolutionary biologists and behavioral psychologists have found neural and, in some cases, genetic evidence of a predisposition to cooperate with our colleagues.

Professor of entrepreneurial studies at Harvard Law School Yochai Benkler indicates, "We are more cooperative and less selfish than most people believe. Organizations should

How do you explain to your students, colleagues, or parents why teacher collaboration time embedded into your workday is such an important part of professional responsibility?

What is the thirty-second explanation you would provide to others?

_____

_____

_____

_____

_____

_____

_____

_____

_____

_____

_____

_____

_____

_____

_____

_____

_____

_____

_____

_____

_____

help us embrace our collaborative sentiments."[70] The idea that we might have an unselfish gene that desires collaboration is contrary to previous beliefs.

Benkler quotes Harvard's mathematical biologist Martin Nowak: "Perhaps the most remarkable aspect of evolution is its ability to generate cooperation in a competitive world."[71] In essence, Benkler indicates that the deep-rooted belief about human selfishness is beginning to change. Think for a minute about the primary purpose for collaboration with your colleagues.

♥ MY HEARTPRINT

Michael Fullan is a professor emeritus at the Ontario Institute for Studies in Education at the University of Toronto. His 2004 book *Leading in a Culture of Change*, followed by his 2008 book *The Six Secrets of Change*, led to a significant impact and shift in my professional teaching and leading response to the question: What is the primary purpose of the alliances and collaboration we are expected to engage in as part of our work at school?

Fullan provides a helpful description with his third secret about great organizations in *The Six Secrets of Change*: capacity building prevails. He further indicates the purpose of forming alliances and collaborative teams is not to pass judgment on or shame one another but rather to build the knowledge capacity of each other.[72] My take on his words is this:

My primary purpose as a teacher is the individual and collective knowledge capacity building of my students and my colleagues toward full engagement in our work.

Do you really believe that statement? For me, this means I will work to develop the knowledge capacity for each of my students and each of my colleagues within my sphere of influence continuously and forever, *together*. It seemed at first like a lot to ask of myself as a professional educator.

Fullan reveals a partial answer to the My Heartprint question[73] when he cites researcher Georg von Krogh and others: "We believe a broad acceptance of the emotional lives of others is crucial for establishing good working relationships—and good relations, in turn, lead to effective knowledge creation."[74]

MY HEARTPRINT

Hmm. This means that for me to effectively build into your knowledge capacity or vice versa, I need to be aware of the general condition of your life. Are you married? Do you have a partner? Do you have children? Do I know birthdates and names? Do I know your hobbies? Do I understand circumstances in your life that might be a drag on the current season you are in? Do I know how you ended up teaching and leading at my school or on my team? Do I know your history and how it shaped you into the person you are today?

As you either have discovered or will discover, the benefits to student learning as a result of your embedded adult learning far exceed anything you can do alone. Your personal knowledge creation and knowledge capacity building and growth, based on real-time evidence of student learning, reveal the genuine purpose of participating in a collaborative and cooperative culture, forging alliances with your colleagues, and coming together and learning from one another. You start sharing and take the time to focus on issues that really matter.

In a strange way, your self-interest is best served as part of a collaborative team that serves an *intrinsic greater good*.

Do not skim over the last three words in that sentence. You and I are most effective as professional educators when we are part of a collaborative team that harnesses our intrinsic motivation—as in, why am I going to work each day and giving my discretionary effort to this job without burning out?

In addition to his comment about the neuroscience evidence of cooperation in the opening quote, Benkler further states:

> [Cooperative] systems that harness intrinsic motivations and self-directed cooperative behaviors don't need to limit themselves to knowledge of what people will do. Every participant becomes his or her own monitor,

What percentage of your colleagues (whether teachers or administrators) do you believe currently view their day-to-day work as building the knowledge capacity of each other and solving work-life-related problems together, each and every week?

How are you trying to help each colleague better understand the benefits of knowledge sharing together?

_____

_____

_____

_____

_____

_____

_____

_____

_____

_____

_____

_____

_____

_____

_____

_____

_____

_____

_____

_____

_____

_____

> bringing insight and initiative to the task—whether or not
> someone is monitoring behavior.[75]

Thus, in the best school systems, the intrinsic motivation Benkler describes springs from your desire to embrace a professional life that is bigger than you. You give everything you have to the week in, week out tasks of the team, because it not only builds into your knowledge development but also allows you to play a role in the greater good for your grade level or course-based team's knowledge development. This mindset becomes part of your heartprint development.

For this exact reason of serving the greater good in my school district, I have spent the majority of my professional career pursuing, teaching, and leading the PLC movement. In the next few chapters, we take a deeper look at exactly what this means and how our alliances within the PLC process help develop intrinsic motivations for our work *and* erase inequities that might exist in student learning.

PLCs: Serving the Greater Good

America's education system has become less a ladder of opportunity than a structure to transmit inequity from one generation to the next.

—Nicholas Kristof

I appreciate the words of Pulitzer Prize–winning journalist Nicholas Kristof in the opening quote,[76] but I think he missed the mark on the last part. It is not from one generation to the next that we transmit inequity.

It is much worse.

In many schools, we transmit inequity from one classroom to the next. We do not mean to. I do not think it is intentional, as I have talked to hundreds of teachers about this issue. Transmitting inequity from one classroom to the next is generally not something we are mindful of or think about as part of our professional heartprint development.

I taught for six years in Room 210 at West Chicago Community HSD 94, right next door to Vera Sorenson in Room 208. We taught mostly the same classes. Not one time in those six years did it occur to me (or to her) that we were the cause of gross inequities in student learning because we chose to work in isolation from each other.

I was unaware at the time that parents would call in to the school and ask for their children to be placed in a class with a different teacher based on community perception of how hard one teacher was compared to another. Or, they might make the request based on the nature of that teacher's grading practices or the difficulty of the exams given (my tests tended to be pretty rigorous, and a lot of students did not like that).

Do a team collaboration check! On a scale of 1 to 10, with 1 not very collaborative and 10 totally collaborative in all aspects of the PLC process just described, give your team a score. Then answer this question:

Why didn't you pick a lower collaboration number for your team or teams?

_____

_____

_____

_____

_____

_____

_____

_____

_____

_____

_____

_____

_____

_____

_____

_____

_____

_____

_____

_____

_____

_____

_____

Vera and I were friends and liked each other. Yet, Vera had no idea which standards I taught out of our textbook or how hard my lessons were. I had no idea about the rigor of her tasks and homework, or how much she graded and counted that homework. We thought these were decisions that we were supposed to make alone. It never occurred to us that we should work as part of a collaborative team around evidence of student learning in our course.

But, what exactly is the PLC process?

According to the AllThingsPLC website (www .allthingsplc.info):

> [The PLC culture is] an ongoing process in which educators work collaboratively in recurring cycles of collective inquiry and action research to achieve better results for the students they serve. Professional learning communities operate under the assumption that the key to improved learning for students is continuous job-embedded learning for educators.[77]

This description of the nature of PLCs is insightful. Let's break it down into six characteristics.

1. Educators work collaboratively—*Okay, I got it! Isolation is obsolete!*
2. In recurring cycles—*How often? Oh yes, before, during, and after a unit of study.*
3. Of collective inquiry—*You ask, "Do you think our strategies will work? Let's try!"*
4. To achieve better student results—*Is there evidence of learning in our classrooms?*
5. To serve—*I serve the students and colleagues? Yes, by teaching and leading others.*
6. Job-embedded adult learning that impacts student learning—*The end!*

 # MY HEARTPRINT

Collaboration then, is a continuous job-embedded learning process. Your collaboration efforts with colleagues are for the purpose of developing your knowledge and the knowledge of each team member— at each moment during the school year in which you plan to use that knowledge and the evidence of student learning based on that knowledge, for the units of study taught in your school.

Responding to the lower collaboration number question in the My Heartprint on the previous page reveals the efforts you are making to validate your team's move toward alliances and a more interdependent, collaborative team culture that takes *collective action* every day. And, according to Benkler, neuroscience shows "a reward circuit is triggered in our brains when we cooperate with one another."[78] You and I benefit from our collaborative efforts with others.

The PLC process—and the effort your team makes when working together around the issues that impact student learning—serves a greater good. It eventually helped Vera and me to examine the unintentional inequities in student learning and performance created by the many decisions we made in private for the students randomly assigned to us.

The idea that our routines and daily work-life decisions, when made in isolation from our colleagues, could be a primary contributor to inequities in student learning in our school had not yet become part of our heartprint on each other. But we were willing to try.

In what aspects of your current teaching do you make instruction and assessment decisions in isolation from other team members? Are other teachers unaware of your makeup policies, methods of scoring an assessment, or expectations for how students embrace their errors when you pass back a quiz, test, project, or report?

MY HEARTPRINT 💜

The good news is that your collaborative team is capable of improving itself. Good teams attack inequities that isolated decision making can cause and seek out magnified impact far greater than any individual on the team could ever achieve.

You and your team do more than rely on discussion and debate by sharing information and best-practice perspectives. You agree to use discrete teamwork products, such as common assessments, projects, homework assignments, and lesson-design elements,

What steps can you take to become more aware of the routine practices of other teachers on your team and erase any inequities—even if unintentional?

_____
_____
_____
_____
_____
_____
_____
_____
_____
_____
_____
_____
_____
_____
_____
_____
_____
_____
_____
_____
_____
_____
_____
_____
_____
_____
_____
_____

produced through the joint real contributions of each team member, as the promise of your magnified impact becomes tapped.

Mrs. V. was my daughter's fifth-grade teacher. Mrs. V. reminded me of the axiom that great teaching is always a form of love. She was well on her way to becoming a fully formed professional.

However, Mrs. V. did not yet understand the unintentional inequities she caused for the students in her school, because she worked in isolation from other fifth-grade teachers. She had not yet reached a *magnified impact* point in her career.

Her strength and love were in science. During the year, she assigned her class a powerful science project. This project required evidence of research and proper sourcing of the information. Mrs. V. provided clear guidelines as to the scoring rubric and expectations in order to receive full credit on the final report, and she offered several formative opportunities for feedback as the project progressed. It was a positive learning experience and opportunity in science for my daughter— both for its requirements to be creative and its structure to keep the ideas and presentation focused on the most essential standards.

At the same time, my daughter had a best friend also in fifth grade at the same school, but with a different teacher (there were three fifth-grade teachers). Her friend was not doing the science project, at least not at the same time as my daughter. On the surface, this bothered me, because I kept thinking about next year. If every one of these students is enrolled in sixth-grade science (most likely on a middle school campus) and two of the fifth-grade classes do not do the month-long project, then how will they be equitably prepared for sixth-grade science standards?

So, I went to see Mrs. V. and again indicated what a great teacher I thought she was. I also praised the effort and energy it must have taken to place together the details and expectations for the science project.

Then, I asked the $64,000 question that has a basis in PLC culture: "Will the other two sections of fifth-grade students also be doing this project and meeting these science standards?"

The answer was *no*. She had a special interest in science, and this was one of her special projects. I then asked her if the other teachers would at least be teaching and assessing the same standards as this project. Again, the answer was no because there just was not enough time due to prep for the mathematics and English language arts state exams.

I then asked her, "Have you thought about having a more magnified professional impact during your career?"

I continued by showing her the four critical questions every collaborative grade level, course-based, or leadership team in a PLC at Work culture asks and answers on a unit-by-unit basis as they pursue coherence in student work.[79]

1. What do we want all students to know and be able to do? (essential learning standards, tasks, and projects)
2. How will we know if they know it? (assessment instruments and tasks used to inform student learning and progress)
3. How will we respond if they don't know it? (formative feedback and action processes established)
4. How will we respond if they do know it? (formative feedback and action processes established)

Without realizing it, Mrs. V. was violating the intent of critical question 1: What do we want all students to know and be able to do? By choosing to be the only fifth-grade teacher addressing certain science standards and providing a remarkable project for her students, she was creating an inequity among all students in fifth grade. As I pointed out to her, there were sixty-five students that would not have access to learning those standards and the benefits of engaging in such a powerful project.

I indicated the real victory would be to magnify her impact by engaging her other fifth-grade colleagues in discussions about how to use the science project and how to teach the essential science standards. Part of her role as a collaborative team member was to develop the knowledge capacity of others.

Today, Mrs. V. is the fifth-grade team leader and, although the conversations and the work are sometimes difficult, the teachers on her team are experiencing the magnified impact that comes from engaging in each other's knowledge and understanding. And the fifth-grade students in her school are the beneficiaries of that impact.

Using the four critical questions of a PLC, you can bring coherence to your work, begin your equity pursuit for each student, and address together any potential inequity places. The next chapter examines a few of those places you might want to look!

Oh, the Inequity
Places We'll Go!

H   E   🅐   R   T

*I refuse to accept the idea that the "isness" of man's present
nature makes him morally incapable of reaching up for the
eternal "oughtness" that forever confronts him.*

—Martin Luther King Jr.

The first time I saw this Martin Luther King Jr. quote,[80] I was fourteen years old and attending a Chicago White Sox boys sports camp on Lake Winnebago, just north of Fond du Lac, Wisconsin.

During that summer, I worked at a traveling street carnival and circus, setting up and tearing down every week, as we went from one Midwest town to the next. My dad was the promotion manager, and my stepmom, Connie, and I ran a concession stand together. And most days, I also worked a four-corner ring-tossing booth. I made ten dollars a day, plus an extra ten dollars on teardown day. It was the summer of 1965, and that White Sox camp cost $210 for two weeks. Sixteen days of work, and I could go!

In some ways, those days were my first real introduction to social justice issues of the times. I became more aware that not everyone was like me, as the carnival workers were not an easy bunch of men and women to be around. I had to grow up pretty fast.

At the White Sox camp, I had a lot of friends who, like me, just wanted to play sports. Yet, we came from all kinds of poverty and backgrounds for our two weeks together. My bunkmate was a kid from the south side of Chicago. Robbie was the first one to introduce me to Martin Luther King Jr. and his 1964 Nobel peace prize speech in Oslo, Norway: "I refuse to accept the idea that the 'isness' of man's present nature makes him morally incapable of reaching up for the eternal 'oughtness' that forever confronts him."[81]

I remember thinking at the time, what is the *ought* of a better day I should fight for in my life? I remember too, it made me more determined than ever to go to college—a goal that was not a serious consideration in my family due to financial restraints and other cultural issues.

What about you? What is the *oughtness* you are pursuing this season?

Fourteen years later, my very first experience at erasing and creating inequities in student learning occurred during my one year of teaching (while in graduate school) at Illinois State University in 1979–1980. The course was MAT 121: Business Calculus. My graduate school advisor coauthored the book. He was a teacher of the course along with three other professors from the Illinois State University mathematics department and me. Offered mostly to freshmen, the course was primarily for business majors and was considered a tough course, as it acted as a sorting "separator" for potential business majors.

The five of us worked as a team, and I was the rookie member. We used the same common syllabus for course standard expectations and grading decisions. We met once a month to check on our progress toward those common and essential standards and to discuss the grading for all common tests for the course. We did not share student scores until our last meeting before the common final exam for the 285 students enrolled in the course. At the time, the idea of a common assessment given by each member of the team was progressive for that era of our profession.

And then, we met in late November of 1979, two weeks before the final exam. There was one agenda item: to examine the grade distributions of each team member before the final exam. Specifically, the other professors were upset with my grade distribution. It was too good, they claimed. "You have too many As and Bs." And it was true. They each had less than half my rate of As and Bs and double my rate of Ds and Fs.

How could this occur and, why were they upset with me? Simple— the *fear of grade inflation.*

My colleagues were convinced I was grading way too easy and did not understand the rigor expectations of the course. "If we give out too many As and Bs, the Illinois State University business department will not consider the course to be rigorous enough. There is no way your students can score that well on our final exam. You have been warned!"

Gulp!

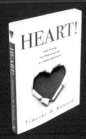 ## Exclusive Videos from
Timothy D. Kanold, Eric Twadell,
Mike Mattos, & Sharon V. Kramer

Enrich your study of *HEART!* with this curated playlist designed to help you foster productive, heart-centered classrooms.

THE MAKING OF *HEART!*

The Making of *HEART!* – Timothy D. Kanold

4:56

The Voices of *HEART!* – Timothy D. Kanold

3:17

Other videos available online

PART 1: *DEVELOPING HEART—H Is for Happiness*

HEART: The Role of Compassion – Timothy D. Kanold

2:55

Are You Engaged? – Timothy D. Kanold

14:29

PART 2: *DEVELOPING HEART—E Is for Engagement*

Avoiding the Drift Into High Negative Energy – Timothy D. Kanold

13:24

Engaged and Balanced – Timothy D. Kanold

6:31

PART 3: *DEVELOPING HEART—A Is for Alliances*

What's at Stake – Timothy D. Kanold

 *3:41*

HEART: Celebration – Timothy D. Kanold, Eric Twadell

7:18

Other videos available online

PART 4: *DEVELOPING HEART—R Is for Risk*

Alliances – Timothy D. Kanold

6:44

HEART: More than Collaboration – Timothy D. Kanold

4:44

Other videos available online

PART 5: *DEVELOPING HEART—T Is for Thought*

Giving Corrective Feedback to Students – Mike Mattos

1:23

Using Student Assessment Data – Sharon V. Kramer

3:07

Other videos available online

Ahh, the hidden meaning of the team meeting was revealed. The real purpose and current *isness* (as Dr. King would say) of the course was to select and sort students out of the course and not expect each and every student to reach successful completion of the course. Some Ds and Fs were required!

They told me there was no way all 285 students would pass the course and the exam. It would not be possible. In essence, the course was designed to be norm referenced, meaning a given number of students (those getting Ds and Fs) should match equally with those getting As and Bs. I was upsetting the bell curve for normal grade distribution regarding student performance in the course, they said.

The plan was for our team members to give the final exam (seventy-five multiple-choice questions), come together to create a team score distribution based on the results, and then ensure that the bottom 30 percent of student test takers, regardless of how low or high they scored, would get a D or an F on the exam.

Without ever really announcing it, we were in the *selecting-and-sorting business*!

We didn't want each and every student enrolled in MAT 121 to succeed. We wanted there to be a normal distribution of Fs. We did not want every student to make it over a qualifying and measurable performance bar.

Don't be too quick to judge us, though. It was a different time period in our profession. It was only in the late 1980s and early to mid-1990s (when an explosion of assessment research was assembled) that the idea of criterion-referenced assessments became the norm.

One way to erase these grading inequities is to use a criterion-referenced assessment that expects each student to demonstrate evidence of learning the essential standard criteria. Your team establishes a proficiency "bar of performance" revealed to all students in advance of any exam. Students are expected to make it over that bar and demonstrate learning of the essential standards on each assessment. This proficiency bar should not be a changing target dependent on a comparison of students taking the exam (called setting a curve and thus lowering or raising the bar based on students' individual performances) or the random decision by a different teacher on the team. We are expected to take responsibility to help each student make it over the proficiency bar.

Think about your bar of expected student performance for each grade level or course in your school. What is your collective adult response when the students of various grade levels or courses do not learn and fail to make it over the bar?

Is the bar for assessment performance a moving target for your team? Does everyone on your team keep that bar high and then help each and every student make it over the bar as an indicator of his or her grade?

 # MY HEARTPRINT

Let's take a deeper look into some of the possible inequity places from my Illinois State University experience on the MAT 121: Business Calculus team in order to help with your own search at your school.

First, consider the inequity revealed by PLC critical question 1 (see chapter 16, page 109): *What do we want all students to know and be able to do?* To a casual outsider, our MAT 121 course team did not have this inequity issue per se. All five members of our team taught the same essential learning standards, right?

Right, but we did not teach the standards with the same level of *rigor*. True, we felt students deserved access to the same essential learning standards. What we failed to do, however, was talk more deeply together about the places of inequity we were causing.

For example, our MAT 121 team did not discuss why each standard was relevant or how to make it meaningful for the type of students enrolled in the course. Technology was just emerging as a useful tool back then, and I embraced its use, while others on our team thought it would hamper student learning. Thus, unintentionally, I created an equity and access learning gap, as my students had a calculator benefit other MAT 121 students did not receive.

For our daily lesson-design elements that unpacked the standards to be taught, I had a simple teaching weapon that the other professors did not use: *student-engaged learning*. I rarely lectured for more than ten minutes before I placed my students into small groups and engaged them in meaningful peer-to-peer discourse (hard to do in a large lecture hall). Mostly I just did not want my students' brains to be overwhelmed. Today, we are more aware of the high impact on student learning when teachers use effective peer-to-peer communication during a lesson. So, it is more understandable that my students might have had a learning advantage back then.

Reflect for a moment about the essential learning standards taught in your grade level, course, or school. Do you know if each member of your team is teaching those standards with the same level of rigor, using technology in an appropriate way, and engaging students in the standards with the right pacing? You can use the My Heartprint prompts for a deep introspection into your current practices with your colleagues.

MY HEARTPRINT ♥

Give your team a score of 1, 5, or 10, with 1 being low (you have not addressed this inequity place at all) and 10 being high (you have erased this inequity in your grade level, course, department, or school completely). Be sure to write the reasons!

To erase standards inequity places, our team asks deep questions such as:

1. How do we explain why each standard is so essential to learn (relevance)?

2. How do we ensure the context for the lesson contains elements that create meaning, reasoning, and sense making for the student (meaningfulness)?

3. How do we connect to the various demographic and personal characteristics of our students?

4. How do we suggest and provide accommodations and modifications for English learners that support access to learning?

5. How do we access and understand home language and culture in order to facilitate learning?

6. How will students' prior knowledge be addressed when designing our lessons?

7. How do we keep students highly engaged during the lesson?

8. How do we access technology for deep student learning and support (for example, websites, discussion groups, or webinars)?

Second, consider how critical question 3 (see chapter 16, page 109) could cause inequity: *How will we respond if [students] don't know [the essential learning standards]?* When my Illinois State University MAT 121 team sat at the table, waiting for my response as to why I had such a grading inequity compared to the rest of them, I suppose I should have been more intimidated. I was the new one on the team. I could have caved in and lowered some of my grades, but I knew the grades were well deserved. I knew my students had worked hard for those grades. In my mind though, I was thinking, "What if I was wrong?"

Instead, I said, "First, these grades are deserved. Every student showed up for my class. And if they didn't, I showed up at their dorm rooms later. They learned quickly to come to class. Second, I have allowed them to make up errors on their tests to improve their grade as long as they showed up in our tutoring center to do so. Third, I made it clear that not doing their work was a failure to commit to me, to the course, to their parents' money, and to the university. I often ask my students, 'Where the heck is your Redbird pride?'" These were my responses to critical question 3. It never occurred to me that they would not learn the content of the course. Eventually though, I discovered that what determined a student's grade in MAT 121 was widely variant for each professor and teacher on our team.

My colleague and author Sarah Schuhl reminded me about this reality in a memo:

> During a recent experience at a Nevada middle school, I discovered that the teacher teams were grading very different things from teacher to teacher. Some teachers graded home-work, and others didn't. Some graded classwork, and others did not. Some counted and used computer work or projects, and others did not. Some teachers gave out grade points for participation, and some did not. There was no clarity among the team of teachers about how a student taking seventh-grade mathematics or eighth-grade mathematics should be graded. There had been no discussion about the elements of a grade based on proficiency of learning the standards, and much less agreement on how to gain clarity and coherence on how to implement those elements together. (S. Schuhl, personal communication, August 14, 2016)

Reflect for a moment on the clarity issues Sarah describes. How do her words connect to your current work situation? You can use the My Heartprint prompts for a deep introspection into your current grading practices with your colleagues. Consider answering the questions by yourself first, and then use them as part of a team discussion.

MY HEARTPRINT ♥

Give your team a score of 1, 5, or 10, with 1 being low (you have not addressed this inequity place at all) and 10 being high (you have erased this inequity place in your grade level, course, department, or school completely). Be sure to write the reasons!

1. Do we have complete agreement on the elements to be used to establish a grade for our grade level or course, and do we each apply those elements with fidelity based on our team agreements? Do we have agreement on our make-up work policies?

2. Do we write and use our common end-of-unit assessments?

3. Do we grade and double score some of our unit assessments together?

4. What will be our formative response, and how will we ensure students reflect, refine, and act on any work that is graded and passed back?

5. Have we created and do we use a student goal-setting, response-to-errors process on assessments and allow those responses to improve a student's grade?

In short, do you expect and seek the grading-inequity places of your grade level or course that may be preventing a student from getting up and over the essential standards learning bar? To help you in eradicating potential places of grading inequity, I recommend the research and helpful writing of thought leader and colleague Tom Schimmer in his 2016 book *Grading From the Inside Out: Bringing Accuracy to Student Assessment Through a Standards-Based Mindset.*[82]

Back to December 1979: the MAT 121 business calculus final exam results were in.

The multiple-choice exam would count for 25 percent of the students' grades. In some respects, 25 percent was an indicator of an equity we had erased. At least all of us would count the exam as 25 percent of students' grades, and this wouldn't vary depending on which professor students had for the course.

Grade submission deadlines were waiting. This final team meeting was critical. Remember, I was "Mr. Too Many As and Bs."

Well, my students pulled me through and proved me right. The same number of students who received As and Bs before the final exam received As and Bs on the final exam. My teaching reputation was saved!

In this time and in this moment of your professional life, do not let your present *isness* get in the way of your *oughtness*. Go after any inequities caused by teacher isolation—or lack of clarity on the important issues for inspiring student opportunities to learn—and watch the *oughtness* of your life become your new reality!

Know this: there might just be a few headaches along the way, as you reduce the noise of your professional work together.

Reduce Our
Professional Noise

In the world's greatest school systems . . . [there is] a set of invisible forces ensuring that no teacher is left alone to invent solutions to complicated and ever involving challenges of helping students learn.

–Elizabeth Green

Elizabeth Green is cofounder, CEO, and editor in chief of Chalkbeat, a nonprofit education news organization. She authored the 2014 book *Building a Better Teacher: How Teaching Works (and How to Teach It to Everyone)* based on her investigations of teaching in the United States and Japan. The book received recognition as a 2014 *New York Times* Book Review notable book.[83]

To summarize one of her primary points about our profession, or at least the one that made so much sense to me, much of our work as educators is based on a two-hundred-year practice of teaching in isolation. It is time to no longer think of our professional work as a private practice and reframe our mindset into thinking of our profession as a series of public performances.[84]

When we work in isolation and invent our own solutions to the problems and issues we face each day, it can create a wide variance in the practice of your team members. Our profession, the education of students, is considered a "noisy" profession, according to Princeton University's Daniel Kahneman and his colleagues. By noise they mean:

> The problem is that humans are unreliable decision makers; their judgments are strongly influenced by irrelevant factors, such as their current mood, the time since their last meal, and the weather.

Consider your personal response to Aaron's powerful words. How do his comments connect with your current school culture and your team's collective power to create a bigger difference in student learning than any individual member of the team?

_____

_____

_____

_____

_____

_____

_____

_____

_____

_____

_____

_____

_____

_____

_____

_____

_____

_____

_____

_____

The unavoidable conclusion is that professionals often make decisions that deviate significantly from their peers, from their own prior decisions and from rules they claim to follow.[85]

I asked my colleague Aaron Hansen, a wise professional educator, about how to achieve magnified impact within any team and cut through the noise of widely variant professional judgments. Aaron is a teacher and author and was named Nevada's 2009 Innovative Educator of the Year. He responded:

> It's a universal truth that it is through commitment and the discipline of adhering to self-set boundaries that we achieve true autonomy. This is easily evident in personal relationships, like a marriage. It's less obvious when talking about professional relationships like teams, but true nonetheless.
>
> When members of a team truly commit to the process of working with each other in the pursuit of a worthy cause that they really care about, they make a trade. They trade in the immediate gratification of being able to make all their own decisions for faith in the team's collective power to make a bigger difference. The sense of freedom comes as teams actually achieve goals they couldn't have reached on their own. In my mind, that's the essence of true autonomy—when you give up some immediate freedom in order to get something that means more. (A. Hansen, personal communication, July 12, 2016)

Aaron's words are poetic. Can you feel their value to the power of your team? Can you see how making decisions together might reduce the noisiness of your work?

 # MY HEARTPRINT

Kahneman and his team further suggest we conduct a noise audit for our teams by identifying differences and inconsistencies in our daily practices, diagnosing why we have so much noise (variant judgment) on issues for student learning, and then acting to harmonize the noise, so to speak.

Kahneman further indicates that your team could conduct a noise audit by creating a realistic scenario, diagnosing the sources of your noise, and working toward being more consistent as a team as you buy into actions that might reduce the noisy nature of the issues and how you generally respond.[86]

As an example of a situation that needed a noise audit, consider this real-life scenario.

For twelve years, as the director of mathematics and science at Stevenson, my routine during our Monday morning team time was generally pretty calm. Every Monday, thirty-three course-based teams would meet for collaboration time, as we discussed and prepared lessons, assessments, and materials for our units of study throughout the year. I would often rotate from one team to the next during team time, providing feedback as needed.

Then one morning, a teacher came running into my office and yelled, "Come quick, I think Maureen (not her real name) is dying! Call the paramedics; call the nurse!" I ran to the biology lab where that team was meeting, and ignoring my training about blood-borne pathogens, I jumped on Maureen and applied pressure with my hands on her face to stem the flow of blood until the paramedics and nurse could get there. It was quite a scene. Maureen ended up in the hospital, and several stitches later, came back to work.

"Maybe this collaboration idea isn't quite so easy," I thought. So, I asked the rest of Maureen's team, "What happened?" It seems that the team was trying to work out *common* homework assignments for the next unit of study in biology (erasing one of those inequity places you can go). When one of the team members got upset about the nature of common homework assignments (some application problems that did not pass her judgment or desire to assign, yet she was expected to honor since it was a team agreement), she threw her book at Maureen and knocked her out of the chair. I decided this team needed some conflict resolution support, something milder than book tossing, as they reduced the noise around the homework situation for their course!

The story itself is insightful in terms of this team's lack of understanding of how to reach consensus on important decisions, such as homework, when trying to reduce the noise and eliminate the inequity in this area of their work. What could the biology team have done differently to better engage in consensus development? How do we reach consensus on issues that reveal places of inequity?

Are there any areas of wide variance your team needs to work on this week or in this unit? Any places of inequity or noise you might be causing by not discussing and sharing with one another? What are those areas of your professional work, and how might you approach the effort with your team to reduce the noise and focus on the magnified impact on student learning?

_____

_____

_____

_____

_____

_____

_____

_____

_____

_____

_____

_____

_____

_____

_____

_____

_____

_____

_____

From a practical point of view, it starts by making sure everyone understands an operational definition of consensus: *everyone's voice on the team is heard, and the will of the group prevails.*

I would add to this definition, however, that the voice of each individual needs to be an *informed* voice and not just an opinion. As I told my faculty teams many times over the years, your voice needs to support practices that have evidence bigger than your opinion, and our practices must demonstrate evidence of an increase in student learning. Our choice to reduce the noisy nature of our work should always be an informed judgment and decision.

Can you think of a current noisy judgment issue for your school or team that needs to be resolved?

 # MY HEARTPRINT

To paraphrase Aaron Hansen's words: There is a sense of power and freedom that comes when members of your team achieve student learning goals they couldn't have reached on their own.

Despite my best efforts at collaboration for more than twenty years now, I have had several stumbles along the way. How about you? In my innocence, I just thought making our work more public with one another would be easy peasy, as some of my students like to say.

I was very wrong.

When I make my work more public, my greatest strengths and hidden weaknesses are revealed. My personal decision-making process and my personal judgment process are interrupted. Decisions well in advance of a unit of study are now more public. I might be a "prepare the lesson at the last minute" kind of guy! You and I might not agree, and now I must spend time integrating my ideas with yours. You might be a person with crazy ideas and whims (or you might think that of me).

Your pursuit over time of the ideals of a PLC culture is a pursuit to reduce the noise and the potential for wide variance and inequitable practices in your professional work. Working together has a great benefit.

MY HEARTPRINT 🩶

Of course, participating in these difficult "reducing the noisiness of our work" conversations requires a certain relational intelligence. We need a desire to not reach the book-throwing stage of my biology team members.

In the next chapter, you will discover the power of developing your social intelligence and improving your relationships with your colleagues and teams.

Reflect on the most difficult aspects of making your daily work more transparent and public with your colleagues. Do you easily invite others into your classroom and your work-life decisions?

_____

_____

_____

_____

_____

_____

_____

_____

_____

_____

_____

_____

_____

_____

_____

_____

_____

_____

_____

_____

_____

_____

_____

_____

_____

Relational Intelligence Required

We might think of "social intelligence" as a shorthand term for being intelligent not just about our relationships but also in them.

—Daniel Goleman

Did you know you and I are wired to connect with others? We are! Seriously!

In this chapter, we examine our relational capabilities more closely through the lens of behavioral scientist and world-renowned bestselling author, Daniel Goleman. As the author of *Social Intelligence: The New Science of Human Relationships*, Goleman reveals the incredible impact of our professional and personal relationships: "Nourishing relationships have a beneficial impact on our health, while toxic ones can act like slow poison in our bodies."[87]

You are most likely familiar with the term *intelligence quotient* or *IQ*. IQ tests were designed to predict success in school and "model the sorts of things which children do in school."[88]

Just as we have an IQ, we also have an EQ, or *emotional quotient*, sometimes referred to as our EI, for *emotional intelligence*.

With the release of his 1995 book *Emotional Intelligence*, and based on earlier work of Peter Salovey and John Mayer, Goleman described an extensive definition of EI.[89] By 1997, Salovey and Mayer more succinctly defined *emotional intelligence* as:

> The ability to perceive accurately, appraise, and express emotion; the ability to access and/or generate feelings when they facilitate thought; the ability to understand emotion and emotional knowledge; and the ability to regulate emotions to promote emotional and intellectual growth.[90]

Do you have any nourishing relationships at work? Do you have any toxic ones? How do those relationships affect your emotional state on a daily basis?

_____

_____

_____

_____

_____

_____

_____

_____

_____

_____

_____

_____

_____

_____

_____

_____

_____

_____

_____

_____

_____

_____

_____

_____

That definition is a handful! That is a whole lot of emotion going on.

According to Goleman, emotionally intelligent people give praise, create a climate of positivity, criticize well, provide direction, support people's needs, and "frame the group's mission in ways that give more meaning to each person's contribution—or not. . . . All these acts help determine a leader's primal emotional impact."[91]

Sweet, sign me up to work with that person!

 # MY HEARTPRINT

Furthermore, a positive emotional climate at work drives performance results, and your emotional intelligence drives how people on your team feel and perform. The more relationally demanding the work environment, the more these skills are needed. The more stressful the situation—such as working in chronically low-performing schools, working in a district with severe budget cutbacks, elimination of viable and necessary support programs, and the stress of public scrutiny—the more essential EI is for you and your colleagues. (If you are interested in learning more about Goleman's work, see the online links provided at the end of part 3 on page 150.)

By 2006, Goleman revealed evidence from an emerging field of social neuroscience when he published his book *Social Intelligence*. Going beyond IQ and EQ, he describes the intelligence of our social interactions and how they can reshape our brain through neuroplasticity: "The way repeated experiences sculpt the shape, size, and number of neurons and their synaptic connections. . . . Our relationships have subtle, yet powerful, lifelong impacts on us."[92]

Wow! Our repeated daily social interactions with one another have a lifelong impact on our overall health.

∞

John Dossey was, in fact, the first educator in my life who really noticed me. Dr. Dossey was one of my favorite professors in college. He was an associate professor of mathematics by age twenty-seven—my junior year in undergraduate school at Illinois State University—so, he and I were not too far apart in age, which may have helped our initial friendship. John and I shared a connection you might have with someone on your team: it felt pleasant, engaged, and easy.

Not surprisingly, when you are in rapport with a colleague, you are able to be more creative and efficient when making decisions. You become a valuable asset to each other as part of your daily work. And for this reason, I returned to graduate school, for a chance to once again work with and learn from John.

He was unique in that he made it clear to me that as graduate student and professor, we would learn from each other. There would be reciprocity to our work together. He also made it clear he expected me to do high-quality work every day.

John was the first teacher I had that helped me understand Goleman's quote at the opening of this chapter.[93] Developing my relational or social intelligence required me to go deeper than just meeting with him and doing our work. It was about commitment to the work, to my colleagues in the mathematics department at the university, and to my students. It was about being in the relationships at work. It was about developing a rapport with my students, listening to them, demonstrating empathy for them, and exhibiting a passion for their work and effort, just as John was modeling for me.

Much of what we do well in life comes down to our feelings of well-being and happiness. Goleman cites Nobel Prize–winning economist Daniel Kahneman's four-item list (in order) of the people in our lives that we most desire to socialize with in a more mutually nourishing way.[94]

1. First friends, and then relatives
2. Then spouse or partner, and then children
3. Then students or parents, and then coworkers or colleagues
4. Then your boss

Do you find Kahneman's ordered list consistent with your own life? Do you most desire to socialize with your friends, relatives, spouse or partner, children, students and parents, colleagues, and finally boss—in that order?

Coworkers are pretty far down on the list. No wonder despite being wired to relate with others, the desire to socialize with colleagues may be lower than we think, unless we elevate them to friend status.

MY HEARTPRINT 💜

Using these same mutually nourishing categories, write your own ordered list of those you most desire to socialize with. Does your list match Daniel Kahneman's?

Do you agree with Goleman's statement about the good life? Describe the nature of the nourishing relationships in your life these days.

_____

_____

_____

_____

_____

_____

_____

_____

_____

_____

_____

_____

_____

_____

_____

_____

_____

_____

_____

_____

_____

At the time that John was in my life, he was mostly a boss-type person for me. I was his graduate student, and I was working for him. I did not view our relationship as coworkers, and yet John did. In a strange way, he treated me like an emotional equal and as a friend. Yet, he taught and modeled for me how to be more thoughtful and noticing of the effort of others along the way.

Goleman states, "Among people around the world, nourishing relationships are the single most universally agreed-on feature of the good life."[95]

MY HEARTPRINT

We should build relationally with others. And for some educators this is a much easier pursuit than for others. Trying hard to be more relational just doesn't come as naturally for some of us.

Over the years, I have had several faculty members who wanted to be team leaders, grade-level leaders, district coordinators, instructional coaches, assistant principals, or principals—and they were fairly well skilled in the nature of the work—yet they were not relationally strong enough with other adults, often offending other colleagues or not having what we might term a high relational intelligence and emotional awareness of others.

I knew if I allowed individuals with low-level emotional intelligence to be placed into an expanded leadership position, it would create problems for everyone else in their sphere of influence.

I have several colleagues, some whom I worked with at Stevenson, who claim you cannot get better relationally. It is not a skill you can improve with deliberate practice. You either have the ability to relate well or you don't (as if it is about talent and not effort). You either have the EI to develop knowledge, self-awareness, and relational capacity in yourself and others, or you don't.

I suspect that, like me, Goleman would disagree. In *The Emotionally Intelligent Workplace*, he indicates a framework for emotional and social intelligence, which includes specific competencies for improvement, such as empathy, service orientation, development of others' needs, conflict management, teamwork, and collaboration. These competencies are key ingredients of a successful workplace, and the development of these competencies begins with the model and then the subsequent influence of team members toward building these competencies with other colleagues on your team.[96]

Your team members' success is predicated on their relationship with you and the emotional climate you create and support. It is possible that with sheer will alone, you may not be as strong or confident relationally as you want to be. Or you may fluctuate between good and bad relational days. Goleman provides guidelines for how to become a stronger educator relationally. The four practices listed in the next My Heartprint provide a great basis for measuring how you and those on your team are doing. You can become a more intimate teacher and relate better to others.

MY HEARTPRINT ♥

Examine the following four criteria for improving your relational intelligence. Choose one you know needs some work during your current school season. Decide one action you can take to get better at the EI practice you choose.

Consider asking a trusted colleague to tell you which one he or she thinks you need to work on, and see if it matches with your choice. My experience is it most likely will not.

1. *Listen without interrupting.* Record your next leadership or teacher team meeting. How often do your team members interrupt one another?

2. *Practice empathy through deliberate inquiry.* How often do your team members seek first to understand the meaning and intent of the words of others? How often do you hear the phrase, "Tell me more," or "How could I support you in this work?" in your daily conversations?

3. *Never betray a private conversation.* Is the fine line between what is for public knowledge and what is for private knowledge crystal clear for your leadership or teacher team? As teams pursue greater transparency, how well does everyone respect the confidences of private conversations, including team conversations?

4. *Exhibit genuine passion for the people you serve.* How well do members of your leadership team exhibit genuine interest and pay private and personal attention to the individuals in their sphere of influence?

_____

_____

_____

_____

_____

_____

_____

_____

_____

Reread Goleman's words
about IQ and social intelligence.
It took me three tries before his
words began to gather meaning
for me. What is your take on his
comments for your work life?

_____

_____

_____

_____

_____

_____

_____

_____

_____

_____

_____

_____

_____

_____

_____

_____

_____

_____

_____

_____

_____

In 2005, Goleman updated his book, *Emotional Intelligence: Why It Can Matter More Than IQ.*[97] He detailed a powerful finding initially revealed in his earlier book *Social Intelligence.*

> In a little-remarked scientific embarrassment, IQ tests themselves have no underlying theoretical rationale supporting them. Rather they were designed ad hoc, to predict success in the classroom. . . . The more powerful force in the brain's architecture is arguably the need to navigate the social world, not the need to get A's. . . . Those who would say that social intelligence amounts to little more than general intelligence applied to social situations might do better to reason the other way around: to consider that general intelligence is merely a derivative of social intelligence.[98]

 # MY HEARTPRINT

Here is my takeaway: your relational improvement effort, your emotional grit, so to speak, has an impact on developing your talent and level of achievement in our profession.

One final reflection I have often asked of myself: *Would you like to work with you?*

In a June 2016 *Harvard Business Review* article, renowned cellist Yo-Yo Ma reflected on the keys to effective collaboration. He summed up the nature of effective collaboration as two words: *ego management.* Ma claims, "It's easy to get locked into 'in my world' or 'this is the way I see it,' so you have to move your brain to a different time or structure . . . a somewhat spongelike state, as opposed to a judging one."[99] He then states, "If you think differently than I do, then let me put myself in your shoes and see what's successful according to you, and then you do the same for me."[100]

As to what Ma looks for if he was to collaborate with you: "First I look for generosity; second, mutual respect and admiration."[101]

I read his words and thought about how hard it is to show empathy when I am on a team with someone whom I do not respect or admire or who judges me harshly. Being mindful of treating each other well, however, becomes a priority of our relational and professional work-life responsibilities. The beneficiaries of our relational intelligence improvement are our students. This is why expert teachers and leaders exhaust themselves trying to cross the line of education as a *private practice* and move over to education as a series of *public performances* with one another.

Expert educators understand there is a strength and no shame in crossing that line.

What Are Those Black Boxes?

So we beat on, boats against the current, borne back ceaselessly into the past.

—F. Scott Fitzgerald

Just as we are how we treat each other, we also are how we choose to learn from one another. In "Bringing Minds Together," author and cofounder of Boston Scientific, John Abele, describes essential elements of building community with our colleagues.

Although talking in the context of the medical field, Abele makes a point that applies just as well to you and me in our profession, when he states:

> Community building begins with convincing people who don't need to work together that they should.

> This depends on:

> - Inspiring them with a vision for change that is beyond any of their powers to bring about individually

> - Convincing them that the other collaborators are vital to the effort and equal to the challenge

> - Preventing any one person from benefiting so much that the others feel their contributions are being exploited[102]

Abele establishes that the community builder (you as a team leader or as a team member) is responsible for ensuring that these three community-building success criteria are protected. How would you rate your current grade-level teams, course-based teams, or school-based teams on these criteria?

Abele also describes the importance of live demonstration and audience interaction as part of building community together. This fits well with the notion of team lesson study as a way to be more public with each other and to learn from one another.

Enter Alex Chicos, the director of the Cardiac Electrophysiology Laboratory at Northwestern Memorial Hospital in Chicago. I first met Dr. Chicos due to a recurring problem with atrial fibrillation. It is not necessarily life-threatening, but it gives you a deep malaise, as your resting heart rate sits in the range of one hundred to one hundred twenty beats per minute. After two failed attempts at what is called a catheter ablation (essentially a mapping of your heart and then zapping the areas that might be causing the electrical circuits to misfire), I finally went to Northwestern Memorial Hospital to seek a solution with Dr. Chicos.

He convinced me to try one more time, letting me know they had sort of a road map to work from based on my previous failed attempts. I was pretty loopy and drifting in and out during the six-hour procedure. I thought I was pretty funny too. I kept telling the medical team working on me how much I loved them, and the ceiling tiles seemed to me to be moving like a wave washing over me.

I also noticed some angels in the gallery with black boxes in their hands. Strange!

The key component of this story is the team of doctors and nurses during and after the procedure. These doctors take a team approach to treating atrial fibrillation patients undergoing catheter ablation procedures. I was in a dedicated electrophysiology laboratory with an entire team of heart rhythm specialists, cardiac surgeons, cardiologists, cardiac electrophysiologists, nurses, and other experts, who coordinated their efforts for my procedure.

In a post-operation follow-up two weeks later, I asked Dr. Chicos about the angels with the black boxes I saw during the procedure. He explained that the angels were residents and interns with iPad-like devices to take notes about my procedure. My procedure was recorded for review after it was completed. During the procedure, the observers were able to take notes for feedback and discussion later—all with the aim to improve the next ablation procedure patient who may have similar heart symptoms as mine.

I thanked Dr. Chicos for his time and his leadership in helping me experience a more normal life (I have had no symptoms since), walked out of his office, and thought to myself, "Man, we do not do anything like that in my profession."

Consider this professional idea: we design and record a lesson, we ask five to six teachers to observe the lesson using iPads, yellow pads, or any type of notepad, and take notes while observing both teacher and student behavior. Within twenty-four hours, the team meets to discuss specifics about what worked and what did not work for successful student engagement and learning and decides how to improve the lesson for the next set of students.

That would be a fantasy world for our profession. The idea we could and would willingly make our work public to one another and learn from each other is so essential to our growth. I hope this is part of who you are becoming these days. Those "learning from one another" alliances matter. They help us become more connected to our work.

MY HEARTPRINT ♥

As educators, we build the bridge of great teaching and leading as we learn to walk on it. We do not and most likely never will have the exact answers to our work. That is why there is an *art* to our profession. We always try to improve our behavior and inspire improved student performance. And, we build that learning bridge together. We connect, one piece at a time. We look back, and we see the impact of our work. And we see change in ourselves.

Who do you need to become so that others would want to connect with and learn from you? You can become someone who is proactive and not reactive in your decision-making process. You can become someone who demonstrates enthusiasm, persistence, and inspiration and pushes the team for the desired and expected student performance results.

This is how you'll know when you are not connecting with your students and colleagues.

- You only do your work out of obligation or compulsion.
- You feel unusually overwhelmed by your usual workload.
- Your concerns are mostly self-focused.
- Your ego gets in the way of sharing with others.

List the first action you currently take to stay connected to your colleagues and to learn from them every week in a *public sharing* of your daily work, professional practice, and action.

_____

_____

_____

_____

_____

_____

_____

_____

_____

_____

_____

_____

_____

_____

_____

_____

_____

_____

_____

_____

_____

_____

_____

_____

_____

_____

Examine the seven personal barriers from the list that might cause you to disconnect from the work of your team.

Choose one starting point from the list, and write about what you might do to improve your connectedness with others on your team.

———————————————

———————————————

———————————————

———————————————

———————————————

———————————————

———————————————

———————————————

———————————————

———————————————

———————————————

———————————————

———————————————

———————————————

———————————————

———————————————

———————————————

———————————————

———————————————

———————————————

———————————————

———————————————

———————————————

———————————————

- ◆ You wonder if you are making any impact on your team's work results and effort.
- ◆ You are reactive rather than proactive when making decisions in class or with your team.
- ◆ You would rather maintain the status quo than take risks and make changes to current practice.

MY HEARTPRINT

In reflection, realities surrounding your current work situation usually prompt your selection—such as the reality of your present job, your current school year, a recent set of personal circumstances that have cropped up in your life, or your wiring or temperament (for example, when I was a teacher in my twenties, I could have used a dose of surrendered ego—sometimes my own ego and desire to be right got in the way of listening to and sharing good ideas with others).

Sometimes, our profession can feel like a string of endless days beating us down, hammering hard on the hope of our better tomorrow. But it is in the building of the bridge as we walk it each day, as a community, that we overcome the events that conspire against us. As indicated in the ending to *The Great Gatsby*: "So we beat on, boats against the current, borne back ceaselessly into the past."[103]

By rowing the boat together and belonging to a team, you and I overcome the currents of our work life that sometimes beat against us. Don't let the currents win.

On a personal parallel, by rowing the boat together with my wife Susan, I have overcome so many of the currents that have beat on me in this lifetime. There is no other way to honor her other than be in the boat with her.

As you and your colleagues pursue the steady heartbeat of becoming a fully formed professional, the benefits of connecting and belonging in both your professional and personal life become deep and real. You meet this aspect of your professional heartprint through understanding and embracing the power of celebration in your work life.

That's next.

Celebration: Making *Above and Beyond the Norm* the Norm

H   E   A   R   T

Celebrations infuse life with passion and purpose. They summon the human spirit.

—Terrence E. Deal and M. K. Key

I suspect you and your team will have one regret if you do not become intentional about this most important element of the alliances you forge in your life. You will look back and realize you did not celebrate nearly enough. I have never heard any team of educators complain that their work, effort, behavior, or results were celebrated too much.

If anything, the complaint is too little. Far too little.

At Stevenson, Rick DuFour understood the importance of radical and authentic public celebration long before I did at our leadership team meetings. Early on in my teaching and leading career, I was often the voice that would argue against public celebration. I felt we would invariably forget to mention someone who had accomplished something and then feelings would be hurt.

How would we know whom to celebrate? Would the rest of the staff really enjoy celebrating colleagues who did things better than they did? This type of deficit thinking is sometimes known as the tall poppy syndrome—a pejorative term used to describe a social phenomenon in which people of genuine merit are resented, attacked, cut down, or criticized because their behavior, effort, grit, and achievements elevate them above or distinguish them from their peers.[104]

But I was very wrong.

Over the years at Stevenson, we systemically began to think of celebration as an important aspect of our culture for continuous growth as a profession, and our community eventually became one of taller poppies—every one of our adults. As a school organization, our incremental pursuit of greatness was often best revealed during these celebration moments. We would reach critical milestones and ask, "Can we get taller?"

At Stevenson, celebrations became a public event three times per year. We would plan for public celebrations with all adults at the start of the year on opening day, during mid-year between semesters, and at the end of the school year before the summer break. We would share and celebrate our trend data and student achievement data at the start of the year. We would celebrate our student satisfaction data (student survey results), during mid-year, and we would celebrate our Super Pats (we were the Patriots) at mid-year and end of the year.

As principal, Rick DuFour would stand on our stage in the Performing Arts Center, and in front of about 450 school district faculty and staff, celebrate the accomplishments of many. His tone of voice and sincere presence would cause everyone to focus and listen as he read story after story of celebration. An example of one such story follows.

When a colleague's spouse was critically ill for an extended period of time, these two teachers stepped in to help out in a big way. In their efforts to ensure that no student fell behind due to the extended absence of the teacher, these two individuals created sub plans, shared teaching responsibilities, wrote and scored assessments, and provided her students with extra help as needed. Their superior efforts helped to minimize the impact of their colleague's absence by continuing to provide students with quality instruction and feedback on their performance. Their willingness to go above and beyond has earned them this recognition. This Super Pat goes to _____.

The Super Pat Award would be handed out to these teachers or teacher teams, and Rick would move on to celebrate the next story of effort and achievement special and unique to our school culture. Rick taught all of us how to use celebration as a tool to *build* community. He was an insightful leader who used celebration to connect us to our shared purpose and to create a sense of belonging among the faculty, staff, and students.

Consider these behind-the-scenes planning elements for successful public celebrations.

- *Effective identification:* Two months before the celebration event, the administrative team, faculty, and staff would submit names of individuals and teams worthy of a Super Pat.
- *Effective criteria:* The award would be given based on any above-and-beyond adult actions that moved the school closer to its vision, values, and desired results.
- *Effective rewards:* Awardees received a variety of Super Pat hardware, from a paperweight and bookends to a book that might reflect their hobbies or interests.
- *Effective storytelling:* Important elements of the process included connecting the story to student success, describing the predicament that was solved, highlighting the details and effects of the adult actions, and saving the names of the awardees until the end.

Business school authors at Santa Clara University and world-renowned leadership gurus Jim Kouzes and Barry Posner capture the essence of presence and identity in team celebration, quoting Harvard professor Howard Gardner. Gardner, as cited by Kouzes and Posner, emphasizes:

> The artful creation and articulation of stories constitutes a fundamental part of the teacher's vocation. Stories speak to both parts of the human mind—its reason and emotion. And I suggest, further, that it is stories of identity—narratives that help individuals think about and feel who they are, where they come from, and where they are headed—that constitute the single most powerful weapon in the teacher's literary arsenal.[105]

MY HEARTPRINT ♥

Gardner nails the celebration point, doesn't he? For our colleagues and our students to be successful, they need to reason and feel that success. They (and we) need to see themselves in the narrative of our work.

What is your reaction to the Howard Gardner quote? Do your current celebrations meet some of his listed criteria?

_____

_____

_____

_____

_____

_____

_____

_____

_____

_____

_____

_____

_____

_____

_____

_____

_____

_____

_____

_____

_____

_____

_____

_____

_____

_____

_____

_____

_____

_____

_____

Scott Carr is an exceptional middle school teacher, administrator, and leader at Liberty Junior High School in Clay County, Missouri, which was recognized as the 2007 Outstanding School of the Year by the Missouri Center for School Reform. The Liberty culture embraces the importance of radical celebration. I asked Scott about the storytelling nature of a positive school culture. Here is what he said:

> I believe that storytelling is one of the most powerful tools we use in education. I love telling stories but I also love to listen to a good story. Many times, I will ask teams to share their stories rather than expect them to listen to mine. There is something magical that happens to a team when they get to convey their journey through a narrative. They become very proud of who they are as a team and what they hope to become. They begin to add a future to their current story by contemplating where they are heading next and what it will take to get there. Once they start sharing, there's no stopping them! Stories and celebration drive the culture in our school. I am constantly looking for ways to get my staff to share with one another and the community. Everyone needs to hear a good story! (S. Carr, personal communication, June 16, 2016)

So, here is my challenge to you. Raise your noticing quotient. Notice the incredible small victories you and your team are experiencing every day, and share them. Scott's words seem to promote the idea of being fully present with one another—whether it be public or private.

In his essay, "Waiting for Us to Notice Them," James Lang reveals the idea of working with a pedagogy of presence.[106] I really like that phrase as a life motto. Does it connect with you?

Am I fully present in this conversation with you today? Am I fully present with my students during the lesson? Do I walk through the day honoring others by being present with them in the moment we are in? Am I fully present with my family and friends at home?

Or, is my face in my phone?

Lang means, I think, are we aware of how we are engaging with our colleagues and classroom of students? Are we really noticing the students or just going through the motions of another lesson? Are we aware of our colleagues and their well-being—on this day? Do we exhibit to others a pedagogy of presence?

In the mid-1990s, I made a promise to myself to notice my students and colleagues more. I decided I would write note cards every day for the rest of my life, either to a family member, colleague, or student.

The card would celebrate and thank the person for actions that we place high value on either in our family or our work. I wanted to celebrate those making the discretionary effort toward a professional life reflecting *above and beyond the norm* as the norm.

I knew that for my notes to have meaning, they needed to be sincere as well, from my heart. Over time, those note cards became a bit more electronic and sent via email, text, or WhatsApp.

There have been a lot of folks who told me that my note came at just the right moment for them. There was even one surprise. It was time for our annual retirement party, and one of the faculty members retiring was someone I had battled a lot over the years. We didn't exactly see eye to eye on the vision of our work and how to best move that work forward.

During the retirement ceremony, this colleague came up to me with a small notebook and said, "I just wanted you to know how grateful I am for all of the time you took to invest in my teaching and my work." Since this was the first time this person had ever said anything remotely like that, it took me quite by surprise.

"I want to show you something," my colleague opened the notebook to show me five handwritten notes I had given over the years. The colleague mentioned that the notes had helped on days when the job was a struggle. We hugged, and I walked away realizing you never really know the impact that noticing others may have on the world we live in.

So, spend your life working to develop a radical celebration plan with your family, colleagues, and students. Begin publicly and privately celebrating now. Don't delay. Don't make excuses. Don't say you are too busy. Don't take the efforts of those around you for granted. Celebrate small day-to-day efforts that are above and beyond the norm for expectations at work, and make sure you celebrate the heroes that bring the meaningful moments of student learning into a reality.

Notice your significant other, children, friends, or colleagues at work, and give them the public and private encouragement and support they need. Do it tonight. Don't wait until tomorrow. Write notes or send pictures; take the time to celebrate the people in your life.

Be intentional, mindful, and purposeful with your quiet celebrations as you build an authentic professional learning community with all the students and colleagues in your professional life.

My advice? Have a radical celebration plan every day. Raise your awareness of the effort of others, and watch your relationships improve!

FINAL THOUGHTS

Why Helping Others Drives Our Success

H　　E　　♥　　R　　T

Meet Adam Grant. Grant is an author and a professor at the Wharton School of the University of Pennsylvania. He wrote an engaging and helpful *New York Times* bestselling book, *Give and Take: Why Helping Others Drives Our Success.* If you are interested in the topic, I highly recommend his book for an in-depth look at the nature of the colleagues you work with every day.

In the book, Grant establishes three fundamental reciprocity styles of social interaction: giving, taking, and matching. Grant describes each style as having a descriptive signature.[107]

1. *Takers* like to get more than they give. They place their own interests ahead of others' needs.
2. *Givers* prefer to give more than they get. They are other-focused, placing more attention on what other people need from them.
3. *Matchers* prefer to keep a score and keep things balanced. They are focused on a principle of fairness and an even exchange of favors.

Which of these three fundamental styles of social interaction or reciprocity styles do you believe is most successful?

The results that Grant reveals may surprise you, as the science of how we behave continues to be revealed. Grant does say it is possible for all three styles to achieve some degree of success.

The least successful style, however, is the givers. Does that surprise you?

Givers on a team achieve less success because they place making others better off ahead of their own self-interest. They also set themselves up for burnout and potential resentment.

Which reciprocity styles do you most like working with in your colleagues? Which style describes your primary behavior with colleagues?

_____

_____

_____

_____

_____

_____

_____

_____

_____

_____

_____

_____

_____

_____

_____

_____

_____

_____

_____

_____

_____

_____

_____

_____

So, who is at the top of the success ladder then? Get ready!

It also is the *givers*.

The givers on your team, when balancing the nature of their giving, are the most successful teachers and leaders in your school. To quote Grant:

> When takers win, there's usually someone else who loses. Research shows that people tend to envy successful takers and look for ways to knock them down a notch. In contrast, when givers win, people are rooting for them and supporting them, rather than gunning for them. Givers succeed in a way that creates a ripple effect, enhancing the success of people around them. You'll see the difference lies in how giver success creates value, instead of just claiming it.[108]

I sat with that next-to-last sentence in the quote for quite a long time: "Givers succeed in a way that creates a ripple effect, enhancing the success of people around them."

 # MY HEARTPRINT

Sign me up! Put me on a team of balanced givers, and we could change the world! That is just how I feel. However, if you are to be a successful giver, and not one of those that falls on the trash heap, then heed these two cautions.

1. *Embrace high other-interest and high self-interest:* Make sure you take care of your own self-interest along the way. As Grant indicates, "Successful givers weren't just more other-oriented than their peers; they were also more self-interested . . . just as ambitious as takers and matchers."[109]

2. *Get and give impact feedback:* Giver burnout has less to do with compassion fatigue and more to do with knowing whether or not there is an impact as a result of the giving. Did a colleague's behavior change in the classroom? Did student learning increase during this unit of study? Grant describes this frustration for

teachers: "Even though teachers interact with their students on a daily basis, it can take many years for their impact to sink in. By then, the students have moved on, and teachers are left wondering did my work actually matter?"[110]

We began part 3 of the book with why we should collaborate and finished with the idea of celebrating each incremental team success as part of our heartprint. In the Grant quote, we discover that to be successful professionals we need to collaborate but also be mindful of not being taken advantage of by our colleagues. In the end, mindful collaboration is worth the energy and effort required, as we see and feel our impact on student learning on a weekly, if not daily basis. Alliances then, become part of our professional story.

We opened part 3 with the essential heartprint question: Are you a person open to influence and shared values, able to become relationally intelligent and interdependent with others?

I close with this heartprint comment: the *C*, in PLC, *community*, is worth fighting for.

To do so means we honor the agreements and covenants of our teams, give in to our self-interest, and unleash our unselfish gene, but not to the point we let others take advantage of us. We cut through the noise of our work and erase student-learning inequities caused by our own isolated behaviors. We push to improve our EI, we treat our students and colleagues with grace, and we practice the pedagogy of being fully present each day.

Take a moment to reflect on part 3, "A Is for Alliances," and the past seven chapters. What are your primary takeaways? Include two or three possible actions you can take as you continue your journey in this important aspect of your work life. Think of the next steps as *I will*. . . statements, and write them down as you measure your personal heartprint during this stage of your career.

MY HEARTPRINT ♥

_____

_____

_____

_____

_____

_____

_____

_____

_____

_____

_____

_____

_____

The following resources are instrumental in the support of our work together in part 3. Depending on your personal interests, you may use these resources as you continue to expand your knowledge base and the knowledge base of your colleagues. You may also visit **go.SolutionTree.com/HEART** to access direct links to the websites and download three additional chapters related to part 3.

Part 3: A Is for Alliances

Resources

Abele, J. (2011). Bringing minds together. *Harvard Business Review, 89*(7–8). Accessed at https://hbr.org/2011/07/bringing-minds-together on September 1, 2016.

Beard, A. (2016). Yo-Yo Ma on successful creative collaboration. *Harvard Business Review.* Accessed at https://hbr.org/ideacast/2016/05/yo-yo-ma-on-successful-creative-collaboration on August 1, 2016.

Benkler, Y. (2011a). *The penguin and the leviathan: How cooperation triumphs over self-interest.* New York: Crown Business.

Benkler, Y. (2011b). The unselfish gene. *Harvard Business Review, 89*(7–8). Accessed at https://hbr.org/2011/07/the-unselfish-gene on September 1, 2016.

DuFour, R. (2015). *In praise of American educators: And how they can become even better* (pp. 121–136). Bloomington, IN: Solution Tree Press.

DuFour, R., DuFour, R., Eaker, R., Many, T. W., & Mattos, M. (2016). *Learning by doing: A handbook for Professional Learning Communities at Work* (3rd ed.). Bloomington, IN: Solution Tree Press.

Grant, A. (2014). *Give and take: Why helping others drives our success.* New York: Penguin.

Guskey, T. (2015). *On your mark: Challenging the conventions of grading and reporting.* Bloomington, IN: Solution Tree Press.

Kahneman, D., Rosenfield, A., Gandhi, L., & Blaser, T. (2016). Noise. *Harvard Business Review, 94*(10), 38–46.

Mattos, M., DuFour, R., DuFour, R., Eaker, R., & Many, T. W. (2016). *Concise answers to frequently asked questions about Professional Learning Communities at Work.* Bloomington, IN: Solution Tree Press.

Schimmer, T. (2016). *Grading from the inside out: Bringing accuracy to student assessment through a standards-based mindset.* Bloomington, IN: Solution Tree Press.

Additional Resources

More on the PLC at Work process: http://allthingsplc.info

More on the work of Elizabeth Green and transparency in our work: www.chalkbeat.org

More on Daniel Goleman and emotional intelligence: www.danielgoleman.info and www.danielgoleman.info/topics/emotional-intelligence

A free online quiz to test your emotional intelligence: www.ihhp.com/free-eq-quiz

PART 4

DEVELOPING HEART

R

Is for Risk

Essential Heartprint Question: Are you a person of vision-focused risk taking for sustainable change, with a growth and data-driven mindset for learning and life?

It is a way of thinking: "My role, as a teacher, is to evaluate the effect I have on my students." It is to "know thy impact," it is to understand this impact, and it is to act on this knowing and understanding. This requires that teachers gather defensible and dependable evidence from many sources, and hold collaborative discussions with colleagues and students about this evidence, thus making the effect of their teaching visible to themselves and to others.

—John Hattie

In part 4, "R Is for Risk," we explore the role that risk and risk taking play in our pursuit of a fully informed and reflective professional life—a life that results in meaningful and sustained change that demonstrates an impact on student learning. It is through this type of focused change we become efficiently pulled forward in our work.

I have dedicated my entire professional life to better understanding risk taking and change and have written much about it in previous work. This much I know. Taking risks brings out a very emotional and often visceral response in us. Some of us are averse to risk due to many factors, including some of the energy and engagement drain factors discussed in part 2 of this book, or some of the relationally draining alliance factors described in part 3.

For some, to change and take on one more new idea or action this year or take a risk in one more area of your work, it will just be too much. Risk taking is not a positive emotion for you. At least not right now.

Others are risk seekers. "Let's try it!" you say. You are willing to embrace any new idea or action and often are ready to move on to something new and different in order to maintain interest in your work. Risk taking is generally a very positive emotion for you, and you are not fazed by the possible failure of the risks you take.

And, just as our profession is dedicated to helping students take risks and develop new knowledge and understanding, so does our profession expect us to take risks and improve in our learning and understanding of our work throughout our entire career. However, the call to become a risk taker within our profession is a call to become a measured risk taker throughout our life.

First, measured risk taking is based on evidence of student and adult learning and evidence of our impact on others. This means our risk-taking moves are based on feedback from student performance coupled with a reflective response to the strategies we use to enhance student learning, subsequently taking risks toward improved strategies for the future. In some ways, the results and evidence of our work cause us to reflect and *look backward* at our daily actions.

Second, measured risk taking is based on a shared vision for decision-making behavior. We pursue effective and deliberate collaboration and examine our risk-taking moves based on our belief that the risks involved will advance our team, school, or district toward its vision for improving student learning.

In this sense, a shared vision pulls us *forward* as we risk and take actions in our work that we believe will advance the shared vision, and provide eventual evidence of student learning. *Shared vision* provides a focus for our risk-taking efforts, and *results* become evidence of success or failure in the risks we take. Thus, vision and risk taking become a connected duo during our collaboration and personal growth efforts. This duo helps to minimize the potential negative emotions of taking risks.

Part 4, "R Is for Risk," is a very grown-up (think maturing) aspect of our work. We could be great at each of the HEART elements of happiness, energy, and alliances, but then we must ask a most difficult question: *Does our lifetime of work and effort as educators matter?*

As we grow in our understanding of being a fully formed professional working within the context of a collaborative learning community, a key phrase of the PLC process will continuously crop up: *Is there evidence of student learning based on the risks our team has taken?* Essentially, we risk and measure our success based on evidence of student learning that resides in the aftermath of our effort.

MY HEARTPRINT 💜

Why take risks? Because, we seek to continuously discover our full potential through *reflection, refinement, and action* based on student results.

Does that seem like a strange response? Ultimately, no matter how much we achieve as educators, we will always be merely good relative to what we can become—our greatest potential. And, ultimately, our students' performance measures the impact of that potential.

Our success resides in their hands. Did they learn?

We are all in a state of creating great, and better, seasons of teaching and learning—one school year at a time. Greatness as a teacher and leader is an inherently dynamic process, not an end point. Greatness lies in our ability to make a distinctive impact on student learning over a long period of time. The moment you or I think we are great, that we have made it in our profession, our slide toward entropy has already begun.

The seven chapters in part 4 begin with understanding how to set targets for student learning that connect the risks you take to the results of your

What does *evidence of student learning* as an aspect of the risk-taking culture in your team or school mean to you? What evidence of learning do you use to measure your risk-taking efforts as a team?

_____

_____

_____

_____

_____

_____

_____

_____

_____

_____

_____

_____

_____

_____

_____

_____

_____

_____

_____

_____

_____

_____

work, examine your beliefs about whether each student can achieve those learning targets, and connect your risk-taking efforts to both improving your work and improving student results.

These chapters then provide insight into how to sustain your risk-taking efforts and minimize the negative emotions that can come with risk and failure. How can we become more intentional as risk takers by developing trust with our colleagues? Part 4 concludes with wise words from Rick DuFour and a promise to avoid the subtleness of entropy that most assuredly awaits us if we don't stay focused on meaningful change in our daily practice.

It is my hope these chapters will help you become a more confident and measured professional risk taker and change agent—forever.

What's in a Goal?

> *Of all the things I've done, the most vital is coordinating the*
> *talents of those who work for us and pointing them toward a*
> *certain goal.*
>
> —Walt Disney

As I work on this chapter, I am at Disney World in Orlando. The opening quote I chose many months ago for this chapter is from Walt Disney. I am here to observe a colleague, Nathan Lang, speak and to provide him with feedback for his professional life goals. As always, I am here to learn from him as well.

Interesting word—*goals.*

Those of you familiar with the writing or the creating process for any type of project know that it is painful and slower than you would like. There will be a lot of reflection and refinement moments. For example, as I work on this chapter, it is now my eleventh try to clean it up and get it right. Would it be appropriate to say my goal is to keep taking risks with the words and rewriting the chapter until I get it to a point where I hope it will connect to you, the reader?

Well, it depends on what we mean by a goal in our profession. What does the word *goal* mean to you? Did you notice the word in the Walt Disney quote? He ends with ". . . and pointing them toward a certain goal."[111] I wonder what he really meant? What pops into our heads when we hear the word *goal?*

One common use of the word *goal* is to indicate an activity or action related to our work life or our personal life. For example:

- This year it is our goal to implement the new reading curriculum.
- My goal today is to teach division of fractions.
- Our third-grade team goal is to develop common homework assignments this year.
- Our district goal is to provide training to all faculty on school safety.

- My goal is to run a half marathon this year.
- My goal is to start that diet—tomorrow.

These goals are admirable and do require some risk, as they require that we take action and complete them. Yet, they are limited in that they do not take the risk of connecting us to either the emotion of our work or the outcomes of our work. They are not measurable goals in terms of quality.

A second use of the word *goal* is to indicate a *measurable outcome* or result due to our work effort and actions. This then more directly connects our risk-taking actions to the results of our work.

- This year, as a result of implementing the new reading curriculum, our goal for reading scores will improve from 68 percent proficient at grade level, to 80 percent proficient at grade level.
- As a result of today's lesson on fraction division, my goal is for 100 percent of my students to demonstrate understanding based on the exit task we created.
- Our team goal this year is to increase the number of students completing daily homework assignments from 65 percent to 90 percent.
- My goal is to improve my half-marathon time to under two hours this year.
- My goal is to have a perfect attendance record this year.

Do you see the difference in the two lists? The first goal list has no measurable outcomes attached to it. It is a list of stuff you plan to do (you can check tasks off as you do them). The second list is *measurable* in the sense that it is based on *evidence* of learning or evidence of behavioral outcomes achieved. It sets a results target, connects us more deeply to the outcomes of our work, and helps us to know if our actions do or do not make a difference for improved student learning and behavior. When we connect our efforts to results, this places us at a more personal and emotional risk.

When we pursue becoming a fully formed professional, we tie our heartprint to the results of our effort, and we do not stop at our effort alone. In our profession, our effort, all the things we *do*, is not an end. Our energy and effort are the means to achieving the end results and measure if the effort and risk actually made a difference in student learning.

I consider the first list of goals as a nice set of actions or effort, but the list does not represent measurable learning goals. Goals, when referenced as part of the PLC process, are the *results* of our work effort.

Thus, goals represent the measurable outcomes of our effort and action. Goals connect our profession to the ultimate recipients of our actions—our students' performance and our colleagues' improvement.

By creating the potential for our personal failure (we might not reach a measurable goal or target that beckons, as I like to call it), we attach ourselves more emotionally to our work. "Did I actually make a difference in student learning?" is a much tougher standard by which to measure your success, because students have to participate. Your success as a teacher and leader in the school rests in the hands of your students and in your ability, as Walt Disney states, to coordinate their talent (at whatever level that talent may be) and their effort (the power of deliberate practice à la Duckworth), toward a certain goal. And, that can be a very challenging reality.

Evidence of student learning is on me personally? Yes, it is—you and your team.

John Hattie is a New Zealand researcher and professor at the University of Melbourne in Australia. He has often been cited in our profession due to his extensive meta-analysis of specific actions and efforts of teachers that make a significant impact on student learning. Essentially, he has identified adult behaviors that impact student learning.

His 2009 book *Visible Learning: A Synthesis of Over 800 Meta-Analyses Relating to Achievement*[112] was followed by *Visible Learning for Teachers: Maximizing Impact on Learning*, which is the source of the opening quote to part 4.[113] In 2014, Hattie extended his work with *Visible Learning and the Science of How We Learn* coauthored with cognitive psychologist Gregory Yates.[114]

In *Visible Learning for Teachers*, Hattie states:

> It is a way of thinking: "My role, as a teacher, is to evaluate the effect I have on my students." . . . This requires that teachers gather defensible and dependable evidence from many sources, and hold collaborative discussions with colleagues and students about this evidence, thus making the effect of their teaching visible to themselves and to others.[115]

Taking risks as part of our professional responsibility is important to our heartprint because we spend a lifetime of teaching others, and that teaching becomes a lifetime of you and me getting better based on the goals we set for evidence of student learning, reflecting on those results, and then taking measured risks designed to improve those results.

Provide a one-minute

story you might share with some-one that describes how you evaluate the effect you have on your students—the defensible and dependable evidence you currently collect for your teach-ing success. How do the student learning outcomes for your team or school become more visible to your colleagues?

_____
_____
_____
_____
_____
_____
_____
_____
_____
_____
_____
_____
_____
_____
_____
_____
_____
_____
_____
_____
_____

 # MY HEARTPRINT

Simply stated, think of goals as the *outcomes* of all your work and effort.

When my son Adam was thirteen, I coached the local Babe Ruth traveling baseball team. We had a good team (not great), with a wide variety of charac-ters. Think about it—they were all thirteen-year-old boys and about to be eighth graders. I am already drawing sympathy from the middle school teacher readers! My assistant coach, Pat Maguire, also had a son on our team, and we spent the summer trying to help these kids learn the game of baseball as well as learn lessons about life.

We instinctively knew we had two outcomes (goals) to fulfill. First, we needed evidence that skill-wise, the boys were becoming better baseball players. We were developing their talent to play the game. And second, we needed to ensure they were becoming better young men. They were developing their skill at becoming more positive and polite human beings. You might ask what would be the evidence that we were achieving these measurable outcomes, and that would be a perfect risk-taking question to ask.

I won't get into the details here, but Pat and I had created a list for measuring both their skill at base-ball (as measured by intensive drills we created) and their behavior as young men (as measured by their reactions and responses to various adults during the stress of practice or games). Their success or failure toward these outcomes would, of course, be based on the risks we took as their teachers and coaches with the strategies we used to teach these skills.

Notice we did not base our outcomes on our win-loss record. We saw our record as a reflection of our work and effort *if* we were measuring and then responding to the other outcomes as described.

Imagine this picture. It is our final tournament of the summer season. It's 95ºF or more, hot and humid, in Chicago. It's the championship game. We are losing the game 2–1 in the sixth inning (we only play seven innings at that age level). Pat is standing next to me in the dugout. His son Danny is pitching. I look over at Pat, and he is a nervous wreck. Our entire four-month season was coming to an end against a bitter rival.

He looked a bit green, so I asked Pat, "Are you okay?" He said, "No! My entire sense of well-being is resting in the hands of a bunch of crazy thirteen-year-old boys! This is killing me. My stomach is in knots! And what's wrong with you, anyway? You can't be this calm!"

At the time, I did not respond. There was a lot going on in the game, and I was signaling the pitches for Danny from the dugout. But I remember thinking, "Man, I wish I could capture that feeling of connectedness he had at the moment." I have told this story before, and someone in the audience always wants to know our final record. That summer it was 34–27. And we did win that final game 3–2. Pat could take a breather! But to look at that summer of 1997 as a success or failure based on the record would miss the point.

All of these boys are now grown men. Most likely, none of these men could tell you what our record was that year. But all of them can tell you (for good or bad) the heartprint we left on them based on the risks we took to help them grow and improve. Pat and I must both ask and be judged by, "What is the residue of the human assets we left behind with these young men?"

Pat's sense of humor served him so well as a teacher. He had a sense of achievement as a teacher (and coach) that was tied to his students' (his players') performance as young men. He understood that his success, the risks he took, were measured by their success. He cared that much about how well they did or did not do. It took me a long time to make that crossover to being that emotionally connected to the results of my students' work, effort, energy, and commitment to my class or my school; to connect to their pain when they failed and share that failure as my failure too.

MY HEARTPRINT 💜

Are you connected to the work, effort, and performance results of your students? Does their success still give you thrills? Does their failure break your heart? Do you experience the emotional risk of connecting your effort and action to their success or failure?

Only you know what lies inside your risk-taking heart for your work when students do not learn.

_____

_____

_____

_____

_____

_____

_____

_____

_____

_____

_____

_____

_____

_____

_____

_____

_____

_____

_____

It was late in the summer, right before the new school year was to begin, and my cell phone rang. A good friend and long-time mathematics colleague of mine from Florida was on the line. She was excited and wanted to talk about the new K–8 mathematics curriculum program her district was about to implement. It included a lot of really great actions. Teachers would receive close to forty-five hours of professional development on the program during the school year. The local university was going to work with the district to provide deep training and unpacking of standards for the K–5 teachers. The district was committed to one hour a week of collaborative team time just for mathematics implementation work.

And, it was exciting! It had been a lot of work with the mathematics task force to get it to this point. She was calling me for advice on the team expectations and proposed product development priorities during the team meetings. The new school year was about to start. I listened for almost half an hour, and as she was talking, I also skimmed the proposal and the expected adult effort online.

When she finished (remember, she was a good friend), she asked me what I thought. I simply said, *"So what?"*

There was silence on the phone for five or six seconds, and then she asked, "What do you mean?"

I responded (with a kind tone, I think), "It seems to me like a lot of hoops for the faculty to jump through. It seems to me like a lot of meetings and a whole lot of new energy and effort will be required, and I am wondering, what results or outcomes do you expect to get better because you ask the teachers to take risks and jump through these hoops?"

I continued, "Nowhere in your proposal do I see the expected teacher and teacher team 'effort' tied to any evidence of student learning. How will the teachers know if their actions have an impact? What data do you expect will get better? The goal is not to 'do a new curriculum.' The goal, the outcome, is to improve student learning, so what exactly do you expect will be the student learning results of your work? How will you measure if this effort is successful? What then, exactly is your . . . *so what?*"

A bit more silence. This was not the response she was hoping for. At the moment, I was being a bit of a killjoy. As the title of this chapter suggests, she needed to connect her awesome proposal to some measurable goals: to *evidence of learning*. I told her that if I was her superintendent and agreed to a five-million-dollar mathematics program implementation, I would definitely want to know the projected evidence of student learning based on the implementation of the new program. What outcomes did she and the task force seek?

Over the next few weeks, we went back and forth as I helped her integrate *student achievement* goals into her risk-taking plan. I also explained to her that the small victories of results and movement toward measuring our success are how we know we can celebrate, eat cake, and drive hard to keep the momentum of risk taking required for moving forward week after week once the school season starts. Teachers, I explained, need to know they are winning the day, week, unit, and year with their students. It helps them to keep trying and risking and experimenting with the new curriculum.

MY HEARTPRINT ♥

When you can clearly focus on measurable goals being first and foremost about the outcomes (evidence of student learning) connected to your risk-taking actions, then you are well on your way toward understanding why you are willing to take risks. You hope your risks result in improved learning for the students in your classroom or your school.

The danger and the emotional risk in setting measurable goals and connecting yourself —like Pat Maguire did—to the students expected to achieve those goals lie in whether or not you believe each and every student in your classroom or your school can achieve those goals. In the next chapter, we examine those beliefs and how they impact your willingness to take risks. Read cautiously!

How would you answer the *so what?* question for your risk-taking work effort in this season of your teaching life? What are the results (no matter how small or big) that let you know every unit, week, month, and school year your work and effort will result in success? What will be the evidence of student learning you will analyze and seek out with others?

_____

_____

_____

_____

_____

_____

_____

_____

_____

_____

_____

_____

_____

_____

_____

_____

_____

_____

_____

_____

_____

_____

Shared Purpose: Each and Every Child Can Learn

A shared purpose is not the verbiage on a poster or in a document,
and it doesn't come via charismatic leaders' pronouncements.

—Paul Adler

The interdependent processes of collaboration discussed in part 3 require measuring the risks you take against the backdrop of your basic beliefs as an educator. There is an ethic of contribution by each team member based on an often-undeclared mission or *shared purpose*. And purpose is all about your beliefs. Do you really believe in the most fundamental and basic educational purpose?

Do you believe that *each and every child can and will learn*?

Early on at Stevenson, as we were embracing and designing the PLC process, we used an opening activity with all new members of our faculty. I have adapted it slightly for the purposes of this book, and I am asking you to respond. Which one of the four statements in the My Heartprint best represents your belief about the students you teach? Be sure to explain why.

A shared mission or purpose (why your job or your school exists) articulates how your team or school positions itself in relation to other teams or schools and, ultimately, how you define your success. Your choice from the list in the My Heartprint illustrates whether your *shared purpose* for risk taking will be more robust than your own self-interest.

The first two choices are conditional.

1. Each and every child can learn *if* he or she has the ability.
2. Each and every child can learn *if* he or she works and makes the effort.

If this is your belief or the belief of your team, then you will always be in the blame mode and not take full ownership of the results of your risk-taking efforts. You might hear phrases such as, "It is not my fault they aren't learning," "They just can't learn," or "They just don't do their work" in your school or on your team.

Teams with this mindset position themselves to accept the lack of student success toward measurable performance goals as a result of student effort. In effect, you yield the power and ownership of learning entirely to students and minimize the honest potential of your impact.

The second two choices are not conditional, but one of them is unintentionally disingenuous.

3. Each and every child can learn, *and* we will accept responsibility for ensuring his or her growth.
4. Each and every child can learn, *and* we will establish high standards of learning that we expect all students to achieve.

Can you see the subtle difference between beliefs 3 and 4? Belief 3 is a positive purpose, in the sense that you or your team share the purpose of being responsible for student learning. Yet, in this purpose, there can be a tendency to lower the bar of expectations in order to help each child succeed. This should never be acceptable to you.

MY HEARTPRINT ♥

Choose the one statement that best represents your personal belief about the idea that each and every child can learn, and explain your choice.

Each and every child can learn . . .

1. Based on his or her ability
2. If he or she takes advantage of the opportunity to learn
3. And we will accept responsibility for ensuring his or her growth
4. And we will establish high standards of learning that we expect all students to achieve

_____

_____

_____

_____

_____

_____

_____

_____

_____

_____

_____

_____

_____

_____

Can you think of a current individual, team, or school practice that might unintentionally lower the bar and require less from some of your students?

The next example illustrates for you my response to the last My Heartprint prompt as I describe how I unintentionally created an inequity in my work with students at Stevenson.

I was a member of an AP calculus team consisting of four teachers. I was a coauthor of the book we were using, and I had hired two of the three other teachers on the team. I was not the team leader and did my best just to serve the team as needed. We had a lot of success. Close to 91 percent of our students received honor grades on the AP exam at the end of the year (compared to 57 percent nationally at that time). We were a smooth-functioning, "fun to be with" team!

MY HEARTPRINT ♥

But I had a problem, and no one really knew it. My students performed poorly on one major section of the exam, an essential learning standard: Volumes by Cross Section. Sounds exciting, I bet!

Imagine an essential learning standard in the grade level or course you teach, or in your school, in which your students just don't seem to perform well year in and year out. The evidence of learning is weak. The result of your risk taking is weak. If you can imagine that standard, then you can understand my problem. I had three years worth of AP data that verified my students could not pass this section of the AP exam. It was my weak performer.

Did this mean I was a bad teacher? Did it mean I did not know the content? Not necessarily. It did mean, however, that the *strategy* I was using to teach the standard wasn't connecting for my students. It wasn't an *effective* strategy.

I do believe our team had embraced our shared purpose as the one previously indicated in belief 4: *Each and every child can learn,* and *we will establish high standards of learning that we expect all students to achieve.*

List some barriers that limit the risks you take and cause an inequity in learning expectations (lowering the bar) for certain student populations or demographics in your school.

—————————————

—————————————

—————————————

—————————————

—————————————

—————————————

—————————————

—————————————

—————————————

—————————————

—————————————

—————————————

—————————————

—————————————

—————————————

—————————————

—————————————

—————————————

—————————————

—————————————

—————————————

But, for our team, only three of us were achieving the *each and every child* part for that standard, since my students were not learning the standard. And that is unacceptable when you commit to a shared purpose and you really mean it.

So, I (finally) took my problem to the team. *I took the risk* of letting them know that I had an area of weakness and needed their help. I asked them for strategies they used to teach *volumes by cross section*. I needed to know—if we were to achieve our shared purpose as a team.

Team member Chris Kelly shared with our team a teaching strategy that worked for her. She asked students to construct physical models to represent the standard using cardboard, play dough, construction paper, scissors, and markers. The strategy was so good that my students' performance on this standard soared. I just wish I had taken the risk and asked her about that strategy three years earlier (so do those students, I'm sure).

This cycle of focused *risk and reflection* (where I identify my strengths and weaknesses), *refinement* (what different strategies I might try for teaching that standard to students or colleagues), and *action* (okay, I'll try it) is a dynamic that separates expert educators and teams from good educators and teams, and great schools from mediocre schools.

Eventually you, your team, your department, your school, and your district must decide how far to stretch your measurable goal-setting and risk-tasking efforts and to honor both your goals for learning and the vision of your work effort for your school.

MY HEARTPRINT 💙

Consider the standards you
teach. Are there one or two standards that challenge you every year? No matter what you try, students seem to struggle to demonstrate learning? Name each standard. Who can you talk to (take a risk) about a different strategy to try the next time you teach the standards, so *each and every child* might have a chance to learn them?

_____

_____

_____

_____

_____

_____

_____

_____

_____

_____

_____

_____

_____

_____

Results or Persons?

H   E   A   **R**   T

Stretch goals need to be high enough to inspire extraordinary effort but can't appear so unreasonable or unattainable as to discourage people from reaching them. Good stretch goals move people's focus from a determination to be as good as we have to be and [ask] instead, how good can we be?

—Noel Tichy

It's funny. In preparing to write this chapter, I had to go back to my 2005 calendar. The quickest way to do that was to take my iCalendar, go to Year and, within seconds I was able to scroll back more than a decade. And there it was, just like that, Thursday, August 18, 2005. Eleven plus years backward in eight seconds!

It felt strange to watch the blur of the years scroll by so quickly, realizing that every one of those school seasons was a labor of love, sweat, tears, arguments, hard work, really hard work, risk taking, and growth; and that they were *over*.

I couldn't get them back, although they seemed like yesterday—close enough to touch. I could see all of my activity right there on the calendar. Yet the years also seemed far away—distant memories. Does that make sense to you? Are your school seasons deep in the rearview mirror, while at the same time unfolding one day, one week, or one hard challenging moment at a time? All at once, those calendars represent what will be and what is becoming the heartprint of your life. *Again, you are building your career as you live it.*

Back to August 18, 2005, opening day. Five hundred faculty and staff were in the auditorium, and some of them were new to our district. We were about to launch a new school season: 2005–2006! And I had great news to share. We had hit a ten-year-old stretch goal (student achievement outcome) over the summer. Moreover, this stretch goal represented data that had been heading north for almost two decades. So, I decided on a theme of true north. I provided everyone with a note card, pencil, and a compass

What is more important,

student results that reflect the quality and the risk-taking actions of your work? Or, is it the educators, such as you and your colleagues, the adults responsible for taking the risks to achieve those results?

_____

_____

_____

_____

_____

_____

_____

_____

_____

_____

_____

_____

_____

_____

_____

_____

_____

_____

_____

_____

_____

_____

keychain that said *True North* on the back as faculty and staff walked into the auditorium.

I also had a massive cake on the stage. One of my primary methods of radical celebration was always to "let them eat cake"! I only had one problem. Over the summer, a faculty union committee had come to visit with me, concerned that we—the administration— were placing too much emphasis on student achievement results. My discussions with them reminded me of Tichy's quote at the opening of this chapter: good stretch goals move people to ask, "How good *can* we be?"[116] not "How good do we *have* to be?" so no one will notice. Measurable outcomes must be high enough to inspire extraordinary effort but can't appear so unreasonable or unattainable as to discourage people from reaching them.

Due to our passionate pursuit of improved student learning results (both our mission at Stevenson and our reason for much of our risk taking), the committee was concerned that maybe our faculty and staff as persons were getting lost in the work. Essentially, they were asking me, what is more important: student achievement results or the faculty taking the risks that lead to those significantly improved student results?

I spent the summer dwelling on this concern. And I suppose this is also one of those heartprint check moments for you too. How would you describe this conflict of results (the measurable student outcomes of your work effort) or the persons (the educators taking the risks) in the culture of your school and your personal pursuit of a fully formed professional life?

 # MY HEARTPRINT

With this dilemma weighing on my mind, I wrote this letter and related a version of this message to my colleagues for opening day 2005–2006. I titled the message *True North*. In this slightly abridged version of the message, you can be the judge as to whether I decided results or persons were most important at Stevenson.

August 18, 2005

Dear Colleagues,

In 1983, a group of sixty adults—parents, teachers, support staff members, administrators, students, and board members—came together to write our first vision document, *A Portrait of Excellence*.

From this document, we generated our focused vision for excellence in student learning at Stevenson HSD 125. We were challenged to "head north" on a quest for the "best practice" knowledge in curriculum, instruction, and assessment for student learning, and to chart a risk-taking course toward the social, emotional, academic, and personal growth of every student.

The 1983 task force knew that our school needed to become markedly different if we were to seriously pursue successful college preparatory performance for all our students, including those in the bottom 50 percent of their class, or those on IEPs, in EL classes, or others severely unprepared for the academic rigors and expectations of college. The harbor of limitations was left behind. There would be no more quotas for honors classes, no "ceilings" on performance, preparation, access, or opportunity. And gradually, student achievement results began to head north and climb, reflecting the risk-taking effort and hard work of so many in this auditorium today.

For our college-bound students in the bottom half of their class, the ACT became a high-stakes exam. A good score was essential to college entrance. During the 1980s, our student ACT performance was subject to an artificial "ceiling" of a 22.0 composite score. Our students just couldn't seem to break that barrier. Then in 1990, they broke through the 22 barrier and headed for 23. Six years later, in 1996, they broke the 23 barrier with a composite score of 24.0.

Nine years later, our students have slowly climbed toward the target of 25.0, a possibility of achievement that was only a dream twenty years ago. The 25.1 composite score achieved by the Class of 2005 is another ceiling breaker, showing the unlimited potential and possibility of our students.

Most assuredly, the celebration is not for the number 25.1. The celebration is for the journey and for you, believing in the possibility of our persons—students and colleagues—to achieve a greater good.

The celebration is for the risk-taking efforts of thousands of adults who have helped Stevenson HSD 125 maintain a heading of *True North*, as we become a place of "no limitations" possibility. Every adult that received the compass has played or will play a role in opening the doors of possibility for our students.

Regardless of your role in our school—from operations and support to classroom teaching and learning—you have helped to create a culture of expected excellence, equity, safety, understanding, engagement, and community. Our learning community culture has been nurtured by all, not just a few—the result of so many who refuse to say *no* to the passion of possibility.

So what is next? What barrier will we shatter by 2015? Or 2025? I don't know for sure, but I do know we will break through future barriers others thought impossible—for that is the Stevenson way.

And as also is the Stevenson way, we now have set a new goal for our school: an ACT composite score of 26.0. I do not know when and if we will succeed in obtaining that stretch goal, but I suspect that when it does happen, it will be because of the extreme

CONTINUED →

effort made by so many here today and by our students and parents—and by all of the persons involved in this educational enterprise. If you are new to our faculty and staff this year, welcome aboard a train that refuses to deny the fierce urgency of now.

In the meantime, I hope each of you have a year of unlimited possibility, and I personally thank you for your risk-taking efforts to keep our school culture focused on persons and on student results—on a heading of *True North*.

Most sincerely,

Timothy D. Kanold, PhD
Superintendent

Respond to the three

cultural values listed. How do you honor the ideals of mutual interest, interdependence, and interlocking contributions for risk taking and success in your school and on your team?

_____

_____

_____

_____

_____

_____

_____

_____

_____

_____

_____

_____

_____

_____

_____

_____

_____

_____

So, what do you think? Was my message to our faculty on the stage that day about results *or* about the value of the persons in our school organization?

In great organizations, I believe it is always about both. It is an *and*, not an *or* proposition. It is about persons *and* results.

How do we honor and develop each person: the faculty, students, parents, and the greater school community? By making sure there is a common thread of mutual interest (each and every student can learn), interdependence in the work (we work together), and interlocking contributions (your success depends on me and vice versa).

Examine your current teaching and leading life against these cultural elements in your school. Are they fully present?

+ A common thread of mutual interest (each and every student can learn)
+ An interdependence in the work (we work together)
+ Interlocking contributions (your risk taking success depends on me and vice versa)

 # MY HEARTPRINT

Your commitment to care for the persons in your school—the students, your colleagues, and your parents—will always result in improved student learning, especially as you focus on the risk-taking actions (such as my decision to try a different teaching strategy in my calculus class, as described in the previous chapter) you take together.

∞

My observations of teacher teams, schools, or districts that are considered on a quest for greatness exhibit a focused journey for the work, without much yaw in the focus of their risk-taking actions. *Yaw* is a sixteenth century century word meaning "movement off course."[117]

This can happen to you and your team or your school if you are not careful. You will drift off course, and the risks you take can actually be counter-productive as one change (a risk-taking initiative) undoes another. You will behave in ways that take you away from focused risk-taking efforts that work in concert with one another. When you lose your focus, it takes quite a bit of work to do a midcourse correction during the school year. *So what can you do?*

First, do not lose sight of those stretch goals and outcomes discussed in chapter 22! They are the targets that focus the direction of your work. You and your team, by working together to examine evidence of learning regarding the impact of your work, should relentlessly track data that allow you to shatter barriers you previously thought impossible.

Your team does this by setting both short-term and long-term measures for levels of future student learning; and you eat cake every time you inch the results forward! You look back in your calendar and realize you have accomplished great things. Those student achievements are your achievements too and become part of your heartprint on all those in your path.

Second, never lose sight of why you take certain risks. Take risks with actions in your daily work that you believe will advance those student learning targets. This prevents the yaw that most assuredly will occur if you take risks just for risk taking's sake.

A final thought from that August day in 2005. I wanted to avoid the yaw that can pull our work and our risk-taking efforts off course, from that compass heading of true north.

As our faculty and staff were about to leave, I asked each person to write on one side of a note card, one *I will . . .* action he or she was planning to take that school season to advance our school closer to the new ACT target goal of 26.0. On the other side of the card, I asked members to state one *I will . . .* risk-taking action that advances the work and the skills of one of their colleagues. I collected the cards as they left the auditorium.

During our mid-year celebration in January, I used pictures and video of our faculty and staff from a variety of settings, and our staff created a video set to Nichole Nordeman's song "Legacy." To the video, we added streams of *I will . . .* phrases—actions and commitments our faculty promised to make over the course of the school season. We used the moment to recognize our persons (the heart and soul of who we were) and our results.

I wanted to connect us as colleagues to our collective heartprint. If we love what we do, and if we can see the day-to-day wins from our risk-taking efforts around a vision of social justice for each and every student, then great long-term results will just happen.

It is not persons *or* results. In a healthy school culture, it is always about persons *and* results. Risk taking connects our actions to the results of our work. It is how we measure our success. However, that risk taking should always be connected to the shared vision for our work.

The Risk-Vision Dependency

H   E   A   Ⓡ   T

A TPOV [teachable point of view] is a cohesive set of ideas and concepts that a person is able to articulate clearly to others.
—Noel Tichy

I walked into the principal's office and asked her a simple question: "Does this unit exam meet your vision for seventh-grade assessment in this middle school?"

She took a look at the test and asked, "What do you mean?" I replied, "Does this unit exam meet your assessment 'teachable point of view' that you are articulating to your faculty and staff?"

There was a bit of silence. And then I stated, "Your school could become great at sustaining change by using a focused assessment risk-taking process—can I help?"

In our conversation that followed, we discussed her teachable point of view, or TPOV (as referenced in the opening quote by leadership author and thought leader, Noel Tichy), for assessment.[118]

What were the deeply held beliefs and values about assessment in her school? What exactly was she teaching her faculty? And what were the teachers teaching to the students—about the assessment vision for the school? How could all the adults in the school help sustain the change needed to take risks and move toward that assessment vision; and if we asked members of her faculty, was there clarity regarding the risks needed to achieve that vision?

These were a whole lot of assessment questions for 7 a.m. And yet, these are important questions that focus our risk-taking efforts, at least in the case of the assessment process your team or school uses.

And then, I asked her one more question: "Is the *vision* (for assessment in this case) deeply rooted in the clearly defined purpose of the school—*each and every child can and will learn*?" We discussed how teacher team actions that move the school toward a clearly defined vision are where we discover the meaningfulness of our work.

Our work then becomes much more than stuff to get done—like getting a unit test ready—and more about how we believe the test makes a difference toward improving evidence of increased student learning.

Vision, or the *what you are trying to become*, is a powerful heartprint tool to help you measure what you are supposed to be changing *toward* (it is not just about the results discussed in previous chapters of part 4). A well-articulated and understood vision places boundaries on our risk-taking behaviors and provides the direction in which we need to go to make good judgments and decisions.

Vision is the *compelling picture you paint for your students that produces energy, passion, and action in yourself and others.*[119] It is what we teach others; it is our teachable point of view about our expectations of how we take risks at work.

Every risk-taking step we take cannot be random action stuff. It should be interdependent with the vision. It should be focused on the belief that the changes we make will advance us toward our vision for teaching and learning in our classroom or school.

During my conversation with the middle school principal, I asked her to describe how faculty members currently make choices for daily student work and lesson design, unit assessments, and the activities designed for independent practice (homework). I asked her if her faculty members make assessment decisions in the privacy of their homes or workspace or in the public practice of team discussions.

Are assessment decisions tied to a teachable point of view for instruction and assessment in her school? And, how did she know? Did she think every member of the faculty and staff could articulate the same teachable point of view clearly?

We also discussed the need to make sure the vision or teachable point of view for assessment was based on reliable sources or on evidence about actions bigger than our personal opinion! Our risk-taking efforts should not be wasted on actions that do not improve student learning, I suggested. Were the changes and risks taking place in her school based on *reliable sources*?

During the next week of work, connect your daily decision making to any sources that inform that decision-making process. Write down every decision you make—large or small. Next to that decision, write down the factors or reasons for that decision and list the source that informed that specific decision. For example, was the source educational research, a mentor, a national or state-level recommendation, a field-based observation, a core personal belief, or something else?

MY HEART PRINT 💚

Over the years, I have discovered that one of the biggest assessment problems schools experience is the lack of a coherent vision regarding the actual assessment practices carried out by the teachers and teacher teams in the school.

Your schoolwide coherent vision for assessment should reflect the many personal visions of the stakeholders in your school and be informed by reliable sources. You can use the following vision activity for discovering your school or your teams' teachable point of view or vision for assessment.

First, describe the two to three most vital adult behaviors (non-negotiable behaviors you believe each member of your team should embrace) as an aspect of effective assessment practices in your grade level, course, department, or school.

Draw a circle in the center of a piece of poster paper. Each person at the table writes his or her own list of vital assessment behaviors outside the circle. Write your own list on the paper and initiate a small-group discussion. Remember, do not write inside the circle!

Second, create your team vision or point of view for highly effective assessment practices.

Using eighteen words or fewer, capture the essence of what you believe must become the effective assessment practices in your school. You also may use a symbol or picture. Place this "vision statement" or picture, which represents the vital behaviors listed by each person, inside the center of the circle.

When you complete your assessment vision poster, look closely at what is inside the circle. Do your current risk-taking efforts advance the vision for assessment you have stated or not?

So, why do this vision activity? Consider how you would respond to this question: Who is the voice of authority in your school? You know, the person with the final say in what you should and will do? Can you name the person or persons? What is his or her job title?

No matter how you responded, the first thing to know is this: I asked you to respond to a terribly unfair

At the end of one week, what do you notice about the patterns in your decision making as a teacher and leader? What sources inform those decisions?

Are those sources reliable and steeped in field-based research from reliable organizations?

_____

_____

_____

_____

_____

_____

_____

_____

_____

_____

_____

_____

_____

_____

_____

_____

_____

_____

_____

_____

_____

_____

_____

_____

_____

Take time to answer these vision questions for your school and team.

- What is the vision for assessment in your school?
- What are your reliable sources that inform that vision?
- How does that vision impact your risk-taking actions?

_____

_____

_____

_____

_____

_____

_____

_____

_____

_____

_____

_____

_____

_____

_____

_____

_____

question. In a healthy school culture, it is the wrong question to ask when it comes to authority. The question is not, nor should it ever be: Who is the voice of authority in your school? The question *should* be: What is the voice of authority in your school? The intrinsic motivation of shared vision and values is always more powerful than the extrinsic motivation provided by a boss-type person telling us what to do in our work life.

The vision for assessment you create—that teachable point of view—becomes your professional voice of authority for you, your team, and your school to measure your risk-taking behaviors against. Once the vision is established, we now have a professional obligation to behave in ways we believe advance that vision.

To be sure, a vision is ultimately evaluated against other possible choices and directions for you, your students, and your students' parents and whether there will be evidence and an impact on student learning. Your vision for teaching and learning should paint a picture that is better than current practice. It should be more energizing and more inspiring. The vision, just like the targets that beckon, pulls your behavior forward at the same time it establishes boundaries on your behavior.

Any sustainable change initiative should be connected to and aligned with actions you believe advance the shared vision created inside your circle. The vision brings coherence and focus to your work together.

Risk-taking efforts should be designed to advance various elements of your vision.

Imagine if I could walk into your school and ask any educator, "Tell me your thirty-second vision for the assessment of students in this school. Tell me the reliable sources beyond your opinion that the vision is based on." Imagine that each person I interviewed could easily teach me with great clarity the established vision for effective assessment practices in the school. How awesome would that be?

 MY H E A R T P R I N T

I eventually came to understand that if I was to effectively take risks as an ongoing part of my personal improvement, then I had two markers on which to evaluate the quality of those risks (and thus my change effort) I would pursue, whether large or small.

One marker forced me to *look forward* and determine if the risk-taking actions would connect to and honor our vision for instruction or assessment.

The other marker required me to *look back* and examine the improved evidence on student learning outcomes, if I took those risks. Did my students achieve those measurable learning goals?

I look back and look forward simultaneously all season long as I make hundreds of daily decisions that affect my students—and sometimes my colleagues' students.

MY HEARTPRINT 💟

Building this type of ongoing risk-taking action is eventually built on a culture of mutual trust and emotional connection to our work. In fact, the millennials demand it!

Stop and ask yourself this question: What am I better at doing, looking forward (based on the vision) or looking backward (based on results)? How can I make them both equally strong traits?

_____

_____

_____

_____

_____

_____

_____

_____

_____

_____

_____

_____

_____

_____

_____

_____

_____

_____

_____

_____

_____

_____

Build Trust the Millennial Way

Trust can only arise where people have deep intense interest in each other . . . to know which aspects of one another are special and worth trusting.

—Peter Senge

In 2008, Gallup surveyed adults over eighteen about their views on leadership by asking the questions: "What leader has the most positive influence in your daily life?" and "What three words best describe what this person contributes to your life?" The survey produced four categories of responses. The first category was *compassion* (see chapter 4). The second was *hope* (see chapter 5), and the third was *stability* (see chapter 6). The fourth and final category was *trust*.[120]

I struggled in my commitment to write this chapter. Trust is very difficult to write about, and we often avoid it as a professional development topic in general. Yet trust is essential to effective risk taking with your colleagues. Trust is just such an elusive part of our heartprint.

Trust is dynamic. And it is never fully achieved. We will spend our entire careers trying to build and earn trust with others each and every day.

Trust is hard to define exactly and much harder to carry out. And I suppose it is earned, which means you will not trust me until my actions demonstrate you can. And all it takes is one moment of being fully human, and I may lose your trust forever.

Yet trust is exactly what we must work toward. Trust diminishes negative emotions when we take risks, sometimes fail, and then try new strategies throughout our career.

Name a colleague to

your north. Do you work with
this person more like a coach or
a manager? Do you help each
other build on your strengths? Do
you trust that he or she has your
best interest at heart? Do you
think this person has an interest in
you and understands what makes
you special?

_____

_____

_____

_____

_____

_____

_____

_____

_____

_____

_____

_____

_____

_____

_____

_____

The 2016 Gallup report *How Millennials Want to Work and Live* discovers:

> Millennials don't want bosses—they want coaches. The role of an old-style boss is command and control. Millennials care about having managers [colleagues] who can coach them, who value them as both people and employees, and who help them understand and build their strengths.[121]

Think about colleagues at work to your north: a team leader, an administrator, or a team member that may have more experience than you. Or, maybe you are to his or her north. Review the Gallup comments about what millennials want from bosses, and then reflect on those findings in the My Heartprint section.

♥ MY HEARTPRINT

In essence, millennials expect and demand to exist in a working environment that is more meaningful—a work environment built on trust and mutual interest.

In turn, as trust builds with our colleagues, we are more likely to take risks without fear of the failure that might come from trying something different in our work. When asked what trust meant, respondents in the Gallup survey used words such as *honesty, integrity,* and *respect.*[122]

For you to be deemed trustworthy, you must exhibit three trust-building characteristics.

- *Trust is about honesty:* Will you mentor me and coach me with sincerity?
- *Trust is about integrity:* Will you build into my strengths without bias?
- *Trust is about respect:* Will you value me as a person?

Think about these three descriptors and check them off as part of your My Heartprint response. How would your students or colleagues rank you on each of these heartprint trust characteristics? Do others deem you as trustworthy? You also may consider completing this My Heartprint activity with a trusted colleague.

MY HEARTPRINT ♥

My wife would claim that I do not get easily agitated or so upset that my first, second, or third response to any issue would be aggression. And yet, when I first began my work at Stevenson, I became unglued one afternoon at our weekly leadership team meeting. We were just starting the process of analyzing data to help our teacher teams focus their risk-taking efforts based on evidence of student learning.

This effort was taking place during an era of early technology for student data-management systems. Today, student performance data are instantly available online to a wide range of stakeholders such as parents, students, teachers, counselors, and support personnel. But not back then. Student data performance was a very private affair, and not many of our colleagues knew the what or the how of our student data until report cards were released. We did not yet trust one another to share our data and look at our results *together*. There was a fear of judgment from our peers and from those in the administration that could make data sharing (evidence of student learning) emotionally risky.

In addition, I felt strongly that if the faculty would willingly choose to share their student data with each other (to create ownership as a learning tool), and move into meaningful conversations about more effective strategies for student learning (based on comparative evidence), then I needed to build a culture of trust among team members as they looked at their data.

So, imagine a long rectangular table about three feet across and eighteen feet long. The principal was sitting at one end of the table and leading our team administrative meeting. I was sitting in the middle on one side of the table, and one of my colleagues was sitting directly across the table from me. The agenda item we were debating was the best way to help our teacher teams effectively share their data and use the data as part of an ongoing cycle of informed risk taking, reflection, and action as part of the team's work.

My colleague across the table stated, "Well, I for one am tired of this crap. I think the best thing we can do

Consider the following trust characteristics and give yourself a 1, 5, or 10, with 1 being not very good, 10 being awesome, and 5 meaning you are working on it.

Trust is about honesty: Will you mentor me and coach me with sincerity?

Trust is about integrity: Will you build into my strengths without bias?

Trust is about respect: Will you value me as a person?

_____

_____

_____

_____

_____

_____

_____

_____

_____

_____

_____

_____

_____

_____

_____

_____

_____

_____

_____

is just give everybody the data for their team, and the personal data of every other team member for comparison. Let them see how bad they are compared to other teachers. Then I am going to place their bad student performance data into their evaluation so they get the message."

I was gathering steam, when he said, "I am going to call my teachers with really low performance into my office and let them know they are failing, and how the data have to improve now or else. If the data are pretty good for the rest of the team members, what's wrong with them? They need to improve now and . . ."

At this point, without quite realizing what I was doing, I leapt out of my chair and drove my body across the table, grabbing him by his tie, inches separating our faces and yelling at him, "We must never do this. Never!"

The room became silent. I had knocked things over. We were both red in the face, and he was, of course, shaken up too.

So, what happened? I instinctively knew that if he meant what he was saying, then he would ruin the trust approach to using data for all of us, not just for his teachers. It would cause such a toxic culture in our school that I might never be able to reach my expectations for creating meaning for our work through trust building, sharing, and ownership of our evidence of learning—the student achievement data for each unit of the grade level or course.

The days of managing by intimidation were over. I had just had enough of his outdated mindset. Was I wrong to act so viscerally? Of course, and I apologized. The irony was that my personal actions at that moment violated my trust with him for a very long time.

Why was I angered with my colleague, though? What was at stake? The willingness of our faculty and staff to take risks was at stake. Take a closer look at the three elements of trust that Gallup outlined.[123]

1. *Trust is about honesty:* You mentor me and coach me with sincerity. It seemed to me, my colleague was more interested in punishing others than being a positive mentor and coach. Telling you to improve is not the same as expecting your results to get better, helping you to do a purposeful self-analysis of the data results, providing specific feedback and advice on how to improve, and then supporting you in doing so.

2. *Trust is about integrity:* You build into my strengths without bias. Rather than focusing on strengths and facilitating work around your strengths, my colleague was only calling you in to shame you about your weaknesses.

3. *Trust is about respect:* You value me as a person. When my colleague asked, "What's wrong with them?," that's when I

lost it. It was at that point I felt he no longer placed value on the persons taking the risks and trying to improve student learning.

Building trust with our colleagues does indeed begin by getting to know them better. Yes, you can build your trust skills. You can inspire trust by how you act each day. You can grow it and restore it. From my perspective, trust rekindles the inner spirit of your work, and it limits the chance for deep regret later. There are some basic practices that help build your trust skills with colleagues, and I hope these help you and your team members at school.

Consider three essential elements of building trust with colleagues.

First, trust is a personal commitment to keep promises. I learned this lesson the hard way early in my leadership career. I would often use the phrase in meetings that "I will try to get it done." Of course, those in my team sphere assumed correctly that I was making a promise to action. However, in my mind, saying, "I will try to get it done" let me off the hook to actually getting it done.

Until one day, my colleague Kathy Rauch came into my office and said to me, "You are losing credibility and trust with the faculty because you keep telling us you are going to get things done, and they aren't done yet. Don't promise if you can't deliver."

And she walked out. I was stunned.

And she was right.

From that moment forward, I was very careful to measure what I promised and made sure I delivered on time what I did promise. Few actions on your part will chip away at trust like broken promises.

In *The Speed of Trust*, Stephen M. R. Covey provides this great trust and honesty tip to guide our daily behavior:

> Tell the truth in a way people can verify. Get real and genuine. Be open and authentic. Err on the side of disclosure. Operate on the premise of "What you see is what you get." Don't have hidden agendas. Don't hide information.[124]

Second, trust is a personal commitment to make good decisions. Can good ideas emerge from anyone or anywhere in your school organization? Can colleagues, regardless of positional authority, speak to the work that must be done? Although team and personal trust can be elusive, trust is earned through your team's daily decision-making progress.

Reflect on your daily decision making: How well do you connect every decision to the vision expectations for your classroom, team, or school?

Describe your latest

decision—big or small. Did you publicly connect it back to elements of the vision for your school? How did you do this with your students or colleagues?

Did you neutralize your judgment of a student or colleague by separating his or her behavior (violated a core value of your school or classroom) from who he or she is as a person (still worthy of your love)?

_____

_____

_____

_____

_____

_____

_____

_____

_____

_____

_____

_____

_____

_____

_____

_____

_____

_____

_____

_____

_____

_____

 # MY HEARTPRINT

Third, trust is a personal commitment to value others. Everyone matters—every student, parent, and colleague. Respect occurs when you understand the strengths and weaknesses of others and help them build into their strengths. Trust does not mean indifference to the work of others; it means respecting the risk-taking effort required to improve, listening first, and really noticing what is going on. Did the risks advance the vision and impact student learning or not?

A key element of building trust is making sure your students and colleagues feel respected without being judged. What could be better than an environment of trust where students and colleagues alike feel strong, know who they are, and know how they can contribute?

The *vision* of the school organization serves as the neutral authority that allows trust to flourish. When difficult conversations can be diverted away from the person and toward whether risk-taking actions are inconsistent with the vision, then you become a more trusted person. You are not out to get me as much as you are out to protect the moral purpose of the school's organizational work.

Trust also means no surprises. Be sure to communicate any change initiatives to your students or colleagues well in advance.

The phrase *Make good choices* has been adopted in my family as an occasional way of saying "I trust you" as we say goodbye. Trust is a very difficult pursuit—yet essential to a healthy, risk-taking culture.

May you make good choices today!

Fixed or Growth Mindset?

Research has shown that it's never too late to develop a growth mindset about your abilities. The first step is to get in touch with your fixed mindset. We all have some of it tucked away somewhere, and it's important to acknowledge that.

—Carol Dweck

As you have worked your way through this book, have you been able to connect the ideas directly to your current professional practice? Have your reflections within the My Heartprint sections of this book had any impact on your choices and actions at work? If the answer is *yes*, then you most likely have chosen a growth mindset for your professional life.

Do you recognize the author of the opening epigraph? Carol Dweck is the Lewis and Virginia Eaton Professor of Psychology at Stanford University and considered one of the world's leading researchers in the fields of personality, social psychology, and developmental psychology. Dweck's 2007 book *Mindset: The New Psychology of Success* has launched a national discussion about how fixed mindsets versus growth mindsets impact student and adult learning.

In her 2015 *Educational Horizons* article, "Teachers' Mindsets: 'Every Student Has Something to Teach Me,'" Dweck indicates that too many teachers have a fixed mindset about the profession—believing either you're born to be a great teacher or you're not. Fixed mindset teachers view teaching as strictly an innate talent and as limited.[125]

The thinking is like this: *I most likely am not going to improve as an educator, ever. So, why try?* Why take risks that will improve my practice as an educator? And this becomes part of our belief system. However, according to Dweck, this does not have to be our belief. We can make the choice to develop a growth mindset in our work and in our lives. And that choice begins by recognizing our fixed mindsets. So, what does this mean?

Do you believe you have limited talent in some aspect of your professional life, and it will never get better? It took me a little bit of time to admit this for myself. What is it for you?

_____

_____

_____

_____

_____

_____

_____

_____

_____

_____

_____

_____

_____

_____

_____

_____

_____

_____

_____

_____

_____

_____

_____

"We all have some of it [fixed mindset] tucked away somewhere, and it's important to acknowledge that."[126] Interesting, right? There is something rattling around inside of us that we view with a fixed mindset. There is no chance, we think, that using a *reflect, refine, and act* cycle of risk taking would really matter much at improving our daily work.

♥ MY HEARTPRINT

Does the area of your professional life that you view with a fixed mindset need to stay fixed? No! Dweck indicates it is never too late to develop growth mindsets about your work and your life. As indicated in the opening quote: "The first step is to get in touch with your fixed mindset."[127] Can your students and colleagues really experience a new and improved version of you? The answer is good news: a resounding *yes*!

Here are some examples of fixed mindsets in our profession. Do any of these excuses for not taking risks ring true for you or members of your team?

The *I'll never be able to get these students to learn this* fixed mindset excuse: "You need to join the rest of your colleagues and get started using that technology," I said. "I don't want to," she replied. "Why not?" I asked. "The students won't learn what they need to learn. It will damage the critical-thinking process for them."

The *I'll never be as good as that teacher* fixed mindset excuse: "Would you at least read this research about technology and its positive impact on student learning? Let's meet again next Friday." She agreed. A week later, she said to me, "I am not like those teachers in the article. It just is not how I teach."

The *if I take that risk and it doesn't work out, I'll lose my status, control, or respect* fixed mindset excuse: "Okay," I said. "Will you at least go and watch your colleague Chris teach his class and observe how he makes it work with his students?" She replied, "Chris is a master teacher; if I teach like he does, it will blow up in my face."

To best understand these fixed mindset excuses, a quote from Will Rogers is appropriate. Please remember, he said this a long time ago and uses the word *men* in a generic sense, and these are his words, not mine: "There are three kinds of men. The one that learns by reading. The few who learn by observation. The rest of them have to pee on the electric fence for themselves."[128]

Rogers's comments illustrate the catch-22 of a fixed mindset, and why it can so limit our potential. Essentially a fixed mindset prevents us from trying to take risks, and yet it is in the actual trying and risking that we best learn and grow and discover for ourselves what works and does not work. If we do not take risks we maintain the status quo and stagnate. We lose our sense of relevance with students and colleagues.

How might you know if you generally have a fixed or a growth mindset? A simple test is to examine each of the following statements in the My Heartprint list and indicate whether you personally agree or disagree with each statement.

— MY HEARTPRINT ♥ —

Choose to agree or disagree with each statement, and briefly reflect on your choice.

1. The kind of teacher I am is something very basic about me and can't be changed very much.
2. I can change the way I teach, but I can't really change my true teaching ability.
3. I will be ineffective in some areas no matter how hard I try to improve.
4. No matter how much natural ability I may have, I can always find important ways to improve.
5. Every educator, no matter who they are, can significantly improve their teaching ability (to students or colleagues).
6. The value of trying new teaching methods outweighs the risk of making a mistake.[129]

If you agree with the first three statements, you tend more toward a fixed mindset and possibly get discouraged when encountering new challenges, difficult students, or risk-taking colleagues. Dweck indicates it is hard for you, as a fixed mindset teacher, to roll up your sleeves, use every resource at your disposal, and believe you can only get better.[130]

Educators with a fixed mindset fear being judged negatively and are often reluctant for other colleagues to observe them taking any risks, watch them teach, or collaborate on lesson designs. They assume it is their job to go it alone and that innate talent is the most important factor in personal success.

On the other hand, if you agreed with the last three statements in the My Heartprint, you most likely have a growth mindset.[131] You don't believe that a perfect, error-free lesson defines you as a good teacher; you embrace errors students might make during learning in the lesson; and you use those moments as learning opportunities for reflection and refinement for you and your students. You intentionally view all risk-taking aspects of your work as in a constant cycle of reflection, refinement, and action (growth is forever in your mind).

One way to know if you have left your fixed mindsets behind is to examine behaviors you believed in before but no longer practice. I asked author, PLC at Work leader, and elementary education specialist Sharon Kramer that question: "What are the behaviors you believed in before but no longer practice?"

Here is what she said:

> There have been an endless number of lessons I have learned over the past ten years, the most important of which is a focus on learning. This required a different approach to teaching that eliminated many past practices and shifted my thinking from what I teach to what students actually learn.
>
> So often in the past, my actions were focused on the way I teach best, not on the way the students learned best. Now I understand that for learning to occur it has to be an interactive process facilitated by the teacher, not dominated by the teacher. The type of engagement that leads to students owning their learning is essential for learning to occur.
>
> This meant I had to eliminate students sitting in rows. I also needed to engage students more in the process of understanding learning targets, articulating what they know and what they still need to learn, tracking their learning, and working in collaborative teams, not in isolation.

None of these practices were things I either did myself or taught to colleagues ten years ago. (S. Kramer, personal communication, July 23, 2016)

MY HEARTPRINT 💜

A quick test for you to determine if you have a growth mindset is to reflect on your response when you read a new article, listen to an expert speaker, or have a great conversation with a colleague. If you tend to immediately apply what you are learning to your personal, work-related context, and you can imagine how you could make that idea or some part of the idea work for your teaching, then you most likely have a growth mindset.

You trend toward being a growth mindset teacher if you exhibit these daily behaviors:

- ◆ You engage in ongoing professional development with colleagues, read more professional literature, connect the research to your own work, and constantly pick up ideas and teaching techniques from many sources.
- ◆ You routinely observe other teachers and volunteer to teach demonstration lessons for your colleagues.
- ◆ You confront your teaching problems head-on and ask for feedback from supervisors and colleagues.
- ◆ You believe that every one of your students has the potential to teach you something.
- ◆ You seek new strategies and set revised personal goals as you continuously reflect, refine, and act as part of a risk-taking cycle in your work.

How did you do with this list? Can you say *yes* to each growth mindset behavior?

I also suggest taking Dweck's online mindset test (http://bit.ly/MindsetTest) to discover specific areas in which you can change your thinking about your growth and achievement mindset.

In our profession, it seems that the hope for a better future rests in the hands of growth mindset educators—teachers and leaders just like you. Go get that growth

Take a moment to think about two to three behaviors you believed in before but no longer practice. How have your mindsets about these specific behaviors or areas of your work shifted?

_____

_____

_____

_____

_____

_____

_____

_____

_____

_____

_____

_____

_____

_____

_____

_____

_____

_____

_____

_____

_____

_____

_____

_____

_____

mindset today. It's in there. And everyone around you will love you for it! More important, a growth mindset drives your momentum forward for all your professional life, increasing the likelihood that you will avoid the entropy that sets in if you settle for less than the best version of you!

Warning: Entropy Ahead!

H   E   A   **R**   T

Just as the constant increase of entropy is the basic law of the universe, so it is the basic law of life to be ever more highly structured and to struggle against entropy.

—Václav Havel

What are three words you associate with the word *entropy*? *Merriam-Webster* claims these three: *chaos, disorganization,* and *randomness.*[132]

These are not good words if you have chosen our profession! Part 4, "R Is for Risk," has been about understanding how our professional life should be dedicated to leaving a heartprint that fights against entropy. Entropy should be your biggest fear as an educator. The ideas in the six previous chapters have been designed to nourish your risk-taking heartprint and prevent the drift into chaotic and random professional behavior.

Stop risk taking and you stop *becoming. Entropy sets in.* You leave your unrealized potential at the door.

Your greatest concern as a teacher of others—students or colleagues—should be the fear of no longer being relevant; the fear of not being able to sustain meaningful change in your work; the fear that your voice no longer matters; and ultimately, the fear that you are regressing as others around you continue to move forward.

Remember the essential heartprint question for part 4: *Are you a person of vision-focused risk taking for sustainable change, with a growth and data-driven mindset for learning and life?*

Are we dedicated to avoiding entropy in our work life? And since everything has a tendency to deteriorate, what are signs of entropy settling into our work world? What are the signs that we may have let go of the *reflect, refine, and act* risk-taking cycle of our work life?

Is your team or school engaged in lots of energy-draining "stuff" with no connection to actual evidence of improved student learning? Is your school culture defending the status quo? Is the entropy creep closing in on you?

During the years of my work with Rick DuFour, I witnessed his passion about not letting our Stevenson school district slide back into an era of mediocrity. So, I asked him about important signals of impending deterioration that needed to be recognized and addressed if entropy is to be held in check in a PLC culture. The following is Rick's response:

> One of the surest signs of entropy in a school that has implemented the PLC process is a growing sense that the school has "arrived," and thus can begin to take shortcuts on the process that was instrumental to the school's improvement. Instead of the constant pursuit of the question, "What is the best we can be?," we settle for being the "good enough" school that is content with being as good as we need to be. We want to coast for a while because a commitment to continuous improvement is relentless, and we feel we need a break.
>
> When I had the honor of being in a leadership position at Adlai E. Stevenson High School in Lincolnshire, Illinois, we embraced several strategies to fight against entropy.
>
> 1. We established a few stretch goals that could not be accomplished in the short term and thus required a long-term commitment. For example, we said we wanted to eliminate failure in every course.
>
> 2. Each content team was asked to establish an annual SMART goal to help more of their students achieve at higher levels than the year before.
>
> 3. With the faculty's consent, we continued to apply for the U.S. Department of Education's Blue Ribbon award every four years or so. In applying, we had to demonstrate that we were significantly better than when the USDE had deemed us an "excellent" school when we won our previous award. In other words, we had to show we had improved upon "excellent." The bar continued to rise for each of our four Blue Ribbon awards.
>
> 4. We began every school year with a review of the accomplishments of the previous year and a reminder of the commitments that were instrumental to those accomplishments. Our focus was not on what was to be new in the coming year, but rather a recommitment to the purpose, priorities, and processes that were key to our culture and our success.
>
> 5. We celebrated at every faculty meeting. We called attention to individuals and teams that demonstrated a commitment to continuous improvement.

Think of the culture of your school as a garden. Inattention inevitably results in weeds, which not only are perfectly capable of growing on their own but also are certain to flourish if the garden is left unattended. A strong culture of continuous improvement needs constant attention and nurturing. (R. DuFour, personal communication, April 23, 2016)

My experience over the years is that entropy kicks in at your school twice as fast unless the adults relentlessly attack current student performance—together. As Rick indicates, we need to attend to the garden—each day, each month, and each season of our lives!

MY HEARTPRINT ♥

Take a moment to respond to Rick's five strategies. What are you and your colleagues doing right now, this week, this month, and this moment to tend to your risk-taking culture, your garden, and to avoid the entropy-choking weeds that may want to take over?

The My Heartprint that follows provides a quick *yes* or *no* entropy test. See how you do. Then reflect on any actions in your current professional practice that might need to change.

MY HEARTPRINT ♥

Answer each test question *yes* or *no*, and briefly explain the reasons for your answers.

You are drifting into entropy when you:

1. Have a tendency toward superficiality
2. Have tension with colleagues
3. No longer know your story (why you are a professional educator)
4. Tend to be a problem maker and not a problem solver
5. Do not want the problem solved
6. Seek to control rather than collaborate
7. Speak of your students as an imposition on your time
8. Lose grace and civility with others
9. Demonstrate a loss of confidence in your own judgment and wisdom
10. Forget that vision (what you are trying to become) can never be separated from risk (the actions it will take to get you there)

Over the years, one way I tried to make sure we avoided entropy was to always ask our teams, "Is this still the best way to do _____?" quickly followed by, "Can we achieve better results?" My biggest fear was that we would rest on our past practice.

When someone on our team would explain, "Well, that is just how we have always done it," I expected our school response to be, "Is this still the best way to do it?" The answer could be *yes*, but invariably, the answer was *no*. We could improve. And before you know it, entropy is left behind.

Entropy equals chaos, disorganization, and randomness. Make your professional heartprint one of entropy avoidance as you do the dance of change in your school—this school season, and next, until there are no more seasons left for you to make your mark on others.

A Sense of Urgency

H E A R T

What is the single biggest error people make when they try to change? . . . They did not create enough of a sense of urgency.
—John Kotter

In his 2008 book *A Sense of Urgency, New York Times* bestselling author, John Kotter of Harvard Business School fame, provides excellent insight and advice for the end of this part of the book. He calls us to a sense of urgency: urgency to take risks for improved student learning; urgency for outcomes with greater student access and opportunity; urgency to take focused risks and action that advance the vision for our work; and urgency to erase inequities caused by isolated decision making from our colleagues.

Everything we do feels urgent, because for our students it is. This is the time and the moment for them to pass through your professional life. I like to think of this idea as the *fierce urgency of right now*, the very moment we are working and living in.

Kotter, a deep thinker and thought leader about change issues, provides a warning caveat. Be careful not to fall into the trap of a *false sense of urgency*:

> Those with a false sense of urgency behave in ways that can easily be mistaken for people with a real sense of urgency because they are very active. But with a false sense of urgency, the action is much more activity than productivity. It is frenetic. It is more mindless running to protect themselves or attack others than the purposive focus on critical problems and opportunities. Run-run, meet-meet, talk-talk, defend-defend, and go home exhausted.[133]

Kotter's description would have fit Phoenix Union High School District (PUHSD) in Phoenix, Arizona, to a tee in 2003. *Lots of action, no results:* extremely low state test scores and low student access to college-readiness programs. Very little teacher collaboration, no vision for instruction and assessment, stagnant results, and very few teachers aware of those results or taking risks to improve those results. There were pockets of greatness, and many very good teachers and leaders—but there was not a holistic districtwide, risk-taking culture with a systemic focus.

As an urban district with eleven comprehensive high schools, six small schools, twenty-seven-thousand-plus students, the demographics included: 85.1 percent free and reduced lunch, 81.2 percent Hispanic, 8.6 percent African American, 2.4 percent Native American, with 46.3 percent Spanish as the primary home language. PUHSD is a high-poverty, high-minority school district. It could hide behind these built-in excuses for entropy to rule the day. Yet, as the decade unfolded, the adults in the district, including my colleague, author, and mathematics education leader Mona Toncheff, refused to yield to these excuses.

They chose to give their professional work life deeper meaning, as they pursued two critical signposts for our professional risk-taking work, as described in part 4.

1. *Stay connected to small wins along the way.* We need to know the data that tell us our risk-taking efforts are winning today. Every week, we need to know our effort answered the so what? question through evidence of student learning in that moment. Risk taking must be connected to evidence of student learning.

2. *Stay connected to risk-taking behaviors and actions focused on the shared vision of your work.* Do this rather than giving in to the defensive mantra of "this is how we have always done it around here." Always ask the growth mindset question: "How can we respond to ensure the learning of each and every student?"

In 2003, 60 percent of incoming freshmen at PUHSD were placed in below-grade-level mathematics courses, with no chance to attend college, and only 18 percent of tenth-grade students were passing the state assessments in mathematics. The district vision was updated in the spring of 2008: Preparing every student for success in college, career, and life. The district provided support for collaborative teacher team opportunities, common unit assessments, common analysis of those assessments, and deep content-level mathematics discussions designed to support students matriculating successfully into junior- and senior-level courses. The district also needed to bridge the gap between eighth-grade outcomes and freshman readiness to ensure student success in the first year of high school.

The results of their risk-taking work together? By 2014, only 2 percent of students were placed in below-grade-level mathematics courses, student state performance in mathematics was closing in on the state average performance scores, upper-level mathematics class enrollment had increased from 12 percent to 32.8 percent, and course-based team leaders were identified and trained in every aspect of the PLC process. And, one of the high schools, Metro Tech, applied for and became a PLC at Work model school. You may visit www.allthingsplc.info/evidence/details/id,678 to learn more about its effort.

In 2017, there still is not a complete victory at PUHSD over the effects of poverty and language. But I doubt the teachers and leaders will ever again allow a slide back to the accepted levels from 2003. The adults care too much. They and the students know they can achieve more. And, they continue to feel the fierce urgency of *now*.

MY HEARTPRINT ♥

Take a moment to reflect on the last seven chapters. What are your primary takeaways? Include two or three possible actions you can take to improve the way you and your colleagues reflect, refine, and act in your work around the goals and shared vision you have created with your colleagues. Reflect too on your growth mindset behaviors and how those impact your willingness to trust and take risks moving forward with your colleagues.

We opened part 4 with the essential heartprint question: Are you a person of vision-focused risk taking for sustainable change, with a growth and data-driven mindset for learning and life?

I close with this heartprint comment: *The L in PLC—learning means forever.*

A growth mindset is about accepting that we can increase our talent as professionals—as teachers and leaders, forever. We can learn and get better, forever. Our career-learning path never stops. These are actions of your risk-taking heartprint that illustrate you have also become wiser.

We seek to find and know our voice, our teachable point of view, which allows us to take risks in ways that most likely advance student learning and our learning, and to tie ourselves to the Maguire effect (see page 158)—the emotional connection to actual evidence of student learning and growth. Our students become

Think of these next steps as *I will . . .* statements, and write them down as you measure your personal risk-taking heartprint during this stage of your professional career. Include thoughts about how you celebrate students and colleagues. How do you take risks that honor the vision for the work of your team or school?

_____

_____

_____

_____

_____

_____

_____

_____

_____

_____

_____

_____

_____

_____

_____

_____

_____

_____

_____

_____

_____

_____

_____

_____

the residue of our chosen work. Their success or failure is our success or failure. Nothing else really matters.

Along the journey of this book, I have given many hints as to the gathering wisdom we should pursue for our work. It is almost as if knowledge about teaching has been woven within the tapestry of discussing happiness, engagement, alliances, and risk. In the final part of this book, part 5, we explore the elements of thought and wisdom necessary to become expert educators. We will reflect in ways that help us to find our voice, to know whose voice is speaking for us, and to discover a voice that matters.

The following resources are instrumental in the support of our work together in part 4. Depending on your personal interests, you may use these resources as you continue to expand your knowledge base and the knowledge base of your colleagues. You may also visit **go.SolutionTree.com/HEART** to access direct links to the websites and download three additional chapters related to part 4.

Part 4: R Is for Risk

Resources

Claro, S., Paunesku, D., & Dweck, C. (2016). Growth mindset tempers the effects of poverty on academic achievement. *Proceedings of the National Academy of Sciences of the United States of America, 113*(31), 8664–8668. Accessed at www.pnas.org/content/113/31/8664.abstract on July 1, 2016.

Collins, J. (2005). *Good to great and the social sectors: A monograph to accompany good to great.* New York: HarperCollins.

Dweck, C. (2014, December). *The power of believing that you can improve.* [Video file]. Accessed at www.ted.com/speakers/carol_dweck on August 10, 2016.

Dweck, C. (2015). Teachers' mindsets: "Every student has something to teach me." *Educational Horizons, 93*(2), 10–15.

Gallup. (2016). *How millennials want to work and live.* Washington, DC: Author. Accessed at www.gallup.com/reports/189830/millennials-work-live.aspx on July 1, 2016.

Hattie, J. (2012). *Visible learning for teachers: Maximizing impact on learning.* New York: Routledge.

Hattie, J., & Yates, G. (2014). *Visible learning and the science of how we learn.* New York: Routledge.

Patterson, K., & Grenny, J. (2011). *Crucial conversations: Tools for talking when the stakes are high* (2nd ed.). New York: McGraw-Hill Education.

Tichy, N. M. (1997). *The leadership engine: How winning companies build leaders at every level.* New York: Harper Business.

Yeager, D. S., & Dweck, C. (2012). Mindsets that promote resilience: When students believe that personal characteristics can be developed. *Educational Psychologist, 47*(4), 302–314. Accessed at http://bit.ly/2bWgjKP on October 1, 2016.

Additional Resources

• More on John Hattie's work: http://visible-learning.org
• More on Carol Dweck's mindset work: http://mindsetonline.com
• Carol Dweck's mindset test: http://bit.ly/MindsetTest

PART 5

DEVELOPING HEART

Essential Heartprint Question: Are you a person with surface and deep knowledge capacity, thought, and wisdom?

It is not enough to do your best; you must first know what to do, and then do your best.

—W. Edwards Deming

In part 5, "T Is for Thought," we explore the role that thought—wisdom about knowing what to do—plays in our growth as professional educators. We explore how to find our professional voice: What do we really understand about the content of our curriculum? What do we care about, believe, and expect from others and ourselves each and every day of our work? What are the principles we will defend and teach our students and colleagues throughout our careers?

When you speak, why should we listen? When you teach, why would we follow? You can't teach and lead others—your students or your colleagues—to places you do not want to go to yourself.

If you think about the academic nature of our profession, then you understand we need both surface and deep pedagogical knowledge about our subject area—or in the case of elementary school teachers, across a broad range of subject areas. We should develop our wisdom about the content and the process of our work. We need to know the best strategies, representations, and ways to make complex ideas simpler.

We can be happy and engaged, form alliances (collaborate well), and be risk-taking and results oriented—all of those heartprint elements will most likely increase our thought and wisdom. However, we will still fall short of becoming fully accomplished and dynamic teachers without wisdom built out of a knowledgeable voice.

This is exactly what happened to me.

Don't get me wrong; my students loved the other heartprint elements of my teaching. I was generally extremely happy in my work, passionate about student learning, and amazed that I was so fortunate to be part of this great profession. I had started a mathematics competition club, and we were pretty competitive overall in those early days. I had great energy for the work, loved hanging out with high school students, and was a reasonable risk taker. The art of teaching and leading my students was developing within me, but my level of understanding in my content field, mathematics, was still limited.

And so, you and I should also become role models as knowledge workers—persons of wisdom about the content knowledge and competencies of our work. Otherwise, our teaching is at best left with a superficial knowledge impact on students.

Over the years, we had the opportunity to hire a lot of great educators and bring them into our school culture at Stevenson. As we brought new teachers and leaders into our school district, we would debate: Should we honor character, then competence and commitment? Or, competence, *then* character and commitment?

I often referred to this hiring dilemma as part of the *three Cs priority*.

1. *Character* was our search for evidence for the potential of growing in your heartprint around the first four parts of this book.
2. *Competence* was our search for evidence of academic knowledge and wisdom about the content or subject matter for the work.
3. *Commitment* was our search for evidence of personal commitment to the PLC process and desire to seek evidence of student learning.

Of course, you most likely want to work with a colleague who is great in all three of these areas. But, what if you had to choose? *Character* with commitment versus *competence* with commitment?

MY HEART PRINT

At Stevenson, I always chose character over competence every time, knowing that competence with the right character, commitment, and grit could more easily be fully developed in each of us.

I recall the year I hit the trifecta when I hired science teachers Bill McNamara, Tom Kelly, and Kenny Latka. They were educators with great character; they also were extremely competent.

The chapters that follow attempt to provide insight into the workplace thought and wisdom we should pursue. We begin with a close look at the elements of our great professional adventure and examine how our voice reflects superficial or deep knowledge for our work. We will dive deep into two profound knowledge actions that significantly impact student learning—actions worth every ounce of your energy, thought, wisdom, and action throughout your career—your classroom climate, and the use of formative and reflective feedback in every student learning experience. We then conclude part 5 with a necessary call to claim every student in your school as you would one of your own.

Reflect for a moment on how would you choose a professional colleague to work with in the future. Assuming you believe this person will be committed to the work of your team or school, which would you choose? *Character* or *competence*? Which would be your priority, and why?

_____

_____

_____

_____

_____

_____

_____

_____

_____

_____

_____

_____

_____

_____

_____

_____

_____

_____

_____

_____

_____

_____

_____

_____

_____

Your Great Adventure!

H E A R T

Life is either a daring adventure or nothing at all.
—Helen Keller

By 1992, I was on my third job as a teacher and leader. Oddly enough, I had been at each job exactly six years. I was also starting to gain some traction as a national thought leader in my field of study, mathematics.

I knew I had "arrived" as a professional when colleague Steve Leinwand approached me after a keynote address I presented in Philadelphia and mentioned I needed to be careful with what I was saying, as folks were starting to listen to me!

I respected Steve quite a bit, and it took me aback for a second. I had not given much thought to the fact that my wisdom and ideas about our work really mattered much. I was just trying to grow and be part of this great adventure we call teaching. His comments caused me to be more mindful of my thoughts about the wisdom I was teaching to others.

That conversation with Steve was the result of a new message I had created during the early 1990s—I called the message *The Great Adventure*. I used its inspirational (or so I thought) message with all types of education audiences for about five years, and then moved on, and those transparencies gathered dust (no PowerPoint, Keynote, Prezi, PDFs, or Internet back then).

Then a few years ago, my family moved. I uncovered the message and repurposed it for the era we live in now. The message has had a revival of sorts and becomes relevant for the final part of this heartprint-driven book.

My initial presentation was based on the idea that every great adventure movie has five essential parts or elements.

1. There are a *clear mission* and purpose to the great adventure.
2. There are *significant obstacles* and opposition to achieving the mission.

How do you view your work-life thought and wisdom as part of a great adventure movie (see the five essential elements)?

What is your current wisdom about the purpose of your work?

_____
_____
_____
_____
_____
_____
_____
_____
_____
_____
_____
_____
_____
_____
_____
_____
_____
_____
_____
_____
_____
_____
_____
_____

3. A hero or *several heroes* try to overcome the obstacles to the mission.
4. The heroes use thoughtful and *effective strategies* to achieve the mission.
5. There is *victory*, a successful ending to the mission . . . every great adventure movie (in my opinion) ends in a successful outcome.

Write down or think about your favorite great adventure movie. Back then, I would use *Raiders of the Lost Ark* as my sample movie. Think about your movie choice. Does it meet the five-part criteria I have listed as satisfying the qualifications of a great adventure movie?

Once my colleagues connected to this idea of a great adventure movie, I made the parallel connection to our professional career and work-life effort as part of understanding the thought and wisdom needed for our personal great adventure of teaching and leading others—you know, a movie about our professional life!

First, there are a clear mission and purpose to the great adventure. The mission and purpose of teaching and leading are that each and every student can learn. This is the daunting great adventure mission for our work. Every year, we start the new school season, determined to do everything in our power to help, support, and expect each and every student to learn. This is exactly the point of our adventure into teaching and becoming fully formed professional educators. It means we need to pursue the thought and wisdom of several strategies and not just a few, if indeed each and every student we teach is to learn the high standards we expect them to achieve.

 # MY HEARTPRINT

Second, there are significant obstacles and opposition to achieving the mission. You can name them all. On some days, it most likely feels as if there are nothing but obstacles to your success and the success of your students. There is the frustration of knowing you are not always winning the day with each and every student.

Here is a partial list to get you started.

• Teachers working in isolation

- Students not doing their work
- Intervention that is not fluid, required, or successful
- High levels of poverty in your community
- Parents who are not connected to the school community
- Teachers who are not connected to the parent community
- Colleagues who are not fully engaged in their work
- Lack of vision or focus for sustained change by fixed-mindset persons in your school
- Lack of student-engaged lesson designs
- A culture that is not safe for some populations of students

MY HEARTPRINT ♥

Third, a hero or several heroes try to overcome the obstacles to the mission. And the hero is *you.* When your thought process and wisdom development pursue a growth and risk-taking mindset of reflect, refine, and act, you become a hero in your own story. You become an *I will not be a victim* educator. You become an *I refuse to give in to the obstacles of deficit thinking and nonbeliefs that each and every student can learn* educator. You climb over and through the obstacles and make no excuses for anything that falls short of your quest.

You. Are. Awesome.

And it makes me want to work with you—each and every day. We find our victories one student at a time, together.

Mike Mattos, outstanding California educator and co-creator of the RTI at Work™ model and coauthor of the PLC at Work process, is an example of a great adventure hero, as evidenced in his words:

> What I do for each student must be nothing less than what I would want for my own child. Every student we serve is someone's 'apple of their eye' . . . a child so precious that their parents would take a bullet to ensure his or her safety. So I can't think of anything more unethical an educator can do than to make a decision that is good enough for someone

The barriers and obstacles can be endless. List some primary barriers and obstacles you currently face—and hold on to them for a moment. Do any of them correspond to the partial list provided?

_____

_____

_____

_____

_____

_____

_____

_____

_____

_____

_____

_____

_____

_____

_____

_____

_____

_____

_____

_____

_____

_____

What is the most recent "hero move" you made this past week with one student, a small group of students, or perhaps a colleague? Give yourself some credit for making a difference and for relentlessly removing obstacles to student learning.

_____
_____
_____
_____
_____
_____
_____
_____
_____
_____
_____
_____
_____
_____
_____
_____
_____
_____
_____
_____
_____

else's child, yet the same action would not be acceptable for their own.

Throughout my career, I have faced countless times where this belief was in direct conflict with what was directed by my superiors or accepted by my colleagues. I must admit that my actions have occasionally fallen short. Yet, my times of failure have provided my most powerful, lasting learning opportunities. That is the thing about a sword—it is an ideal. It is the standard by which we measure our actions. So even when I miss the target, I am always provided the opportunity to self-assess and, hopefully, inch a bit closer to the educator I hope to be. (M. Mattos, personal communication, June 23, 2016)

Mattos provides an example of the kind of hero every great adventure needs, and the sort of hero our students need us to be.

In your own personal great adventure story as a professional educator, do you see the hero who resides in you? Every day, every effort, every little moment that occurs when no one is looking? You can be a hero, as you reach out each week to change the path of one student at a time.

 MY HEARTPRINT

Fourth, the heroes use thoughtful and effective strategies to achieve the mission. The following are several strategies reflecting deep thought and wisdom we have discussed in this book along the way, and a few others for measuring your progress toward the mission of *every child can learn.*

- You commit to understanding how to deliver a relevant, meaningful, guaranteed, and viable curriculum.
- You commit to a lesson-design process that actively engages all learners every day.
- You commit to a student assessment process that always uses meaningful formative feedback (with expected student action)—you and your students risk, reflect, and refine, as you (and they) find grit.

- You commit to developing opportunities for student reflection, collaboration, and self-efficacy, for reasoning and communicating with their peers, for making connections to other subject areas, and for writing about their thinking.
- You commit to a personal technology growth mindset, and ensure each student learns to become fluent as appropriate in the technology world we now live within.

MY HEARTPRINT ♥

Fifth, there is a victory, a successful ending to the mission. The great adventure of your professional journey ends in a victory for you, your mission, your colleagues, and your students. Successful endings to your professional life movie occur many times every school season in many ways, both large and small. Sometimes the victory occurs at the end of the school season in June and sometimes at the end of a chapter or unit. Sometimes it occurs at the end of a really great but long day. Sometimes it is delayed years, as it takes that long for some students and colleagues to get to a place where they can let you know.

MY HEARTPRINT ♥

For the students in our K–12 system who pass through our lives for a very short time overall, the ending of the movie ultimately occurs during that May or June day when they walk across that graduation stage prepared for the next great adventure of their lives.

How you move along the great adventure road can be wide and varied. The mission that *each and every child can learn*, however, may never change. Do you agree?

Your thought and wisdom are what will change and grow over time. It is in your wisdom development that you find your heart and your voice for this profession and become the hero of your own story—the great adventure of *your* professional life!

What is the best current strategy you use to improve student learning and overcome obstacles for your grade-level or course-based team? How do you communicate this wisdom to your colleagues?

_____

_____

_____

_____

_____

_____

_____

_____

_____

_____

Name a victory you have had in the past few weeks or in the past school season. Describe the story that led to that victory.

_____

_____

_____

_____

_____

_____

_____

_____

_____

_____

_____

It is also in your thought and wisdom development that you are more able to engage me in learning with you. What are you teaching me? Why should I listen to what you are saying, to your voice about our work and our practice? Knowing the thought and wisdom behind your voice for our work is what we examine next.

Your Voice of Wisdom

H E A R

Don't count the days, make the days count.

—Muhammad Ali

It seems only appropriate to honor Muhammad Ali[134] with a quote, as he passed away while I was working on the manuscript for this book. This chapter and the next two are about becoming more aware of the voice of wisdom you teach and defend to others and knowing if your daily thought and wisdom choices make a difference.

How do we make the days of our professional life count?

Several themes were emerging for me during my early years of teaching at Stillman Valley, even if I could not articulate them to you at the time. I was shaping my voice, but I did not really know it. My voice, my themes of beliefs, became more solidified during my middle years of teaching with Rick DuFour (he was my principal) and other colleagues at West Chicago. Rick taught me the importance of being aware of my beliefs and thoughts about teaching and learning, and then viewing those beliefs through the lens of wise behaviors.

In my subsequent years at Stevenson, I referenced those fundamental beliefs as the *swords* I would defend during my entire professional career. That metaphor seemed a bit too graphic to me and, eventually, I thought of it more as just knowing my *voice*.

I have spent a lifetime trying to defend the elements (behaviors) of my voice—teaching them, honoring them, modeling them with my own behavior, and being wise about them. If you worked with me, those behaviors were non-negotiable. We would pursue them—forever. How we achieved them could be highly variable. But whether we would pursue them would not be a choice.

This is a cultural and cold reality of our heartprint on others. Our students and our colleagues have a right to know our voice for sustained and improved learning. And we

Reflect on one element

about student learning essential to your voice. It is so important to you that when others join your team, you make sure they reach clarity on this belief.

_____

_____

_____

_____

_____

_____

_____

_____

_____

_____

_____

How do you create an

engaging, meaningful, and fun place to learn each day?

_____

_____

_____

_____

_____

_____

_____

_____

_____

_____

have a responsibility to make sure it is a voice informed by the thought and wisdom of those who do meaningful research in the field of education.

Do you know your voice? Who are you, anyway?

The secret to knowing your voice is to take a close look at *why* you respond the way you do. Why do you passionately defend certain principles and behaviors?

 # MY HEARTPRINT

The following five elements of my voice—my thought and wisdom—took about fifteen years to shape and unfold for me to be able to teach them to others, use them with clarity, and recognize when they were or were not happening in my classroom or with my colleagues. As we worked together, my voice became integrated with their voices, and their voices became integrated with mine. These elements eventually became our shared voice at Stevenson.

First, the classroom should be a fun and engaging place for each and every student. Every classroom will reveal a relevant, meaningful, and connected curriculum every day. We each should think like elective class teachers! Imagine if students didn't have to enroll in your elementary school grade level or your middle school or high school course? What if it was optional? How could we make students *want* to be in our class each day?

By *relevant*, we want students to learn important content. Why is the content relevant and urgent to learn, and how it is connected to other subject areas?

By *meaningful*, we need the wisdom to present the lesson from the students' point of view and make the topic meaningful to them.

MY HEARTPRINT

Back then, I remember Zalman Usiskin inspiring me. He taught at the University of Chicago and emphasized that all fields of study need to apply to the lives of students and have relevance and meaning every day. And with a twinkle in his eye, he would say students need to work hard, and we need to make it fun to boot! Is your classroom, your school, or your district a fun and engaging place for all?

MY HEARTPRINT ♥

Second, students have the right to be college and career ready. We will ensure that unit assessments are high quality, in common, scored with fidelity, and used for formative student and teacher team learning purposes. This was ingrained in me as I observed a K–12 system that used assessments to sort students as early as fourth grade.

My beloved discipline of mathematics often was the root of that sorting injustice, especially among students from minority groups. I knew it wasn't right. Every student deserves access to the curriculum and the support of a collaborative school culture to achieve success in the college and career readiness curriculum.

MY HEARTPRINT ♥

Third, textbooks cannot be the sole wisdom authority. Every classroom will use student-engaged instruction and learning every day. I have been an author of a major mathematics textbook series since the late 1980s. I believe in what my colleagues and I write, and I also believe that the curriculum we present to teachers can be a tremendous aid to their thoughtful work, development, and content wisdom for the subject. Yet, during my early years at Stillman Valley, I had become so book dependent that my own learning became stunted a bit. I could not think for myself.

The textbook is and should be a great resource, as it is a resource designed by experts in the field. And yet, it is just one of many resources to use as your knowledge and understanding of how to present content develop and mature. I discovered that if I allowed the curriculum to do all the work for me, it took away from my own learning, wisdom, and thought processes for life-long content development.

Are there any areas of your school program in which students are being denied access to the curriculum?

_____

_____

_____

_____

_____

_____

_____

_____

_____

_____

_____

_____

How do you and your team ensure you will be lifelong learners of the content you teach?

_____

_____

_____

_____

_____

_____

_____

_____

_____

_____

_____

_____

_____

_____

We should be sure to use experts we trust to sort through the maze of advice that comes at us. For example, one place I know I can go for reliable teacher-made content lessons and video resources is LearnZillion (https://learnzillion.com). Visit www.youtube.com /user/learnzillionvideo to learn more about it and make your own judgments.

Fourth, students have the right to learn with technology. Every classroom will integrate some type of technology into the student learning experience. When I became an adjunct professor at Loyola University Chicago, the first thing the dean of the graduate school expected from me was my technology integration plan. Good for her!

It was clear the university had a technology voice it expected me to satisfy, and this thrilled me, as it was part of my own personal voice as well. The first course I taught was a doctoral studies course for future superintendents.

In this case, I decided each student would keep a personal blog for the course. All papers and projects would be turned in to the blog. Students would answer questions I posted for class on their blogs, and everyone would have a blog buddy whose submissions he or she would have to review and critique. Students had to read entries on my class blog and then comment on those entries. Since they were timed, I would know the exact date and time the students responded.

In this sense, the technology served the growth, thinking, and debate around the ideas of the class. It was not used just for the sake of using a nice technology.

However, this is where I required a growth mindset if I wanted this practice to become part of my thought and wisdom. I did not know exactly how to do this!

So, I went to Chris Salituro, a social studies teacher and leader at Stevenson, to teach me how to manage and organize the work. I asked my tech tutor and guru Charlene Chausis to come to my class on the first night and help me help my students set up their blogs and trouble-shoot any initial problems. Chris and Charlene served as my tech team!

MY HEARTPRINT ♥

HOW do you help students learn by using technology? How do you ensure that the technology is in the service of student learning?

_____

_____

_____

_____

_____

_____

_____

_____

_____

_____

_____

_____

And this brings me to the final element of my thought and wisdom development. In short, I recognized I did not have enough wisdom to become a better thought leader without the collaboration of those two colleagues.

Fifth, individually, educators never have enough wisdom. Every grade-level and course-based teacher will actively participate in a collaborative, interdependent learning community. In my early years of teaching, we did not have the wisdom and the voice of Carol Dweck and her growth mindset research. Nor did we have the deeply held belief that we can and should work to improve our own knowledge base every day.

I suspect gathering the wisdom of others may be true of you anyway. You most likely would not be reading a book called *HEART!* if you didn't have a heart for this perspective on your work life.

Eventually, these five elements of my professional voice became part of my everyday behavior. They energized me as I used them to focus the work of others. They moved from vaguely hanging around in the back of my mind to impacting every moment of my daily actions as an educator.

So, what is in your wisdom bucket?

MY HEART PRINT ♥

Ultimately, you must ask, "Are my wisdom, my thoughts, my voice, about the right things? What if my voice is wrong? Should you follow me then? How would I know if the critical elements of my professional voice are right?" The next chapter provides some valuable signposts to help validate the beliefs and principles that shape the climate of our professional voice.

What are the commitments and the essential elements of your professional voice? Using simple words or phrases, write three to five elements that, like the five I described, represent your wisdom and beliefs—the principles you are so passionate about that you will defend, teach, and energize others toward them for your entire career.

_____

_____

_____

_____

_____

_____

_____

_____

_____

_____

_____

_____

_____

_____

_____

_____

_____

Clean Up the Climate

H   E   A   R   ♥

Expert teachers are proficient at creating an optimal classroom climate for learning.

—John Hattie

I walked into my colleague's classroom and thought, "Oh no, he has slipped backward in the classroom climate we had worked so hard to improve over the past few months." The students were sitting in rows again, and he was standing at the front of the room. The climate of the classroom appeared to be one of student isolation and teacher lecture.

Each student had a worksheet with five problems on his or her desk. My colleague told them, "Get started." It was quiet in the classroom, and yet the next twenty minutes were to become an example of a great classroom climate for learning. After a few minutes of working on problem one, the teacher announced it was time to rotate. Students left the worksheets on their desks, and then the student in the back of each row moved to the front of the row, and all other students moved one seat back. He then told them they could review the work of the previous student on problem one and fix any mistakes, and then get started on problem two. This seat rotation continued until the students returned to their original seats. My colleague gave them time to correct any mistakes on all five problems. Finally, students paired with partners from a different row to compare responses and debate solutions. Twenty minutes had passed, and these students were *engaged*!

The best way I can describe an optimal classroom climate for you is this: if I walk into your room and watch what your students *do* during the lesson for twenty minutes, would I be able to find evidence of these five student practices?

1. Students are free to make mistakes and view mistakes as an opportunity to learn.
2. Peer-to-peer student discussions take place at least 50 percent of the time as you monitor and provide feedback prompts.

3. There is a welcome admission to errors in the class climate overall, especially from one student to another.

4. Students understand that during a lesson there will be moments of knowing and not knowing, and that is okay if it is used to build confidence in learning.

5. Students rarely shut down and stop working and go no longer than ten minutes just listening before direct instruction stops, and they engage in meaningful peer-to peer, small-group discourse activity.

In short, learning should be fun (and also challenging), as all students are *actively engaged* with you and each other. Do they view other students in the class as valuable and reliable resources for learning?

If you are able to sit and feel what it is like to be in your classroom every day from the students' point of view; if you understand there is a benefit and a need for physical movement during the lesson, and that student attention is a limited resource that deteriorates over time during whole-group discourse, then you are developing your thought and your wisdom about the right classroom climate.[135]

Your thought and wisdom about classroom climate mean you are able to activate the student voice during your lessons. You know that great lessons allow you to both *see and hear* what your students are thinking in an actively engaged way. Your wisdom also allows you to know how to use structures that eliminate rows and understands that asking students to sit together won't be sufficient. Your wisdom expects you to shift the expected communication and discourse for your class.

MY HEARTPRINT ♥

How do these five elements of classroom climate connect with and reflect on your current practice?

Are you able to see and hear what your students are thinking and doing throughout the lesson?

What happens in your classroom when students get stuck? What do you do, and what do they do?

During my years at Stevenson, we had to learn about the thought and wisdom for delivering on the promise of student-engaged learning as part of our daily classroom climate. With time, we better understood the wisdom of this aspect of expert teaching. And as my opening story describes, student feedback and engagement can come in many forms as part of your classroom climate.

In the next chapter, we examine the wisdom of assessment expert and thought leader, UCLA professor emeritus James Popham. This book is not designed to teach you his wisdom in depth, merely to inform the nature of using his wisdom as part of our heartprint on others.

Become a Feedback Fanatic

Recent reviews of more than 4,000 research investigations show clearly that when [the formative assessment] process is well implemented in the classroom, it can essentially double the speed of student learning.

—James Popham

Warning! Danger! There is no going back!

Have you had the experience of returning a rental car? There is this moment as you enter the facility over metal spikes known as tiger teeth, and there is no going back. A sign warns that if you back up, your tires will explode. And it's true! (Don't ask me how I know.)

The thought and wisdom issues we are about to discuss represent one of those *no going back* moments. This chapter represents the one aspect of our work that once you know better, there is no going back.

Seems rather drastic, no? And, yet, it is true. So, here we go!

There is nothing more important to the thought leadership and wisdom of our professional work than our ability to effectively monitor student learning, provide feedback for refinement during the learning process, and then expect our students to act on that feedback. We are expected to become feedback experts with our students and colleagues.

We can view feedback from two perspectives.

1. How do we monitor and provide formative feedback *during the lesson*?
2. How do we monitor and provide formative feedback *on our unit assessments*?

Respond to this question: *Are formative feedback and assessment the same as checking for understanding, either during instruction or when you pass back a unit quiz or test?* Would you say *yes* or *no*? They are different. Yet, in fact, they are related.

To begin, let's take a look at the perspective of formative feedback during the lesson.

Leading assessment thought leader James Popham is professor emeritus in the Graduate School of Education at the University of California, Los Angeles. He provides some guidance and wisdom on the importance of feedback to students.

> Recent reviews of more than 4,000 research investigations show clearly that when [the formative assessment] process is well implemented in the classroom, it can essentially double the speed of student learning. Indeed, when one considers several recent reviews of research regarding the classroom formative-assessment process, it is clear that the process works, it can produce whopping gains in students' achievement, and it is sufficiently robust so that different teachers can use it in diverse ways, yet still get great results with their students.[136]

The formative assessment feedback process for students occurs as you monitor and check for understanding during the lesson and then use what you see and hear students doing to provide timely and specific feedback in class. You then expect students to make adjustments to their initial understanding and learning as they take action on your feedback during class. Eventually, your students also become more able to provide accurate feedback to each other.

Checking for understanding then is the first step in a formative feedback process but only that. One way you can measure your progress on this aspect of lesson design is to examine where you stand in the classroom during the lesson. Are you at the front of the room or mostly out among the students?

Like many teachers, I was not aware of how or when I moved. It was not part of my general planning or thought process. Where did I sit, stand, or walk as I taught parts of the lesson each day? And, how did my ability to provide deep and meaningful feedback to my students depend on where I was standing?

Think about the lessons you design.

Where are you standing? Are you at the front of the room? Do you move your body around? What if your students are doing station rotations? Where are you during that time? Are you standing tall over them or kneeling into their team activity? Are you at the back of the room? Are you out and among the students? What do you hear them saying to each other in small-group conversations?

Do you ever sit in a student desk and imagine what class is like from the lens through which they see the class?

Where will they see you standing? What are you expecting from them? How will students show you they understand the lesson? How will you see and hear their thoughts? How will you provide meaningful feedback that is timely and specific? How will students be expected to take action on your feedback as they work during class?

These types of questions are all part of the thought process you should go through during lesson design. And the answers to the questions should be driven by the wisdom of thought leaders such as Popham and others.

When is the last time you walked into a colleague's classroom and just watched the levels of student engagement and talking? Is there evidence and use of the wisdom of formative feedback and action by each teacher on your team?

The following five questions can help your thought and wisdom development regarding formative feedback as part of your lesson design.

1. How much of the lesson content will be covered through students' peer discussions versus didactic teacher lecture?
2. What types of in-class formative feedback processes will be used to evaluate each lesson's effectiveness?
3. What types of questions and conjectures will students propose in the early stages of the lesson?
4. What kinds of student-led summative exercises will be used to measure student understanding and learning?
5. How will the lesson draw on students' personal experiences to facilitate learning?

MY HEARTPRINT ♥

Reflect on your motion and where you stand as you provide students feedback during the lesson. You can use the questions as prompts to help.

When you are walking around the classroom, how do you provide feedback to students? What do you do if they are stuck to help them persevere?

_____

_____

_____

_____

_____

_____

_____

_____

_____

_____

_____

_____

_____

_____

_____

_____

_____

_____

_____

_____

_____

You enhance student perseverance during a lesson through the use of timely and formative feedback. Wise teachers build this formative feedback process into every lesson.

Recall that earlier in the chapter I mentioned that assessment thought and knowledge can be viewed from two perspectives.

A second formative assessment perspective is: *How do we monitor and provide formative feedback on our unit assessments?* You pass back a quiz, test, or project in your school, and the wise educators ask, *"Now what?"*

It is an important distinction that from a testing perspective, formative assessment is not a type of unit or benchmark test students take. Formative assessment of an actual quiz or test refers to processes that are much different than the assessment instrument itself—used as part of a formative process for learning.

Popham again provides a distinguishing analogy to help us understand the process.

> When teachers are told, inaccurately, that formative assessment is a kind of test, this is akin to telling a would-be surfer that a surfboard is the same as surfing. While a surfboard represents an important ingredient in surfing, it is only that—a part of the surfing process. The entire process involves the surfer's paddling out to an appropriate offshore location, selecting the right wave, choosing the most propitious moment to catch the chosen wave, standing upright on the surfboard, and staying upright while a curling wave rumbles toward shore. The surfboard is a key component of the surfing process, but it is not the entire process.[137]

When we give, grade, score, and pass back common unit assessments to students, what happens in your classroom, team, or school? If the answer is nothing, then these tests are strictly checks for understanding and viewed as summative moments by you. Wise teachers and thought leaders understand that the assessment instrument itself (quiz or test) should primarily be used for a *formative* purpose.

In response to the "Now what?" question, in order to use an assessment for formative purposes when a test is returned, students should:

- Take fifteen to twenty minutes to analyze the parts of the test with errors
- Identify which standards they are or are not proficient in based on those errors
- Create a plan of action for reengaging in the standards that are an area of continued weakness

- Take action on that plan over the next week or two to revisit those areas of weakness and demonstrate learning based on those errors

MY HEARTPRINT ♥

Only then can the test be considered as part of a meaningful formative feedback process, and not just as a diagnostic tool for a summative grade.

Student goal setting based on results from a unit assessment helps to inform your students about their learning progress and direction, and enables them to take ownership of what they do or do not know. Wise teachers make student goal setting happen during and after any unit of study.

You become a wise teacher when you monitor learning, provide formative feedback, and work with your colleagues to address the needs of each and every student in your grade level or course, not just the students in your classroom. I discuss this global ownership of the students in your school in the final chapter on thought and wisdom in our work.

Consider the *now what?* aspect of what happens when you pass back a chapter or unit assessment to your students.

Do you use the test as part of a formative learning process for each student?

What actions are your students expected to do with your feedback on the quiz or test? Are students expected to embrace their errors and learn the standards assessed?

_____

_____

_____

_____

_____

_____

_____

_____

_____

_____

_____

_____

_____

_____

_____

_____

_____

_____

_____

_____

_____

33

Yours, Mine, and Ours

H E A R

So much of America's tragic and costly failure to care for all its children stems from our tendency to distinguish between our own children and other people's children—as if justice was divisible.

—Marian Wright Edelman

You are driving to work and thinking about the day ahead. As you think about the students in your school, do you think you possess an inclusive or exclusive perspective on your work? Do you seek to select and sort out students who do not belong? Or, do you tend to expect all students in your school in your grade level or course to meet the success criteria, including those students you don't teach?

My first experience with this final aspect of wisdom and thought leadership for our profession occurred on my third day on the job at Stevenson. My colleague and fellow teacher Karen (not her real name) came into my office and said, "You gotta get these three kids out of my class right now. They do not belong."

I replied, "Really, how can you know this after three days?"

"Because this happens to me every year. They place these kids that don't belong into my classes."

"Who are *they*?" I asked.

Karen got a little flustered and said, "You know, the guidance department."

I asked, "Can you be more specific, who in the guidance department?"

She walked out of my office angrily and said, "Just get them out of there."

I ran after her, stopped her as she was about to enter the hallway, and asked the question I should have asked in the first place, "What did you mean when you said these kids don't belong? Which kids?"

Her response startled me. Partially because I was new to the district and trying to figure out protocols, partially because of my ingrained sense of social justice, and partially because up until that moment, no one had ever said such a thing out loud.

She replied, "Those special ed kids. I have told the guidance department over and over that they do not belong in my honors course."

Stunned, I just stared at her for a moment. I told her to meet me in my office at 7:30 a.m. the next day, and we would discuss the issue in more detail.

The students were more than qualified to be in our honors program based on their previous performance. Karen's lack of wisdom regarding her belief that each and every student can reach her success criteria was severely shallow. She did not see them as her kids or as "I am in this with other teachers too" kids.

Karen's selecting and sorting perspective was not malicious in the sense that she was a mean person. She just had not thought of her role or believed her role as a teacher was to be more inclusive. She had not yet understood the wisdom of expanding the role of her teaching team to include resource teachers and other school support personnel to help her ensure success for every student in her mainstreamed class.

Take a moment to reflect on your own beliefs and mindset about inclusiveness in the classroom.

MY HEART PRINT ♥

Use the following list to test your own beliefs and wisdom regarding an inclusive mindset. Respond to each statement with *yes* or *no*, and explain your reason.

1. Student intelligence is changeable rather than fixed.
2. Teachers in my school are passionate that all students in their class can attain success.
3. Teachers in my school have the ability to move students through a path of success.
4. Teachers in my school respect students as learners and as people.
5. Teachers in my school demonstrate care and commitment to their students.

How did you do? Do these statements represent your beliefs and the beliefs of the colleagues in your school? Why or why not?

So, what was the solution to Karen's dilemma? It was not to take the three students out of her class. That would have been a selecting and sorting solution, not an inclusive one. Do you agree?

Wisdom in our profession does not support a selecting and sorting mindset. Instead, we kept the three students in her course—an inclusive solution. We added a special education resource teacher to Karen's honors science team. This teacher met with the team every week and provided classroom culture guidance for how to integrate special needs students into the mainstream class culture. We also provided required and immediate intervention and support for any student at risk of failing the course, not just those students with special needs or from an EL background.

At Stevenson, we wanted to give our students access to the curriculum by also providing a box of support to stand on, as needed. We made sure our support was required, meaning if any student was at academic risk in the class, he or she must get this additional support. It had to be fluid, meaning the student was not locked into the support forever. As soon as a student demonstrated understanding of the standards or was able to achieve passing grades, he or she moved on from the support. And, the additional class support needed to be standards driven, meaning students received help and support around the essential learning standards for a grade level or course.

And for all of that to work, as professional educators and as the teachers and leaders making the decisions for everything going on in our school, we each had to personally heed the thought, wisdom, and advice provided by John Hattie:

> Expert teachers believe that all students can reach the success criteria. . . . The picture of expert teachers, then, is one of involvement and respect for the students, of a willingness to be receptive to what the students need, of teachers who demonstrate a sense of responsibility in the learning process, and of teachers who are passionate about ensuring that their students are learning.[138]

Hattie's words take me all the way back to the start of part 5 and our discussion about the great adventure of our work. It was why I was so determined to work with Karen as her colleague. She was so good in so many other areas of her teaching life. Teaching was her calling. I just wanted her professional life as an educator to soar way beyond "Get these three kids outta here."

I wanted her to be the hero of her own story.

I have been in the education profession for a long time. I have found no better secret to becoming the best educator you can be than to tell you to stay in love with your work. When you are in love with your work, you pour your heart into it. It gives you the fire to ignite learning in others.

Karen not only stayed in love with her work, but she also became a champion and role model for helping many students (especially girls) become empowered and confident in science. She decided somewhere along the line to change her heartprint and become an even bigger hero than she already was.

How awesome is that? Whose students are these?

They are yours, mine, and ours.

I suspect that if you have read and made it through all thirty-three chapters of this book, you are just the type of professional educator—teacher and leader—with the right kind of heartprint this next generation of students needs.

Hold the Mayo!

H   E   A   R

Don't cry because it is over, smile because it happened
—Dr. Seuss

"R u available for a quick call?" It was September 16, 2014, at 8:12 p.m. It was an innocent enough text, I suppose. Only I knew different.

This was a text from my friend and colleague Rick DuFour. I had known Rick since 1980 when we worked together at Community High School District 94 outside of Chicago. It wasn't the norm for Rick to send a chit-chat type of message. I was in a meeting, and I was afraid something wasn't quite right.

When I called, he was matter of fact and to the point, as always. "I have cancer."

I paused for a moment, not quite sure what to say. I sat down. I got off the phone, numb to the news and afraid for my friend and fellow educator. We had been through a lot of battles together. This would be the next one.

Perhaps you have heard similar news from a friend or loved one. If so, you understand on a deeper level the balanced beauty and effort required to force away the distractions of doctors, chemo, and drug trials; trips to hospitals; time-consuming scans and surgeries; well-wishers and public speaking; and the hundreds of opinions thrown at you. There becomes this paradox of hope and disappointment, good and bad moments, all within a single day wrapped into one week, and then one month at a time.

Rick further discovered, over time, that he had incurable stage 4 lung cancer. He shared his journey about cancer with the public, so I am not sharing details he did not want known.

Rick was a teacher and leader with great clarity of message and a way of cutting through the fog and educational rhetoric. He was one of those unique individuals who made you far better than you ever dreamed you could be. He pulled you forward into a better professional life: a rare gift.

He wrote the book *In Praise of American Educators* in 2016 while fighting through the cancer. The book reveals the rewards and challenges for educators everywhere to invest their time, energy, and entire beings into work and actions that significantly improve student learning and growth.[139]

On August 10, 2016, Rick gave the keynote address to 1,600 educators at the PLC at Work Institute in Seattle.[140] Despite his deep pain and consistent cough, he spoke with strength and clarity as he relayed how the team of medical personnel had collaborated with one another throughout his cancer journey. He described how they had worked to solve problems together, seeking advice together and learning how to best advise him, together.

He highlighted the mission and principles of the Mayo Clinic as a model for educators to follow.

The Mayo Clinic's Mission and Principles

The needs of the ***patient*** come first.

- We will meet those needs through unsurpassed collaboration.
- No one is big enough to work independently of others.
- The combined wisdom of one's peers is greater than any individual.
- We will use a teamwork approach, share our insights, and take a continuous interest in each other's growth.[141]

Rick then stated: "Replace the word *patient* with *student.*"

The Professional Educator's Mission and Principles

The needs of the ***student*** come first.

- We will meet those needs through unsurpassed collaboration.
- No one is big enough to work independently of others.
- The combined wisdom of one's peers is greater than any individual.
- We will use a teamwork approach, share our insights, and take a continuous interest in each other's growth.

All I can think is: these are the types of adult culture, thought leadership, and wisdom we pursue when we say we want to become fully formed professionals. This culture of unsurpassed collaboration could overcome poverty, selfishness, inequities, arrogance, incompetence, and student fear and failure, and kick any lack of urgency right in the butt.

Rick finished his keynote address with this: "Will you act with a sense of urgency, as if the very lives of your students depend on your action? Because in a very literal sense, more so than at any other time in American history, they do."

Finally, he delivered an emotional moment: "I don't know how much time I can be on this journey with you, but I know you are the greatest generation of American educators, and you can carry on this challenge. I wish you Godspeed."

There was not a dry eye in the house, including mine, as he ended his address to the packed house of educators. The standing ovation was both deserved and well received. He was almost embarrassed by it. It is what made him so remarkable—a driven passion and intensity for those Mayo Clinic values, yet, with a humble spirit toward self. Such wisdom we should heed.

On February 8, 2017, as I was finishing this last part of the book, I received a phone call. After a courageous two-and-one-half year battle, Rick's body finally succumbed to the cancer. He may not be on this journey with us anymore, yet, I know he would want us to hold those Mayo Clinic values very close to our hearts.

Hold the Mayo indeed!

Take a moment to reflect on the five chapters of part 5. What are your primary takeaways? Include two or three possible actions you can take to improve the way you and your colleagues can increase your thought leadership and wisdom for the profession. What thought or wisdom would you add that was not in part 5 of the book?

Think of these next steps as *I will . . .* statements, and write them down as you measure your personal thought and wisdom heartprint during this stage of your professional career.

MY HEARTPRINT ♥

_____

_____

_____

_____

_____

_____

_____

_____

_____

_____

The following resources are instrumental in the support of our work together in part 5. Depending on your personal interests, you may use these resources as you continue to expand your knowledge base and the knowledge base of your colleagues. You may also visit **go.SolutionTree.com/HEART** to access direct links to the websites and download two additional chapters related to part 5.

Part 5: T Is for Thought

Resources

Buffum, A., & Mattos, M. (Eds.). (2015). *It's about time: Planning interventions and extensions in elementary school.* Bloomington, IN: Solution Tree Press.

Hattie, J. (2012). *Visible learning for teachers: Maximizing impact on learning.* New York: Routledge. (This is the research meta-analysis book with most of the information for expert teaching wisdom.)

Hattie, J., Masters, D., & Birch, K. (2016). *Visible learning into action: International case studies of impact.* New York: Routledge.

Hattie, J., & Yates, G. (2014). *Visible learning and the science of how we learn.* New York: Routledge. (The highlights of this book include the "cascading inattention" brain research and how student attention deteriorates during whole-group discourse.)

Popham, J. (2013). *Transformative assessment.* Alexandria, VA: Association for Supervision and Curriculum Development.

Mattos, M., & Buffum, A. (Eds.). (2015). *It's about time: Planning interventions and extensions in secondary school.* Bloomington, IN: Solution Tree Press.

Mayo Clinic. (n.d.). *Mayo Clinic mission and values.* Accessed at www.mayoclinic.org/about-mayo-clinic/mission-values on August 1, 2016.

Additional Resources

LearnZillion: https://learnzillion.com and www.youtube.com/user/learnzillionvideo

Epilogue

The salvation of this human world lies nowhere else than in the human heart, in the human power to reflect, in human meekness and human responsibility.

—Václav Havel

It was early August and late in the afternoon, as I was completing a PLC at Work Institute in Seattle, Washington. I was finishing up the manuscript for this book, and it was going through one more iteration of *reflect, refine, and act*. The words for this epilogue were being added to literally the sixtieth version of the manuscript. The research and writing took close to two years. Writing and revising are painful. I often agonized over whether readers would connect to the ideas and the intent of *HEART!*

As I walked back to the hotel thinking about the upcoming school season, it felt like preseason for the National Football League or Major League Baseball—there is hope in the air. "This school year will be a great one," we say to ourselves. "The best year yet! I can't wait to meet my students!" And then, it is mid-October; you are in the early part of the new season and, for some, it is "I am off to a great start!" For others, it is, "Uh oh. I could be in for a long year."

It was one of those rare and wonderful late-summer days that make you want to be outside and so grateful to be alive. Sunny with a cool breeze, temps in the low seventies, and people everywhere, living their daily lives. As I walked along Sixth Avenue and hit Pike Street, I decided to take it east to Pike Place Market, a Seattle landmark, to take in the sights and sounds and sit by Elliott Bay.

People were everywhere—all shapes, sizes, ethnicities, and, I suspect, spiritual inclinations. I saw jackets, no jackets, hats, scarves, coats, no coats, and lots of sunshine on every face. My surroundings felt very inclusive and safe. As I looked at the people, I couldn't keep myself from thinking each and every one of them had a teacher's heartprint on them. They were all K–12 students once. They have all had teachers—someone just like you and me that existed in their past.

And I was left wondering, "Does it really matter to them, now that they are adults, with all the hammering that comes with the stuff of life?"

They had a third-grade teacher. They had a middle school eighth-grade English class. Maybe they took an art class in high school. They had potentially forty to forty-five teachers during those thirteen years in school. And as they passed by me, going their own way, wearing headphones, talking on a cell phone, casually chatting with friends, or riding a bike yelling "on your left," they each had someone like us in the stream of their story.

I thought to myself, I wonder who they actually remember? Who made a difference? Who fought for them? Who saw potential in them? Who among us left our heartprint on them?

Some seem a bit broken. Others seem confident and carefree. I do not know for sure.

All of them seemed to have a place to go. I thought that was good at least. They seemed to have purpose.

So do we. We have perhaps the greatest purpose there is. No matter all the pressures and all the responsibilities placed on us, we chose a profession of persons. True, our work is a grind, and we have to find the grit and the grace to wind our way through the marathon of our work life, year in and year out.

We get it. It is not a sprint.

True too, the students we are teaching are not yet fully formed individuals (are we ever really fully formed?), but they are our students nonetheless. And thus, they each have value. We have chosen a profession that chooses to honor each and every one of those students and to love them and seek social justice for them, as we would for our own children.

I am so glad I chose our profession. There is no better calling in life than to be called *teacher*. I hope you agree.

And, I hope you will forever see every person who passes you by and realize that he or she was once a student. These students needed you, their teacher. Because of your heartprint on them, they are leaving a heartprint on others.

My lifelong friend and colleague, Grace Kelemanik, gave me the gift of reviewing this book. In her review, she said to me:

> [Readers] need a supportive tribe and space to reflect and reconnect and recommit to teaching. I see your book as providing a tool around which they could gather and share. I was struck by the language in the book. . . . I had to stop, pause, and think.
>
> Maybe that is the point of it all: to read this new and different idea—at times almost even written in a different language—and then use it to reflect. I did, though, want you to know that after a while, I started to feel like I was reading into a new and different culture, with authors, and books, and language with which

I was not familiar. When it was your voice, telling real stories from your life, I felt much more grounded. (G. Kelemanik, personal communication, August 23, 2016)

I hope this book, through its stories and ideas, allowed you to find your story as well—a story that is leaving and weaving a positive heartprint on others as you reflect on your chosen profession and proudly announce to the world:

"I am teacher!"

Acknowledgments

I have always thought acknowledgements are a bit awkward for the reader. On one hand, they give you some insight into the author and the team of people essential to the support and development of a book. On the other hand, acknowledgements usually include a litany of names you just do not recognize. So, I will keep these important thoughts of thanks brief but relevant to the work.

When I first took the idea of *HEART!* to the president and publisher of Solution Tree Press, Douglas Rife, I asked him if this book was worth the time and sacrifice it would require. "Would anyone want to read it?" I asked. I trusted his wisdom so much that if he had said *no*, I would have let the project go. From that moment at the Starbucks in Phoenix, Arizona, Douglas has been my biggest supporter and an ear for this work. He is a special gift to many, including me. My thanks too go to CEO Jeff Jones. He was instrumental in support of this project's nuances from the beginning.

Writing a manuscript for any book has a lot of moving parts and requires editorial support from experts that work to make books accurate and clear. In the best of circumstances, the author is fortunate if the editors care as much about the project and work on it with the same passion and interest as the author. In my case, Christine Hood, Sarah Payne-Mills, Rian Anderson, and the Solution Tree editorial staff were there with me before and during the process of creating both the form and the function of *HEART!* Both the book and the subsequent online chapters are significantly improved because of their effort at collaboration. Thank you!

In the book, I relate the stories of many real-life teaching and leading heroes I had the pleasure to work with over the years. They include positive impact teachers, such as Lee Maciejewski, Mary Layco, and my best friend in this lifetime, the late Jerry Cummins, among many others.

I also describe several colleagues, whose names I changed in order to protect their identity. Like me, these heroes, and the part of their story I tell, represent a moment of struggle and failure perhaps. So, I wanted to protect them. But they left a heartprint on me nonetheless, and I am a better educator today because our paths crossed over the years. Thirty-one colleagues and friends provided depth of feedback, enthusiastic responses, and genuine willingness to engage with me on the original ideas for this book. In almost every case, their ideas and sometimes their exact words show up in various chapters.

Solution Tree and I would like to thank the following reviewers: Brian Butler, Scott Carr, Mike Cyrus, Bill Ferriter, Tom Hoh, Corrine Howe, Chris Jakicic, Sharon Kramer, Tom Many, Suzi Mast, Mignon Smith, Scott Cunningham, Rich Smith, and John Staley. Their feedback made the book so much better!

Special thanks go to colleagues Becky DuFour, Sarah Schuhl, Maria Nielsen, Nathan Lang, Tim Brown, Mona Toncheff, Aaron Hansen, Matt Larson, Luis Cruz, Jessica Kanold-McIntyre, Rick DuFour, Denise Walston, Bob Eaker, Mike Mattos, Grace Kelemanik, and Bill Barnes for responding time and again to my numerous and constant questions during the various stages of the manuscript, despite their own busy schedules. They were more than reviewers, they came along with me on my writing journey, and their voices appear in the book.

I have also been blessed with the support of "behind the scenes" friends, such as Charlene Chausis, Janis Fine, Claudia Wheatley, Diane Briars, Linda Fulmore, Al Foster, Anna Hazinski, Shannon Ritz, Shirley Frye, Kit Norris, and the events and marketing teams at Solution Tree. My thanks to all!

Most acknowledgments end with a nod to the author's family. And, it is no different for me. My wife Susan somehow loves me enough to have endured the eleven months of lost weekends as the writing process unfolded. On our spring break vacation, she was very patient with me as I wrote the beginning ideas of part 2, "E Is for Engagement" (the part about living a balanced life—pretty ironic). She is willing to laugh with me and love me as we walk through these later stages of our lives together. And, as I mention in the book, she is the stabilizing force in our family life and for me. Her ninety-year-old mom, Jean, went through a challenging time in life during the manuscript development, and I want to thank her for asking me how it was going and being interested in my progress, despite her own pain.

In our profession, we dedicate our lives to improving the lives of children, including our own. Jessica, Tim, Adam, Jaclyn, and Anna are carving out their own journeys and finding their way in this world. Thanks for letting me tell a few of your stories. My love, friendship, and heart for you know no bounds. You, above anyone, know my heartprint.

And my final thanks is reserved for you, the reader. It is in your commitment to our great profession, and the process of reading, reflecting, and refining your work, that the story of your professional life unfolds each and every day.

I hope this book helps you in that journey.

Notes

1 Havel, V. (n.d.). *Václav Havel quotes*. Accessed at www.goodreads.com/author/quotes/71441 .V_clav_Havel on September 1, 2016.

2 National Center for Education Statistics. (n.d.). *Fast facts*. Accessed at http://nces.ed.gov /fastfacts/display.asp?id=28 on May 1, 2016.

3 Footprint. (n.d.). In *Merriam-Webster*. Accessed at www.merriam-webster.com/dictionary /footprint on May 1, 2016.

4 Spaulding, T. (2015). *The heart-led leader: How living from the heart will change your organization and your life*. New York: Crown Business, p. 193.

5 Mandela, N. (n.d.). *Nelson Mandela quotes*. Accessed at www.goodreads.com/quotes/49585 -there-is-no-passion-to-be-found-playing-small on September 1, 2016.

6 Williams, P. (2013). Happy. On *Despicable Me 2* original motion picture soundtrack [CD]. Los Angeles: Back Lot Music.

7 Seppälä, E. (2016). *The happiness track: How to apply the science of happiness to accelerate your success*. New York: HarperCollins, p. 8.

8 Seppälä, E. (2016). *The happiness track: How to apply the science of happiness to accelerate your success*. New York: HarperCollins.

9 Seppälä, E. (2016). *The happiness track: How to apply the science of happiness to accelerate your success*. New York: HarperCollins, p. 4.

10 Sanborn, M. (2013). *Fred 2.0: New ideas on how to keep delivering extraordinary results*. Carol Stream, IL: Tyndale House.

11 Passion. (n.d.). In *Merriam-Webster*. Accessed at www.merriam-webster.com/dictionary/passion on June 1, 2016.

12 Hattie, J. (2012). *Visible learning for teachers: Maximizing impact on learning*. New York: Routledge.

13 Day, C. (2004). *A passion for teaching*. New York: Routledge, p. 12.

14 Brown, B. (2012). *Daring greatly: How the courage to be vulnerable transforms the way we live, love, parent, and lead*. New York: Penguin, p. 10.

15 Brown, B. (2012). *Daring greatly: How the courage to be vulnerable transforms the way we live, love, parent, and lead.* New York: Penguin, p. 10.

16 Seppälä, E. (2016). *The happiness track: How to apply the science of happiness to accelerate your success.* New York: HarperCollins.

17 Rath, T., & Conchie, B. (2008). *Strengths based leadership: Great leaders, teams, and why people follow.* New York: Gallup Press, pp. 251–256.

18 Buechner, F. (n.d.). *Frederick Buechner quotes.* Accessed at www.goodreads.com/quotes /126649-compassion-is-the-sometimes-fatal-capacity-for-feeling-what-it on June 1, 2016.

19 Sympathy. (n.d.). In *Merriam-Webster.* Accessed at www.merriam-webster.com/dictionary /sympathy on June 1, 2016.

20 Empathy. (n.d.). In *Merriam-Webster.* Accessed at www.merriam-webster.com/dictionary /empathy on June 1, 2016.

21 King, M. L., Jr. (n.d.). *The drum major instinct.* Accessed at www.mlkonline.net/speeches-the -drum-major-instinct.html on February 24, 2017.

22 Pythagoras. (n.d.). *Pythagoras quotes.* Accessed at www.brainyquote.com/quotes/quotes/p /pythagoras160062.html on May 1, 2016.

23 Piercy, M. (1982). To be of use. In *Circles on the water: Selected poems of Marge Piercy.* New York: Knopf, p. 106.

24 Rath, T., & Clifton, D. O. (2004). *How full is your bucket? Positive strategies for work and life.* New York: Gallup Press, pp. 75–76.

25 Hope. (n.d.). In *Merriam-Webster.* Accessed at www.merriam-webster.com/dictionary/hope on June 1, 2016.

26 Rath, T., & Conchie, B. (2008). *Strengths based leadership: Great leaders, teams, and why people follow.* New York: Gallup Press, pp. 251–256.

27 Brown, B. (2010). *The gifts of imperfection: Let go of who you think you're supposed to be and embrace who you are.* Center City, MN: Hazelden, pp. 77–78.

28 Rath, T., & Conchie, B. (2008). *Strengths based leadership: Great leaders, teams, and why people follow.* New York: Gallup Press, pp. 251–256.

29 Weep. (n.d.). In *Merriam-Webster.* Accessed at www.merriam-webster.com/dictionary/weep on May 1, 2016.

30 Gibran, K. (n.d.). *Kahlil Gibran quotes.* Accessed at www.goodreads.com/author/quotes /6466154.Kahlil_Gibran on September 1, 2016.

31 Gibran, K. (n.d.). *Kahlil Gibran quotes.* Accessed at www.goodreads.com/author/quotes /6466154.Kahlil_Gibran on September 1, 2016.

32 Helliwell, J., Layard, R., & Sachs, J. (Eds.). (2013). *World happiness report 2013.* New York: Sustainable Development Solutions Network, p. 5. Accessed at http://unsdsn.org/wp-content /uploads/2014/02/WorldHappinessReport2013_online.pdf on May 1, 2016.

33 Helliwell, J., Layard, R., & Sachs, J. (Eds.). (2013). *World happiness report 2013.* New York: Sustainable Development Solutions Network, p. 5. Accessed at http://unsdsn.org/wp-content /uploads/2014/02/WorldHappinessReport2013_online.pdf on May 1, 2016.

34 Gallup. (2014). *State of America's schools: The path to winning again in education*. Washington, DC: Author, p. 27. Accessed at www.gallup.com/services/178709/state-america-schools-report.aspx on May 1, 2016.

35 Gallup. (2016). *Recognized as one of the world's most influential Americans*. Washington, DC: Author. Accessed at www.gallup.com/corporate/178136/george-gallup.aspx on November 21, 2016.

36 Gallup. (2014). *State of America's schools: The path to winning again in education*. Washington, DC: Author. Accessed at www.gallup.com/services/178709/state-america-schools-report.aspx on May 1, 2016.

37 Hastings, M., & Agrawal, S. (2015, February 1). *Engaged teachers enjoy personal, professional edge*. Accessed at www.gallup.com/poll/181523/engaged-teachers-enjoy-personal-professional-edge.aspx on May 1, 2016.

38 Hastings, M., & Agrawal, S. (2015, February 1). *Engaged teachers enjoy personal, professional edge*. Accessed at www.gallup.com/poll/181523/engaged-teachers-enjoy-personal-professional-edge.aspx on May 1, 2016.

39 Gallup. (2014). *State of America's schools: The path to winning again in education*. Washington, DC: Author. Accessed at www.gallup.com/services/178709/state-america-schools-report.aspx on May 1, 2016.

40 Gallup. (2017). *Gallup Daily: U.S. employee engagement*. Accessed at www.gallup.com/poll/180404/gallup-daily-employee-engagement.aspx on February 27, 2017.

41 Elementary and Secondary Education Act of 1965, Pub. L. No 89-10, 20 U.S.C. § 6301 (1965). Every Student Succeeds Act of 2015, Pub. L. No 114-95, 20 U.S.C. § 1177 (2015). No Child Left Behind Act of 2001, Pub. L. No 107–110, 20 U.S.C. § 6319 (2002).

42 Adlai E. Stevenson High School. *Students*. (2016). Accessed at http://bit.ly/2fVyQrc on November 21, 2016.

43 Baldoni, J. (2013). Employee engagement does more than boost productivity. *Harvard Business Review*. Accessed at https://hbr.org/2013/07/employee-engagement-does-more on June 1, 2016.

44 Schwartz, T., & McCarthy, C. (2007). Manage your energy, not your time. *Harvard Business Review*, 85(10). Accessed at https://hbr.org/2007/10/manage-your-energy-not-your-time on May 1, 2016.

45 Schwartz, T. (with Gomes, J., & McCarthy, C.). (2010). *The way we're working isn't working: The four forgotten needs that energize great performance*. New York: Free Press, p. 185.

46 Schwartz, T. (with Gomes, J., & McCarthy, C.). (2010). *The way we're working isn't working: The four forgotten needs that energize great performance*. New York: Free Press, p. 196.

47 Loehr, J. (2007). *The power of story: Change your story, change your destiny in business and in life*. New York: Free Press.

48 Kanold, T. D. (2011). *The five disciplines of PLC leaders*. Bloomington, IN: Solution Tree Press, p. 129.

49 Loehr, J. (2007). *The power of story: Change your story, change your destiny in business and in life*. New York: Free Press, p. 74.

50 Loehr, J., & Schwartz, T. (2003). *The power of full engagement: Managing energy, not time, is the key to high performance and personal renewal*. New York: Free Press, p. 10.

51 Kanold, T. D. (2011). *The five disciplines of PLC leaders*. Bloomington, IN: Solution Tree Press, p. 129.

52 Loehr, J. (2007). *The power of story: Change your story, change your destiny in business and in life*. New York: Free Press, p. 84.

53 Rath, T. (2013). *Eat move sleep: How small choices lead to big changes*. Arlington, VA: Missionday, p. 13.

54 Rath, T. (2013). *Eat move sleep: How small choices lead to big changes*. Arlington, VA: Missionday, p. 13.

55 Rath, T. (2013). *Eat move sleep: How small choices lead to big changes*. Arlington, VA: Missionday, pp. 14–15.

56 Segar, M. (2015). *No sweat: How the simple science of motivation can bring you a lifetime of fitness*. New York: AMACOM, p. 193.

57 Rath, T. (2015). *Are you fully charged? The three keys to energizing your work and life*. Arlington, VA: Silicon Guild, p. 140.

58 Rath, T. (2015). *Are you fully charged? The three keys to energizing your work and life*. Arlington, VA: Silicon Guild.

59 Rath, T. (2015). *Are you fully charged? The three keys to energizing your work and life*. Arlington, VA: Silicon Guild.

60 Rath, T. (2015). *Are you fully charged? The three keys to energizing your work and life*. Arlington, VA: Silicon Guild.

61 Thurman, H. (1981). *Meditations of the heart*. Boston: Beacon Press, pp. 95–96.

62 Duckworth, A. (2016). *Grit: The power of passion and perseverance*. New York: Scribner, p. 54.

63 Duckworth, A. (2016). *Grit: The power of passion and perseverance*. New York: Scribner.

64 Duckworth, A. (2016). *Grit: The power of passion and perseverance*. New York: Scribner, pp. 269–270.

65 Perspective. (n.d.). In *Merriam-Webster*. Accessed at www.merriam-webster.com/dictionary /perspective on August 15, 2016.

66 Gardner, J. W. (1992). The secret ailment. *Across the Board*, *12*(8), 42.

67 Segar, M. (2015). *No sweat: How the simple science of motivation can bring you a lifetime of fitness*. New York: AMACOM, p. 188.

68 Frick, D. M., & Spears, L. C. (Eds.). (1996). *On becoming a servant leader: The private writings of Robert K. Greenleaf*. San Francisco: Jossey-Bass, p. 3.

69 Benkler, Y. (2011). The unselfish gene. *Harvard Business Review*, *89*(7–8). Accessed at https://hbr.org/2011/07/the-unselfish-gene on September 1, 2016.

70 Benkler, Y. (2011). The unselfish gene. *Harvard Business Review*, *89*(7–8), p. 77. Accessed at https://hbr.org/2011/07/the-unselfish-gene on September 1, 2016.

71 Benkler, Y. (2011). The unselfish gene. *Harvard Business Review*, *89*(7–8), p. 77. Accessed at https://hbr.org/2011/07/the-unselfish-gene on September 1, 2016.

72 Fullan, M. (2008). *The six secrets of change: What the best leaders do to help their organizations survive and thrive*. San Francisco: Jossey-Bass, p. 57.

73 Fullan, M. (2004). *Leading in a culture of change*. San Francisco: Jossey-Bass.

74 von Krogh, G., Ichijo, K., & Nonaka, I. (2000). *Enabling knowledge creation: How to unlock the mystery of tacit knowledge and release the power of innovation.* New York: Oxford University Press, p. 51.

75 Benkler, Y. (2011). The unselfish gene. *Harvard Business Review, 89*(7–8). Accessed at https://hbr.org/2011/07/the-unselfish-gene on September 1, 2016, p. 80.

76 Kristof, N. (2016). *Nicholas Kristof quotes.* Accessed at www.goodreads.com/quotes/624074 -america-s-education-system-has-become-less-a-ladder-of-opportunity on August 1, 2016.

77 AllThingsPLC. (n.d.). *About PLCs.* Accessed at www.allthingsplc.info/about on September 1, 2016.

78 Benkler, Y. (2011). The unselfish gene. *Harvard Business Review, 89*(7–8). Accessed at https://hbr.org/2011/07/the-unselfish-gene on September 1, 2016.

79 DuFour, R., DuFour, R., Eaker, R., Many, T. W., & Mattos, M. (2016). *Learning by doing: A handbook for professional learning communities at work* (3rd ed.). Bloomington, IN: Solution Tree Press.

80 King, M. L., Jr. (n.d.). *Martin Luther King Jr. quotes.* Accessed at www.goodreads.com /quotes/6070160-i-accept-this-award-today-with-an-abiding-faith-in on August 1, 2016.

81 King, M. L., Jr. (n.d.). *Martin Luther King Jr. quotes.* Accessed at www.goodreads.com /quotes/6070160-i-accept-this-award-today-with-an-abiding-faith-in on August 1, 2016.

82 Schimmer, T. (2016). *Grading from the inside out: Bringing accuracy to student assessment through a standards-based mindset.* Bloomington, IN: Solution Tree Press.

83 Green, E. (2014). *Building a better teacher: How teaching works (and how to teach it to everyone).* New York: Norton.

84 Green, E. (2015, April 15). *Building a better teacher: How teaching works (and how to teach it to everyone).* Keynote address given at the 93rd annual National Council of Teachers of Mathematics meeting and exposition, Boston, MA.

85 Kahneman, D., Rosenfield, A., Gandhi, L., & Blaser, T. (2016, October). Noise: How to overcome the high, hidden cost of inconsistent decision making. *Harvard Business Review, 94*(10), pp. 38–46. Accessed at https://hbr.org/2016/10/noise on October 1, 2016.

86 Kahneman, D., Rosenfield, A., Gandhi, L., & Blaser, T. (2016, October). Noise: How to overcome the high, hidden cost of inconsistent decision making. *Harvard Business Review, 94*(10), pp. 38–46. Accessed at https://hbr.org/2016/10/noise on October 1, 2016.

87 Goleman, D. (2006). *Social intelligence: The new science of human relationships.* New York: Bantam Books, p. 5.

88 Goleman, D. (2006). *Social intelligence: The new science of human relationships.* New York: Bantam Books, p. 334.

89 Goleman, D. (1995). *Emotional intelligence: Why it can matter more than IQ.* New York: Bantam Books.

90 Mayer, J. D., & Salovey, P. (1997). What is emotional intelligence? In P. Salovey & D. J. Sluyter (Eds.), *Emotional development and emotional intelligence: Educational implications* (pp. 3–31). New York: Basic Books, p. 10.

91 Goleman, D., Boyatzis, R., & McKee, A. (2013). *Primal leadership: Unleashing the power of emotional intelligence.* Boston: Harvard Business Review Press, p. 9.

92 Goleman, D. (2006). *Social intelligence: The new science of human relationships.* New York: Bantam Books, pp. 11, 171.

93 Goleman, D. (2006). *Social intelligence: The new science of human relationships*. New York: Bantam Books, p. 11.

94 Goleman, D. (2006). *Social intelligence: The new science of human relationships*. New York: Bantam Books, p. 312.

95 Goleman, D. (2006). *Social intelligence: The new science of human relationships*. New York: Bantam Books, p. 312.

96 Goleman, D. (2001). An EI-based theory of performance. In C. Cherniss & D. Goleman (Eds.), *The emotionally intelligent workplace: How to select for, measure, and improve emotional intelligence in individuals, groups, and organizations* (pp. 27–44). San Francisco: Jossey-Bass.

97 Goleman, D. (2005). *Emotional intelligence: Why it can matter more than IQ*. New York: Bantam Books.

98 Goleman, D. (2006). *Social intelligence: The new science of human relationships*. New York: Bantam Books, p. 334.

99 Beard, A. (2016). Yo-Yo Ma on successful creative collaboration. *Harvard Business Review*. Accessed at https://hbr.org/ideacast/2016/05/yo-yo-ma-on-successful-creative-collaboration on August 1, 2016.

100 Beard, A. (2016). Yo-Yo Ma on successful creative collaboration. *Harvard Business Review*. Accessed at https://hbr.org/ideacast/2016/05/yo-yo-ma-on-successful-creative-collaboration on August 1, 2016.

101 Beard, A. (2016). Yo-Yo Ma on successful creative collaboration. *Harvard Business Review*. Accessed at https://hbr.org/ideacast/2016/05/yo-yo-ma-on-successful-creative-collaboration on August 1, 2016.

102 Abele, J. (2011). Bringing minds together. *Harvard Business Review, 89*(7–8). Accessed at https://hbr.org/2011/07/bringing-minds-together on September 1, 2016.

103 Fitzgerald, F. S. (1925). *The great Gatsby*. New York: Scribner, p. 180.

104 Tall poppy syndrome. (n.d.). In *Urban Dictionary*. Accessed at www.urbandictionary.com/define.php?term=Tall%20poppy%20syndrome on December 4, 2016.

105 Kouzes, J. M., & Posner, B. Z. (1999). *Encouraging the heart: A leader's guide to rewarding and recognizing others*. San Francisco: Jossey-Bass, p. 105.

106 Lang, J. M. (2015, January 19). Waiting for us to notice them. *Chronicle of Higher Education*. Accessed at http://chronicle.com/article/Waiting-for-Us-to-Notice-Them/151255 on May 1, 2016.

107 Grant, A. (2014). *Give and take: Why helping others drives our success*. New York: Penguin.

108 Grant, A. (2014). *Give and take: Why helping others drives our success*. New York: Penguin, p. 10.

109 Grant, A. (2014). *Give and take: Why helping others drives our success*. New York: Penguin, p. 157.

110 Grant, A. (2014). *Give and take: Why helping others drives our success*. New York: Penguin, p. 165.

111 Disney, W. (n.d.). *Walt Disney Company quotes*. Accessed at www.goodreads.com/quotes/287154-of-all-the-things-i-ve-done-the-most-vital-is on July 1, 2016.

112 Hattie, J. (2009). *Visible learning: A synthesis of over 800 meta-analyses relating to achievement*. New York: Routledge.

113 Hattie, J. (2012). *Visible learning for teachers: Maximizing impact on learning*. New York: Routledge, p. 19.

114 Hattie, J., & Yates, G. (2014). *Visible learning and the science of how we learn.* New York: Routledge.

115 Hattie, J. (2012). *Visible learning for teachers: Maximizing impact on learning.* New York: Routledge, p. 19.

116 Tichy, N. M. (1997). *The leadership engine: How winning companies build leaders at every level.* New York: Harper Business, p. 31.

117 Yaw. (n.d.). In *Merriam-Webster.* Accessed at www.merriam-webster.com/dictionary/yaw on September 15, 2016.

118 Tichy, N. M. (1997). *The leadership engine: How winning companies build leaders at every level.* New York: Harper Business, p. 74.

119 Kanold, T. D. (2011). *The five disciplines of PLC leaders.* Bloomington, IN: Solution Tree Press, p. 12.

120 Rath, T., & Conchie, B. (2008). *Strengths based leadership: Great leaders, teams, and why people follow.* New York: Gallup Press, pp. 251–256.

121 Gallup. (2016). *How millennials want to work and live.* Washington, DC: Author. Accessed at www.gallup.com/reports/189830/millennials-work-live.aspx on July 1, 2016.

122 Rath, T., & Conchie, B. (2008). *Strengths based leadership: Great leaders, teams, and why people follow.* New York: Gallup Press.

123 Rath, T., & Conchie, B. (2008). *Strengths based leadership: Great leaders, teams, and why people follow.* New York: Gallup Press.

124 Covey, S. M. R. (with Merrill, R. R.). (2006). *The speed of trust: The one thing that changes everything.* New York: Free Press, p. 157.

125 Dweck, C. (2015). Teachers' mindsets: "Every student has something to teach me." *Educational Horizons, 93*(2), 10–15.

126 Dweck, C. (2015). Teachers' mindsets: "Every student has something to teach me." *Educational Horizons, 93*(2), 10.

127 Dweck, C. (2015). Teachers' mindsets: "Every student has something to teach me." *Educational Horizons, 93*(2), 10.

128 Rogers, W. (n.d.). *Will Rogers quotes.* Accessed at www.goodreads.com/author/quotes/132444.Will_Rogers on September 1, 2016.

129 Kanold, T. (2015, January 10). *Growing your fixed mindsets mid-year!* [Blog post]. Accessed at http://bit.ly/2iWhuMB on November 1, 2016.

130 Dweck, C. (2015). Teachers' mindsets: "Every student has something to teach me." *Educational Horizons, 93*(2), 10–15.

131 Dweck, C. (2015). Teachers' mindsets: "Every student has something to teach me." *Educational Horizons, 93*(2), 10–15.

132 Entropy. (n.d.). In *Merriam-Webster.* Accessed at www.merriam-webster.com/dictionary/entropy on May 1, 2016.

133 Kotter, J. P. (2008). *A sense of urgency.* Boston: Harvard Business School Publishing, p. 25.

134 Ali, M. (n.d.). *Muhammad Ali quotes.* Accessed at www.goodreads.com/quotes/200873-don-t-count-the-days-make-the-days-count on September 1, 2016.

135 Hattie, J., & Yates, G. (2014). *Visible learning and the science of how we learn.* New York: Routledge.

136 Popham, W. J. (2011). Formative assessment: A process, not a test. *Education Week, 30*(21). Accessed at www.edweek.org/ew/articles/2011/02/23/21popham.h30.html on September 1, 2016.

137 Popham, W. J. (2011). Formative assessment: A process, not a test. *Education Week, 30*(21). Accessed at www.edweek.org/ew/articles/2011/02/23/21popham.h30.html on September 1, 2016.

138 Hattie, J. (2012). *Visible learning for teachers: Maximizing impact on learning.* New York: Routledge, pp. 26–27.

139 DuFour, R. (2015). *In praise of American educators: And how they can become even better.* Bloomington, IN: Solution Tree Press.

140 DuFour, R. (2016, August 10). *In praise of American educators.* Keynote address given at the Professional Learning Communities at Work Institute, Seattle, WA.

141 Mayo Clinic. (n.d.). *Mayo Clinic mission and values.* Accessed at www.mayoclinic.org/about -mayo-clinic/mission-values on August 1, 2016.

Index